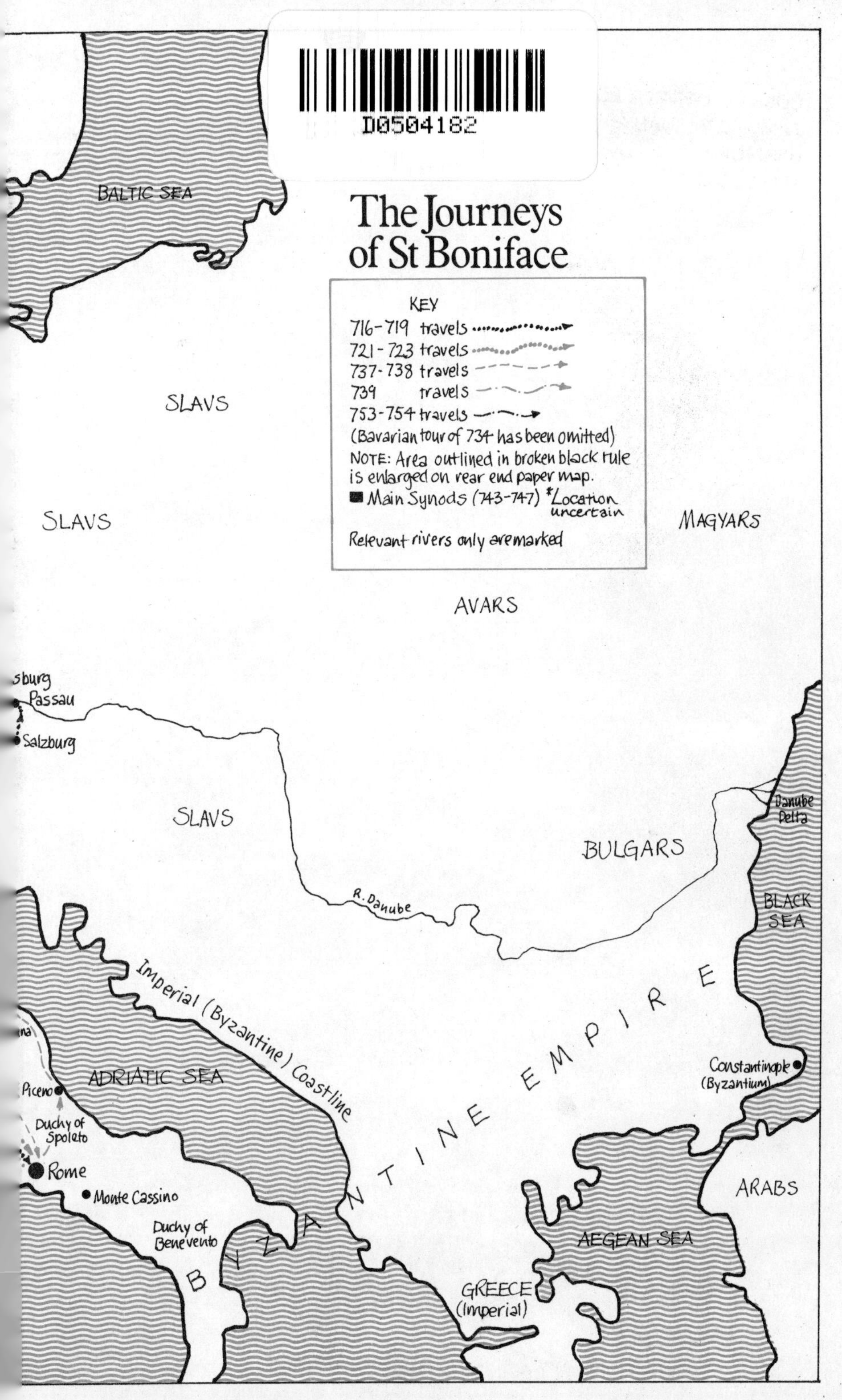
The Journeys of St Boniface
KEY
716-719 travels
721-723 travels
737-738 travels
739 travels
753-754 travels
(Bavarian tour of 734 has been omitted)
NOTE: Area outlined in broken black rule is enlarged on rear end paper map.
Main Synods (743-747) *Location uncertain
Relevant rivers only are marked
BALTIC SEA
SLAVS
SLAVS
MAGYARS
AVARS
Passau
Salzburg
SLAVS
BULGARS
Danube Delta
R. Danube
BLACK SEA
Imperial (Byzantine) Coastline
BYZANTINE EMPIRE
ADRIATIC SEA
Constantinople (Byzantium)
Piceno
Duchy of Spoleto
Rome
Monte Cassino
ARABS
Duchy of Benevento
AEGEAN SEA
GREECE (Imperial)

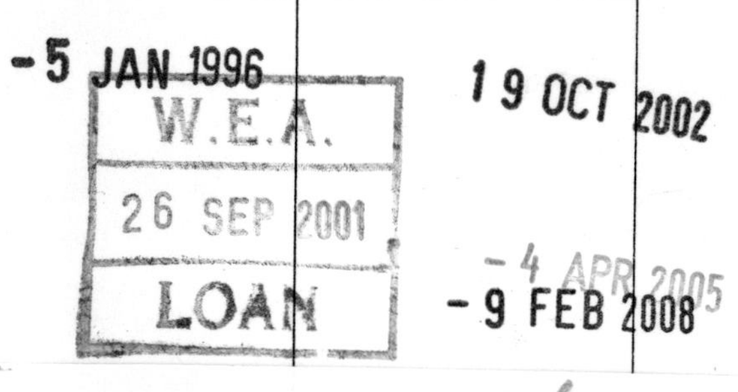

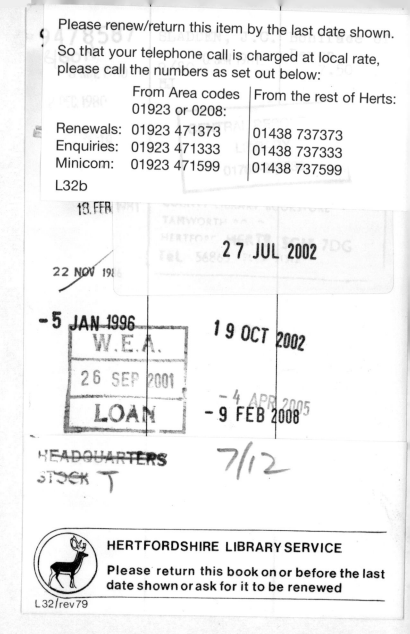

BONIFACE OF DEVON
APOSTLE OF GERMANY

by

John Cyril Sladden, M.A., B.D.

EXETER
THE PATERNOSTER PRESS

ISBN: 0 85364 275 3

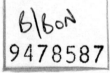

AUSTRALIA:
Emu Book Agencies Pty., Ltd.,
63, Berry St., Granville, 2142, N.S.W.

SOUTH AFRICA:
Oxford University Press,
P.O. Box 1141, Cape Town

British Library Cataloguing in Publication Data

Sladden, John
Boniface of Devon.
1. Boniface, *Saint, Abp of Mainz*
2. Christian saints – Germany, West – Mainz – Biography 3. Mainz – Biography
270.2'092'4 BX4700.B7

ISBN 0–85364–275–3

Typeset by Input Typesetting Ltd
and Printed in Great Britain for The Paternoster Press,
Paternoster House, 3 Mount Radford Crescent, Exeter, Devon
by Butler and Tanner Ltd., Frome, Somerset

CONTENTS

This book is dedicated
to my wife
Mair
without whose
patience,
understanding
and encouragement
it might never have been completed.

FOREWORD

The Anglo-Saxon mission to Europe was hardly known to me until 1966, when I discovered at Seefeld-in-Tirol a parish church in Austria dedicated to an Anglo-Saxon saint, St. Oswald of Northumbria. There was a link here with research in which I was engaged, in the interest of celebrations due to be held in 1969 for the seventh centenary of the church in which I serve, St. Oswald's, Lower Peover. A book which I was intending to write about the life of St. Oswald, king of Northumbria 634-642 AD, was thereupon extended to include the spread of his fame into Europe through the Middle Ages. I read carefully *England and the Continent in the Eighth Century*, by Wilhelm Levison, who came to England from Germany before the Second World War. Willibrord and Boniface figured prominently in this fascinating book. With equal interest I studied C. H. Talbot's *The Anglo-Saxon Missionaries in Germany*, which includes English translations of the earliest 'Life' of Boniface and a selection of his letters. Lives of Willibrord, Leoba, Sturm and Willibald also supplied me with extensive notes made out of sheer interest and beyond what was strictly necessary in relation to St. Oswald. Eventually I set a chapter of the projected book in Echternach in 719, with Willibrord and Boniface involved together. This appeared in a summary of the work, which was circulated to a number of publishers. The summary reached The Paternoster Press just as the need was being felt for an English biography of Boniface, in view of the forthcoming thirteenth centenary celebrations of his birth in Devon. Promptly a letter was sent to me, asking whether I had sufficient interest in Boniface to consider writing about him. Equally promptly I replied: Yes.

Working on the biography disclosed a number of small correspondences. At an early stage I had realised that my birthday (May 15) coincided with the day of the year when Pope Gregory II gave Boniface his 'marching orders', 719. It is also a coincidence that from the window of the house where I was born, the Eton 'Wall Game' could be watched, notably each year on St. Andrew's Day, November 30, the day of the year on which the same Pope consecrated Boniface bishop in 722. In addition, the other chief festival of the school in which I was born and brought up is the eve of St. Boniface's Day, namely the 'Fourth of June'. These facts may imply an alternative account of my interest in Boniface.

I am particularly grateful to the Paternoster Press, both for their original invitation and for the help they have provided from the outset. Thanks are due also to Miss Anthea Cousins for having helped in the correction and emendation of the text. My gratitude goes out to all who, directly or indirectly, have made this book possible, in my family, in the parish and beyond.

John C. Sladden
Lower Peover
October 26th, 1979

Publisher's Note:
Details of the Boniface letters referred to in the text appear in the Chronological Table.

Chapter 1

A WESSEX CRADLE AND A WORLD OF CRISIS

As the leaves turned brown and began to fall, in September, A.D. 680, the immigrant Anglo-Saxon families of Mid-Devon were grateful that another summer had passed without open aggression from the Britons of the Cornish Kingdom. But vigilance was needed at all times. One family in particular was taking care to guard the baby born earlier that year; a boy who, though safely preserved through childhood, would leave home at an early age, and would eventually change the face of Europe.

'The world is a small place', we say today, but in those days, although transport was slow and communications poor, Europe was at least compact enough for events at one end to affect the lives of people at the other. What happened in England, in Rome, in Constantinople, tended to involve everyone including those northern peoples who for centuries had exerted pressure on the Mediterranean scene.

It was in the tongue of land between the Creedy and the Yeo, where Crediton stands today, that the parents of Wynfrith watched over their precious child. We do not know their names. They belonged to the nobility, or at least to the freemen or 'ceorls', of the kingdom of Wessex, the West Saxons. Some years earlier, with encouragement from their king Centwine, they had migrated westward by sea from the Axe basin or beyond to the valley of the Exe. It was a hazardous enterprise, bringing them within the boundaries of King Geraint of Cornwall. Advantage was taken of the sparse population of Britons, many of whose ancestors had left these shores to establish the kingdom of Brittany. Parties of Saxons entering the territory suitably armed, having chosen their time wisely, had a fair chance of gaining and keeping a foothold. This was what Wynfrith's family and some others had done. In due time, according to the degree of success of such ventures, King Centwine intended to mount a full–scale military operation and take over a considerable part of Devon, incorporating it into his own kingdom. This policy was well understood by the courageous migrants, and corresponded with earlier stages of expansion on the part of Wessex.

Wynfrith's parents were Christians, though at present cut off from the ministrations of the Church. The West Saxons had been evangelized almost completely over the forty-six years since the arrival of Birin (St. Birinus) at Portchester in the year 634. The work of Christianisation had been greatly encouraged by the baptism of King Cynegils a year or two later. That had taken place when the Christian King Oswald of Northumbria sought the hand of Cynegil's daughter in marriage. Since then, churches and monastic houses had been founded all over the kingdom. Dorchester-on-Thame had been both capital and cathedral city at first; but owing to the encroachments of Mercia, it was by now Winchester which fulfilled both these roles. Glastonbury and Malmesbury were outstanding among the monastic centres. Both had been adapted to the Benedictine order from the earlier Celtic (British/Irish) discipline. The Church throughout the Anglo-Saxon kingdoms had been unified and strengthened under the great archbishop Theodore of Canterbury. Thus was begun to be forged that 'England' which did not assume a political unity until more than two centuries later.

At this very time, September 680, in another corner of the southern counties (as we would call them), Bishop Heddi of Winchester was in conference with other leaders of the Anglo-Saxon Church under Theodore. It was an important meeting, recorded in history as the Council or Synod of 'Hatfield' or 'Heathfield'. The place may be equivalent to 'Clovesho' or Cliffe-at-Hoo, in the peninsula of Hoo between the Medway and the Thames. This was to become a famous ecclesiastical rendezvous later, as in the year 747, when Clovesho figured in Wynfrith's later life. The gathering in 680 gave evidence of sensitive links between this country and Europe. Both Rome and Constantinople were directly or indirectly involved. A main item on the agenda before Theodore and his fellow-bishops concerned a vital matter about Christ himself. The question may seem to many modern minds to be trivial, though it is not really so; it was in any case a burning issue at that particular stage of the Church's history. Did the incarnate Christ have both a divine *and* a human will, working in unison? Or did he have only one will? It is no part of our present object to follow the controversy in detail. Suffice it to say that Rome, confessing the *two* wills, (di-theletism) was challenging Constantinople where Church and Emperor had been proclaiming the *single* will (mono-theletism), and was seeking an English affirmation of the di-thelete position. A representative of Rome, John the Chanter, was at 'Hatfield' taking note of the proceedings, and due to return immediately to Pope Agatho when the outcome was known.

In Rome itself, in the eastern corner of the city within the Wall of Aurelian, the Pope in his Lateran Palace had these matters much in mind. He was working towards a greater synod than that of 'Hatfield'. After thirty years of division, there was now hope of a reconciliation between Rome and Constantinople over the vexed question already mentioned. A great gathering, representative of the church both east and west, was now planned to be held in the eastern capital. Agatho, going over the whole matter in his mind, could confidently expect John the Chanter to return from England with assurance that there was no disagreement between the English and the Romans. A year earlier, the great and controversial English churchman Wilfrid, a Northumbrian, had been in Rome, largely to plead his own claim to be the rightful bishop of York, and had assured the Pope of his fellow-countrymen's soundness over the doctrinal point that was so topical. Agatho had been impressed with the man, and had sent him back to England with authority to claim York as his. But it had to be admitted that Wilfrid was unusual. How many bishops, on such a journey to Rome, would have delayed to conduct a preaching mission to a heathen tribe, as Wilfrid had done in Frisia? His was a complicated personality. England was not such a simple matter, either, and certainly not always and everywhere compliant with the wishes of the Roman Pontiff. Had not the King of Northumbria, Egfrith, refused to act on the Pope's judgement in Wilfrid's favour?

Wilfrid and Frisia, Rome and the Papacy, issues between east and west, clashes between lay rulers and the spiritual leadership of the church: all these would affect the life of Wynfrith, now in his cradle between the Creedy and the Yeo.

At the very furthest end of Europe, in Constantinople itself, lay the palace of the Emperor Constantine 'Pogonatus' (the bearded one) between the Sea of Marmora and the Golden

Horn. It contained the great 'Trullus' or domed hall, where it was planned to hold the east-west synod of 681, known to history as the Trullan Council. Politics and church life, as so often, were closely linked. Islam, the new religion from Arabia, had aroused in its adherents a passion for military conquest. Those parts of the eastern or 'Byzantine' empire which had favoured the 'mono-thelete' doctrine of Christ had been overrun by Arabs. Constantine was ready to return to the view favoured by Rome, and was making preparations to remove from office the present Patriarch and replace him by another.

The increasing influence of the Moslem Arabs, which brought Rome and Constantinople together at this juncture, was to give rise to another split, which indirectly at least would affect the life of Wynfrith many years later: the controversy over images, 'iconoclasm'.

To complete this survey of circumstances at the time of Wynfrith's infancy, some reference is needed to a great people, the Franks, who dominated large parts of Western Europe by direct government and further regions under some kind of sway. On their northern border were heathens, such as the East Frisians, to whom Wilfrid had preached with little success, and the 'Old Saxons' (as Wynfrith's people were accustomed to call them). Their southern border or that of their dependencies along the Pyrenees would before long be threatened by Arab conquerors coming through North Africa and Spain. At the time of which we are writing, a historic moment was about to arrive. In 681 Pippin of Heristal, great-grandfather of Charlemagne, secured his position as 'Mayor of the Palace' of Eastern Frank-land ('Austrasia'). Six years later he gained effective control of the Western Franks also ('Neustria'). With Pippin's son and grandsons, Wynfrith would be very much concerned.

The first five years of this West-Saxon infant's life were apparently spent in a perfectly normal fashion in and around his home. It was assumed that as he grew up he would become the kind of person his father was. When he was two years old, King Centwine brought his army, and after a number of battles secured territory well to the west of the basin of the Exe. There was general rejoicing. Life gained much in freedom and scope. Christian institutions were soon set up. A group of Benedictine monks settled at Exeter. News of the wider world included vivid stories of Christian preaching among the South Saxons (Sussex), hitherto obstinately heathen. Leading the mission was

Bishop Wilfrid, still banned from his native Northumbria but indefatigable in the service of God. One of Wynfrith's earliest memories may well have been the setting up of a 'preaching cross' by monks of Exeter near to his home. Such stone crosses, a few of which are preserved to this day, were put up at any place where it seemed right to create a focus of Christian proclamation and worship. Only at a later stage, when the population had grown and means could be found, would a church building be erected beside the cross. It is likely that construction of a church at Crediton was preceded by the setting up of a preaching cross, even if we have no direct evidence of the fact. We do know that monks made regular visits to the neighbourhood of Wynfrith's home in his early childhood, and that his parents were fond of entertaining them at their house. What is more probable than that such visits were associated with, and arose out of occasions of ministry at a nearby cross?

Wynfrith early became a favourite with the monks, and they with him. Soon a development occurred for which the young boy's parents were not prepared. He became so attracted by these visitors and their whole way of life that he began to assert a longing to become one of them. It was not unknown in those days for a child to be dedicated to the service of God, with a view to taking full monastic vows at a later stage. Wynfrith's father, though a convinced and consistent Christian, was unwilling indeed to consider parting with his son in this way. The parents strenously dissuaded their son from any such ambition, but made little headway in overcoming his avowed desires.

He was between four and five years old. Physically robust and intellectually advanced for his age, he was regarded by his parents and friends of his family as destined for a great future as a leader of men. What greater waste than for such a promising boy to be shut up in a monastery for the rest of his life! Praying and preaching were high callings, without doubt; but a really bright and strong personality was needed in the service of the earthly kingdom. So they argued. When news came of the death of an older boy in the monastery at Selsey, founded after Wilfrid's mission in Sussex, his parents seized on this as a means of diverting Wynfrith from his declared aim, but with a notable lack of success, for although they were taking care to see less of the monks than formerly, the boy found occasion to question them further on the matter. What he learned might have deterred many, but had a very different effect on him.

The boy in question, being about twelve years old, had fallen a victim to the plague which was rife in that part of Sussex and which had struck down most of the inmates of the monastery, some of whom had nearly died. At the moment when the most desperate prayers were being offered for their recovery, he had been granted a vision. In it he had received a message from heaven, sent by the Apostles Peter and Paul. He was to leave this world and join them and the other saints in heaven; and his death would secure the recovery of all the other sick persons in the house. So it had turned out.

Far from being put off by this story, Wynfrith was fascinated, even attracted. If all that he had learned from the Exeter monks was true (and he believed it without question), then the delights of this life were as nothing beside the joys of heaven; and what a privilege it would be to die for the sake of other people. His ambition to join the monks of Exeter was strengthened by the tale.

Angered by his son's perversity, Wynfrith's father spoke to him with extreme severity. If the boy was prudent enough to refrain, after that, from openly mentioning the subject, it remained clear that his mind was still set in the same direction.

The plague had meanwhile spread, and finally arrived in the Exe valley. Less virulent than in its first outbreak, it affected only a limited number of the local people, and of them, a smaller proportion died. Even this restricted epidemic, however, struck a few of the strongest individuals. One day Wynfrith's father became ill. For what seemed like an age he was close to death. The monks of Exeter, ignoring the coolness which had overtaken his relations with them recently, prayed diligently for his recovery. When eventually the crisis passed, he confessed that he owed his life to them. Giving thanks to God in their presence and with their encouragement, he cast about in his mind to discover by what gift or deed he could adequately express his gratitude. It occurred to him that his sickness and mortal danger had perhaps been a visitation from God, and that he had been resisting God in refusing to countenance Wynfrith's cherished hopes. Speaking to his wife about this, he found her more ready than he had supposed to follow his line of thought. Her maternal instinct, while certainly restraining her from any eagerness to part with her child, at the same time gave her sympathy and understanding towards his desires. She had heard of Hannah and the infant Samuel, and was prepared to regard it as a privilege to give her son into the whole-time service of the Lord.

So it was agreed that in due time Wynfrith would join the monastic house at Exeter.

Chapter 2

EXETER

Wynfrith already had reason to know that the world about him was a troubled place. Plague was but one kind of trouble. There was the need of vigilance and if necessary military defence on the part of Wessex folk against the Cornish to the West and the Mercians to the North. And now, when King Centwine died, there was crisis and an unsettled period as the exiled adventurer Caedwalla came sweeping in from Sussex to seize the West Saxon throne. He was a fourth cousin of Centwine, and he had been trying unsuccessfully to carve out some kind of principality for himself in the territory further east. One of his last acts before re-entering his native kingdom was to murder the King of Sussex, Ethelwalh. Failing to gain support in that region, he took advantage of Centwine's death and obtained his throne by sheer strength. It cannot have been a pleasant time for those citizens of Wessex who preferred more peaceable ways.

Conceivably the state of the kingdom was one factor which helped Wynfrith's father to give way to his younger son's wish. We can well imagine the boy's mother regarding a monastery as a place of quiet and respect in the disturbed environment of the Wessex of that time. As for Wynfrith himself, his character as revealed in later years entirely precludes us from supposing that he himself looked upon the monastic life as a means of avoiding danger. We can more easily see him saying that there was as much, and truer, adventure in the whole-time service of Christ as there was in the life of any of the Caedwallas of this world.

Perhaps in the spring of 686, when he was still under six years of age, Wynfrith was welcomed into the small monastery at Exeter by Wulfhard, its abbot. Wulfhard, though not a man of great learning, doubtless shared the general view that a religious 'house' should educate future members under its own roof from an early age. If there were not already at the Exeter house other boys like Wynfrith, his going there was surely a precedent soon to be followed. As he settled down with his contemporaries, or they with him, he showed himself a thoroughly likeable boy. Although he was the cleverest, he was always modest, and never took advantage of his own abilities in such a way as to appear superior to his fellows.

The full discipline of monastic life, even in that humane form which it had assumed in the Benedictine order, was presumably not shared by the boys until they grew to an age at which they could take the complete vows. Nevertheless from the start Wynfrith was made aware of the whole way of life upon which he had so keenly and voluntarily embarked. He was in no way disappointed by its direct impact, in comparison with descriptions which he had earlier received from the friendly monks. Here were a few dozen men (at the most) living together as one happily family, hard-working and 'fulfilled'. Their working day was earlier, at its beginning and ending, than that of the farmer. Their work was of five kinds. Internally there was, first and foremost, the 'Work of God' in the strict sense (Latin: *opus Dei*), secondly, study, and thirdly, manual labour. Those qualified to do so would go out to preach; but also all would be active in caring for the sick and needy and in hospitality towards travellers.

The 'Work of God' was a daily round of worship which reflected the aspirations of the Psalmist: 'Seven times a day' but also 'in the night season' were praises and prayers to be offered. So there were eight 'offices' or short services. The 'night office', 'Nocturn' (or, strangely, 'Mattins') was held about 2 a.m. According to the time of year the first and last of the seven 'day' offices might also take place in darkness. The first, 'Lauds' ('praises') tended to vary round the seasons, being preferred at cockcrow, or earliest intimation of dawn. 'Prime' followed in full daylight, 'Terce' at the third hour of day (9 a.m. on average), 'Sext' at midday, 'None' at the ninth hour of day at about 3 p.m.; Vespers were taken while reasonably good light remained, or earlier (relatively) in summer, and lastly, before bedtime, 'Compline', that is to say, the completing of the round (Latin: *completorium*). Every day there was a main meal after 'Sext'. On Sundays throughout the year, and on most weekdays except in winter, there was a second meal between Vespers and Compline. In winter, excepting Sundays, and on all official fast-days, only bread and a little drink were allowed at that evening hour. Sleep was not unimportant, and the brotherhood might be mostly asleep between about 7.30 p.m. and 1.30 a.m. Novices and pupils, like Wynfrith in his first eight years at Exeter, might sleep also between Nocturn and Lauds. Whatever had been the custom in St. Benedict's day, about 150 years earlier, by the time of which we are speaking, it was usual for those in full vows to read and study during those early hours.

Sleep might be foregone by some or all on Saturday night, which was regarded as a 'vigil' leading up to the celebration of the Sacrament (or 'Mass') early on Sunday. All partook of the Holy Communion on Sundays. The same could apply at major festivals not falling on a Sunday. On other days there was no 'celebration', but sometimes a distribution of the 'reserved Sacrament' to the brothers.

Reading and study had originally been intended exclusively in the interest of God's Word. Some more general study was necessary even for this purpose. Since worship and the reading of Scripture involved the Latin tongue, a certain skill in language was desirable, beyond what ordinary lay Christians needed for their understanding of the rites of worship. By the end of the seventh century, it had been found useful to include some classical Latin authors among the subjects of study, although the danger of contamination from heathen ideas and standards had to be carefully guarded against. The Greek language, which could have been of great advantage in New Testament study, and in the right development of doctrine, was unfortunately being steadily lost in the Western Church, and only rarely given any attention except (as in Southern Italy) where it was still understood by the native population. The Hebrew of the Old Testament was known to individuals here and there, but was not a regular subject of study. Wynfrith, who showed early promise in language, Scripture and doctrine, could find satisfaction in the small community at Exeter while young. But his inquiring mind would eventually wish to go beyond the limits attainable under the practical, unscholarly Wulfhard. Even if he had no great interest in the 'classics' for their own sake, there was a wealth of Church teaching which he longed to absorb. This was contained in documents affording proper standards, or 'canons', of church life and outlook. All this, in due course, Wynfrith wished to grasp in its entirety as far as one man could. How exactly should the Christian see the mystery of the Holy Trinity? How should he hold together the divine nature and the human nature in the person of the Saviour (*cf.* the 'monothelete' challenge, already mentioned)? How was the authority of the first Apostle handed on and distributed in the later Church with its orders of ministry? How was a monastic house with its abbot related to the diocese with its bishop and to the local Christian community? These were some of the questions answered by the canons. Not least important of course, was the study of the Christian life of virtue, of which the monastic brotherhood was expected to give as perfect an example as could be found on earth.

But the brotherhood had to live, and this meant making its living in terms of food and clothing and shelter. For this it aimed at self-sufficiency, and as far as possible, independence from the community at large: a little more than self-support, in so far as its members sought to serve others beyond its walls. The ideal could not be exactly fulfilled. Someone, a king or landowner, had to make a gift of property, if only the site itself on which a monastic house could be built, and sufficient land for cultivation and livestock to support the brotherhood. The brothers could quarry their own stone and build. Wynfrith may have delighted in such tasks, as Exeter was probably still being developed when he joined. In his day there was no large or elaborate structure, nor formal courtyard or cloister with impressive buildings on each side. There was a simple chapel or 'oratory' with benches and a rough altar. There was a dining room or 'refectory' and a dormitory. In the simplest arrangement the abbot might sleep in the centre and the brothers around him. A similar arrangement could be adopted if a separate room was built for study.

Domestic chores were shared by all, including the abbot. The same applied to the tilling of the soil and the management of flocks and herds. By this time, there were larger monasteries in which more specialisation took place, some monks being set apart as students or a sort of 'clergy', and perhaps the abbot and one or two others as whole time administrators. Exeter is likely to have been conducted along the more primitive lines. The employment of lay servants was likewise a feature known in some larger houses, but probably not seen by Wynfrith until he grew up and travelled. It was good for him to be brought up to regard the simpler and more thoroughgoing monastic ideal as the norm.

Preaching outside the brotherhood was not an original part

of the pattern. It was, however, an inevitable development as monasteries became centres of education in comparatively barbaric lands. (The behaviour of Caedwalla of Wessex shows that England was hardly out of this category!) Barbarism went along with heathenism, broadly speaking, amongst the Germanic or Teutonic peoples of which the Anglo-Saxons formed one group. It was highly desirable for those with the most single-minded dedication to the Christian way to be agents in spreading it by word as well as example.

Equally important, however, if 'example' meant anything, was the care of the sick and needy. This could be considered as an extension of the arrangement within the monastery, for its members; or it may have been derived from early examples in the east, under St. Basil particularly, who had founded the first Christian hospital-cum-hostelry at Caesarea-in-Cappadocia. Exeter in its first decades may have had little need of accommodation for travellers, being almost at the limit of West Saxon territory; but its 'hospital' patients may have been a significant number, swelled occasionally by the wounded after some affray between the local Saxons and the Cornish Celts.

During his sixteen years at Exeter, so close to the border, Wynfrith is likely to have pondered deeply on the question of the Celtic peoples, and how they were to be regarded from the point of view of Christian charity. They were Christians but had strange customs, different in important and inconvenient respects from those encouraged under Augustine and Theodore and under Birinus of Wessex. They did not *deny* primacy to the Bishop of Rome, yet opposed so much that Rome preferred. Columbanus, the Irish missionary, had spoken harshly to the Pope (so it was said) when he had founded Bobbio monastery in Italy a few generations ago. Harshness seemed characteristic of their way. They had monasteries, the rules of which were reputed to be little other than severe lists of punishments. They appeared as unduly negative in their approach. They had bishops, but bishops too unrelated to the general life of the church; not governing, but simply ordaining clergy and consecrating buildings, as needed, and sometimes actually living in a monastery under the authority of an abbot. All appeared to be confusion. The Saxon monk could well be enjoined to pray for the Celt as a brother Christian, even if the King of Cornwall was the earthly enemy of the King of Wessex; but he could not be expected to approve of Celtic practices, taken as a whole.

By no means cut off from world events, the young novice took increasing notice of what was happening beyond the limits of his native kingdom, and not only in connection with the Roman See to which the English monastic tradition was so strongly attached. Indeed, Rome had four popes in five years (682–687). Not until Pope Sergius (687–701) was there a person to express the Roman oversight of the Church in a coherent manner to those far distant from Rome itself. First, Wynfrith 'watched' the completion of the work of Christianising the peoples of this island. With this process he linked the name of that Wilfrid the Northumbrian, whose somewhat strange career had included quarrelling with his king, evangelizing on the Continent, and applying to Rome for support. Wilfrid's return from Rome in the year of Wynfrith's birth had, after a few months of confusion in Northumbria, been followed by his departure to Sussex (681), where he conducted the highly successful mission already referred to. It was under Wilfrid that Caedwalla had, in a vague way at least, accepted Christianity. Six years later (687), Wilfrid, now being in Northumbria again and serving as a bishop, sent two presbyters to the Isle of Wight to evangelize there. This mission resulted from political factors affecting Wessex, Sussex, and Kent, Caedwalla of Wessex helping to open the way. After mainland Sussex, the island was the last stronghold of heathenism to be overthrown. No doubt the monks of Exeter, fulfilling their high duty of interceding for mankind, gave due thanks to God for this achievement when it came about.

'Political factors' is, however, too mild a description of the troubles of Southern England about this time. King Caedwalla's half-brother, known as 'Mule' from his mixed descent, was killed in a raid on Kent, and Caedwalla, already ailing from earlier campaigns, mounted an expedition for purposes of revenge. He suffered badly as a consequence, became suddenly philosophical, resigned his throne and proceeded to Rome. Sorry for his sins, he sought baptism at last, and from the highest quarter. He died, clothed in the white robe of baptism, at Rome, shortly after Easter in the year 689. Many lessons could be drawn by Wulfhard and other monastic teachers from the life and death of the buccaneer-king. Wynfrith and other pupils would receive a deep impression from it all. Caedwalla was about thirty years of age.

The years 690 to 693, bringing Wynfrith well into the second decade of his life, were in many ways formative and instructive for him, particularly as his interests naturally ranged far and wide. We may be permitted to wonder whether this tendency had been strengthened by a fascination with the controversial *Wilfrid*, whose actual name closely resembled, in the language of the time, that of Wynfrith himself, whom German writers to-day call 'Winfrid'. The boy had a fondness for words and word-play, as is known from his earlier literary efforts when he grew up. Not only was he the first Englishman to compile a Latin grammar, but he was also a designer of 'acrostics', a few of which survive. We know also that two of his chief areas of interest, geographically speaking, were Frisia and Rome. English Christianity was at this very time passing from a 'receptive' state to an outgoing one. Archbishop Theodore, after more than twenty years spent in unifying and strengthening the Church throughout England, died in 690. In the very same year Willibrord, a Northumbrian, sailed from Ireland to Frisia as a missionary presbyter, undaunted by the failure of another like himself (Wictbert) to make any impression there. Whether Willibrord's ship called in at any Wessex port on its way to the Rhine delta, we can only guess. At what stage Wynfrith could have heard about him, we cannot tell. But what he eventually learnt, sank in: the more perhaps, as Willibrord had been a pupil of Wilfrid at Ripon.

Wessex itself, meanwhile, was blessed by a truly great king, Ine, fourth cousin to Caedwalla, and more distantly related to Centwine. Ine was strong enough not only to keep Sussex peaceful as a subject province, but beyond that, to extend some sort of authority over the Middlesex area. He called two bishops 'his': Erkenwald of London as well as Heddi of Winchester. Both were present at the promulgation of the famous 'Laws of Ine', probably in 691.

Travellers arriving in England in 693 from Rome brought two sorts of news. Firstly, Pope Sergius had refused to agree with a decision, this time about discipline, taken in Constantinople in 692 at a so-called 'universal' Synod. Secondly, the Western Church was officially disinclined to admit that clergy in the main 'orders' could be married, while the Easterns had re-asserted that presbyters not under monastic vows might, with certain reservations, be married men. The rift between East and West was slowly but relentessly widening. Wynfrith would see more of this in later life. He took the Western view as unquestionable, and (whatever we may judge to be right and wrong) upheld vigorously the standard of clerical celibacy to the very end. The other news from Rome had to do with Willibrord, who had been visiting the Pope, to whom he had reported successes in the Frisian venture under the general patronage of Pippin of Heristal, 'Mayor of the Palace' of the Franks. Wynfrith heard of these things at the end of his first twelve or thirteen years of life: it would be during the last twelve or thirteen years of life (741–754) that he, known widely under another name, would serve another Pippin, grandson of the one in power in the 690s.

At the age of fourteen Wynfrith was admitted to full membership of the monastic community. The modern mind, tending to regard fourteen as too young for confirmation vows, stands aghast at the thought of monastic vows being taken at that tender age. But at that time, puberty and adulthood were literally experienced as one event. If someone from those days spoke with us and said, 'Wynfrith knew what he was doing', we would not be in a position to argue. Almost certainly he did know. His earliest biographer assures us that he mastered successfully the difficulties and temptations with which young men are faced. No doubt he and others like him prayed, while the community also prayed for them, that they might be given grace to be able to develop a fruitful Christian relationship with members of the opposite sex, sublimating carnal desires to divine ends. Wynfrith, and some of those who worked with him later in life, have left evidence that a fine, open, even daring relationship with women (nuns, in fact) could be maintained on a high spiritual plane unsullied by impurity.

During eight further years we envisage this young, studious, well-loved inmate of Exeter proceeding through the 'minor orders' of clerical rank as then envisaged: one step every two years, presumably: doorkeeper, reader, exorcist and acolyte. While the majority at this period remained simple monks, the more articulate and able proceeded into the ranks of the clergy, though they were not normally seconded to what we should call ordinary parochial duties. It would be interesting to know whether anyone at Exeter knew, and could inform Wynfrith, that the year of his birth was just two hundred years after that of the birth of St. Benedict of Nursia, who was coming to be regarded as the father of most of the best in monastic tradition. In actual fact, St. Benedict would have been surprised at much that was taken for granted at this later date, including the progress of monks into the official orders of sacred ministry. Specialization of all kinds had been discouraged by Benedict.

During the years 692 to 694 Abbot Wulfhard was increasingly impressed and delighted, but also perplexed, at the scholarly advances made by the young man from Crediton. How long would it be before that avid brain was satisfied?

The wider outreach of that brain was not infrequently extended during the same period. Wynfrith might have heard from time to time of yet more English missionaries abroad. Suidbert, starting with Willibrord, had come home and been consecrated by Wilfrid as a missionary bishop in 693 (there was no archbishop of Canterbury at the time). He had gone east of the Rhine and done good work with a German tribe, it was said. More sobering, yet glorious, was the news that two companions of similar name, Hewald the Fair and Hewald the Dark, had lost their lives as martyrs while trying to convert the Saxons of Westphalia (694 to 695). 'The blood of the martyrs is the seed of the Church' was a standard quotation from the earliest Latin 'Father', Tertullian. Wynfrith could hope that after such an event those close relations of his own people, namely the continental or 'old' Saxons, would be more receptive to the Gospel, as some of their cousins the Frisians had already begun to be. Willibrord, it was reliably stated, was going from strength to strength: made 'Archbishop of the Frisians' on a second visit to Rome (695), he was soon so busy that he was glad to accept the offer of a site to the south, near the Frankish city of Trier on the Moselle, where he could build a special monastery as a sort of retreat: Echternach was its name (about 698).

As yet his interest in such matters was, apart from the duty of intercessory prayer for the whole Church, a kind of hobby, perhaps no different from word-puzzles. As his main lines of study found less and less stimulus under Wulfhard, some of his time and energy needed to be spent in other ways. By the time he reached the age of twenty two, about the time that he was due to enter the order of sub-deacon, he found the study situation altogether dissatisfying, and asked whether he might be moved elsewhere. This was a serious step, not on the grounds of self-conceit, since he was known as a humble-minded and lovable person, but because in the original ideal a monk lived out his life in the particular 'house' in which he had entered upon his vocation.

Chapter 3

NURSLING AND NEW HORIZONS

'There you have it in a nutshell'. Wynfrith would have appreciated the pun: for 'Nutshell' was the name, or nickname, of a very small place (or of the *monastery* at that place) ten miles to the south-west of Winchester, capital of Wessex, and three miles to the north-west of the rapidly developing port of 'Hamwih' (Southampton). 'It has all that I am looking for, in a nutshell', Wynfrith might well have said. For in fact his request was granted, and he was to move to 'Nutshell' (the modern Nursling) where the opportunity for advanced study was offered by Abbot Winbert. (To be consistent, our English authorities who write 'Wynfrith' should also write 'Wynberht'). Scholarship and devotion were equally renowned features of Nursling at that time. No better choice could have been made. Indeed, such was Wynfrith's reputation that the abbot looked forward to his coming as a prospective teacher, not merely as a senior student.

To go so far eastward meant a further degree of separation from his own family, with whom he had been in fairly constant touch while at Exeter. Of such partings we are told nothing by biographers. It is interesting to wonder whether Wynfrith's girl cousin 'Leoba' (Liobgytha), born 'about 700', was already known to him as an infant before he left the district. Some years later, Leoba, who had been 'consecrated from the womb' in a way that he had not, followed him eastwards as far as Wimborne; and about forty years later again, to the young German church which he by then had set upon its feet; and finally, to a grave under the same roof as his own, in that same land.

The journey of a hundred miles to his new home was a fresh experience for one who during the first quarter of his life of seventy-four years may never have travelled beyond the basin of the river Exe. During nearly another quarter, until he was fully thirty-five, apart from the move to Nursling his journeys would continue to be fairly local, except for one notable excursion to Kent. The remainder of his life would be an almost ceaseless round of travel. The exceptional permission which he received to move from Exeter was like a crack in a floodgate that would later open wide. Nevertheless, his spirit was not restless when he settled in his new surroundings. Nursling was his home continuously for fourteen years.

Abbot Winbert was 'notary', or ecclesiastical secretary to King Ine. He was thus a man fully expert in many aspects of Church affairs. A large library, not easily obtained in those days, was kept at Nursling. Wynfrith could study the interpretation of the Bible in greater depth and breadth. He became adept at the so-called 'tri-partite' understanding of the Scriptures. That is to say, he learned to find up to three 'mystical' kinds of meaning as well as the literal one, particularly in the Old Testament. He became adept, for example, at expounding 'Jerusalem' not merely as the city on which centred the dealings of God with his ancient people Israel, but as a prophetic or mystical reference (1) to the Christian Church on earth (2) to the soul of any and every faithful Christian (*e.g.* as 'a city that is at unity in itself') and (3) to the Heavenly City and the Final Kingdom. With an armoury such as this manifold interpretative scheme provided, a man like Wynfrith who 'had the heart of the matter' could become a colourful exponent of the Bible in preaching and teaching. In both he did in fact excel. Alongside these scriptural studies, but not in any sense sundered from them, he took further his knowledge of the great conciliar findings of Nicaea (A.D. 325) and later representative gatherings of the Church. Doctrine, worship, ministry and morals were all defined by reference to such findings, as the proper understanding of what Scripture required. Wynfrith followed the story of the Church's rejection of one system of false teaching after another down the centuries ('heresies'), and its constant struggle against the intrusion of pagan features alien to the Gospel. Far more than at Exeter he could extend his range of classical studies, developing the art of avoiding 'contamination' while using their contents for purposes of grammar, style, rhetoric and illustration. He became, incidentally, a competent versifier in more than one Latin tradition, an achievement to which he gave occasional expression in later years. At the age of sixty-two he greeted a new Pope (Zacharias) in a felicitous six-fold hexameter, cited and roughly rendered here into English blank verse:–

Te Deus altithronus sancta conservet in aede
Sedis apostolicae rectorem tempore longo;
Melliflua gratum populis doctrina per orbem,
Perficiatque Deo dignum pia gratia Christi.
Splendida percipiat florens sua gaudia mater,
Atque domus Domini laetetur prole fēcunda.

May God on high preserve you in command
For many years, upon the Apostle's seat.
May Christ's sweet lore endear you to all peoples,
And his good grace divine perfection bring.
May Mother Church flourish and find her joy,
And God's household be blessed with progeny.

Apart from the good rhythm and style of the Latin, it is worth remarking that the poet had no compunction about applying to the true God the sort of adjective (*altithronus*) that had characterised Jupiter in the old Roman culture.

We are not told to what extent Wynfrith preached outside the walls of Nursling; but on many grounds we suspect he often did so. The abbot was not inclined to the 'closed order' mentality, by any means. Within the monastery the young monk excelled in every way. He progressed further in the ranks of the clergy, becoming a full deacon about the age of twenty-five and a presbyter at not less than thirty.

Steeped as he was in biblical history, he was likely to regard the age of thirty as a turning point, of which elevation to a rank which could qualify for the celebration of the Sacrament (namely the presbyterate) was only one indication. For the Levitical priesthood, for a prophet such as Ezekiel, for John the Baptist, and most impressively, for the Saviour himself, that was the age when public outgoing ministry began. For Wynfrith, who may have shown signs of incipient restlessness, it heralded a period of six years during which he was given a representative status, attending 'synods' such as were normally held at Winchester (perhaps annually) to set forward church matters in the Kingdom of the West Saxons. (Such meetings may in fact have had more of the character of a national *gemōt.*) He gained such a reputation* that he was chosen, in 713, to take urgent messages from King Ine to the Archbishop of Canterbury, Berhtwald, in connection with a rebellion that had broken out in Wessex. Whatever the exact nature of the ambassage, it was discharged with total success.

Wynfrith was by now famous throughout Wessex and beyond. He in no way allowed fame to go to his head. His brother monks, his tutors and his pupils, all added a proper pride to that love which they already bore towards him.

Bishop Heddi had died in 704. King Ine saw fit to divide his kingdom for church purposes, Winchester being at one end. The new see of Sherborne was thenceforward served by Aldhelm as bishop. Wynfrith's birthplace and also Exeter came into that diocese. Winchester now had Daniel as its bishop. We presume that it was he who ordained Wynfrith to the diaconate (c. 705) as well as to the presbyterate (c. 710). He became his firm friend and remained so for nearly forty years (till his death in 744).

On the wider field, Wynfrith and his fellows had satisfaction from the fact that the northern part of Ireland in 704 began to follow the Roman order, the southern part having done so since 634. Bishop Aldhelm was moved by this, in 705, to write a careful letter to the King of Cornwall, Geraint, in the hope that the Cornish Celts would follow suit. Wynfrith was, as ever, deeply concerned about the Celtic problem.

The fortunes of Wilfrid continued to provide interest until his death in 709. After a further dispute in Northumbria he had spent eleven years as Bishop of Leicester in the Mercian Kingdom (691–702) and after yet further trouble had travelled to Rome again for support, visiting Willibrord in Frisia on the way. After an illness in Gaul, and much debate in England, he was able to return to a Northumbrian see, but only Hexham (not York or Lindisfarne) in 706. Two years later, foreseeing death's approach, he began a final pilgrimage to Rome, but was taken ill in Mercia, and died at Oundle in October 709. Wynfrith, at Nursling in the period of his diaconate (705–10), can be imagined receiving information about all this. The references to Frisia and Rome stuck most firmly in his mind, although at first he may not have seen in this more than an

* So the present author prefers to suppose. The early biographer suggests that Wynfrith did not attend Wessex gatherings until after his visit to Canterbury.

incidental feature of his own receptivity, a mere sign of his lively interest in Christ's Church as a catholic or global family.

Later (as already explained) the attainment of thirty years and the dignity of the presbyterate found him welcoming the occasional call to service beyond the normal round of duty of an ordained monk. The three years following the ambassage to Canterbury in 713 saw a dramatic development in the workings of his mind. Christendom appeared to be under threat from outside and from within. The Arabs or Saracens, with beliefs alien to those of Christians, were marching up through Spain; and after the death of Emperor Justinian II at Constantinople (711) were taking fresh initiatives in the direction of that city. (In 717 they were in a position to besiege it.)

While this pincer movement closed in on Europe as a whole, in Italy the people known as Lombards were growing strong under King Liutprand (712–744), in a manner which was considered hostile to the Apostolic See at Rome. There were rumours in England that the Church in parts of Europe was weak and corrupt. Could these threats be God's challenge to courageous churchmen to rise up and put things right? Since 'the best method of defence is attack', could it be that the conversion of the northern tribes was what God required first?

Chapter 4

FIRST STEPS IN MISSION

It was with astonishment that Abbot Winbert learned from Wynfrith of the 'call' he claimed to have had to service overseas. Wynfrith, at the age of thirty-five, was 'fully formed', outstandingly suited to the work of teaching, preaching and oversight. It was because of his unusual gifts that he had been allowed to move from one Wessex monastery to another. Was he now to be allowed to move again, out of Wessex, out of England? Winbert had lavished much care on the development of the young man's talents over thirteen years. Could it really be true that those talents were to be employed in distant and dangerous places? Was this well-loved tutor and pastor, this able and diplomatic person to be permitted to go and leave an un-fillable gap in the community of Nursling and in the Church life of the kingdom? Surely this could not be. Winbert consulted the brothers of the house solemnly. They found it hard to believe as he. Here was a man who had given precision and shape to their thinking as Christians. As individuals and as a brotherhood they had received continual inspiration from Wynfrith. He had enabled them to know the full glory of membership of the Church of Christ, the 'one, holy, catholic, apostolic Church'. The Church was 'one', and therefore must foster an agreed understanding of the Holy Scripture for the avoidance of false and misleading doctrine. In the same way the Church must have an ordered structure and discipline held commonly throughout. Wynfrith had helped them to see the ways of their Celtic neighbours as lacking in important respects, while reminding them that Christian charity required them to love the heretic while hating the heresy. (Wynfrith confessed that this was often hard!) The Church was 'holy'; and while holy marriage was a genuinely Christian estate, God needed bands of men and women devoted to the single life as a powerful token and instrument of holiness, reminding others that Christ's kingdom was not of this world. So Wynfrith had impressed his fellows with the importance of their own celibate vocation: and so also he had insisted that Rome was right, against Constantinople, in requiring all clergy, particularly bishops and presbyters but also deacons and subdeacons, to be men who had forsworn the married state. The Church was 'catholic', not only because the Gospel was addressed to all mankind, geographically speaking, but because that Gospel was directed to the redeeming and transforming and uplifting of all the aspects of human life and culture. The old cultures (such as classical Rome) thus had something to offer to the Christian. Moreover the structure of the Church was to be such as would hold together the different kinds of people – with a blend of order and freedom. The Catholic order as it had crystallized during the centuries, defined and cemented by the 'canons' of great Councils or Synods, was admirably suited to this. To use later terminology, we may say that Wynfrith expounded with conviction the merits of the system of the priest in his parish, the bishop in his diocese, the 'metropolitan' or archbishop (like Canterbury) in his province, each with his proper authority, function and relationship. The monastery, though having cross-links with others like itself, was essentially within the same order, the abbot being a presbyter or priest under the bishop's oversight, and the community a sort of parish, but also a peculiar centre and focus of spiritual power and influence in one way and another. Not least, as a sort of keystone under Christ, was the Bishop of Rome in his 'Apostolic See'; Rome, with the tombs of the Apostles Peter and Paul, and relics of them and many other 'saints' and martyrs: Rome, where the decisions of universal Councils were carefully preserved and studied: Rome, for so long the centre of the civilized world (for which reason these other factors also applied): Rome, whose bishop was regarded as speaking with the authority of Peter himself. Wynfrith had a straightforward, almost naive view of the papal position, not unreasonably, given the history of the English Church. In recent years Theodore, sent from Rome, had integrated the Celtic and the Roman over most of England. Theodore had set the seal on the work of Augustine, the (at first reluctant) missionary sent by Pope Gregory the Great.

Wynfrith had not, in his teachings, distinguished carefully between the church's 'apostolic' character as expressed in the figure of the Pope and that same character as involving the call to evangelize the world. Though this involved a generalisation greater than could be supported by sober history, the two aspects went together in his mind. Evangelism, duly and properly undertaken, was Rome's concern wherever it took place. Not only Augustine of Kent a hundred years ago, but Willibrord even now, was considered as invested in missionary enterprise with the authority of St. Peter. This simple understanding of things was to be put to a severe test during the remainder of Wynfrith's life; and in the end he would leave the scene of his earthly struggle wondering whether his unquestioning faith in Rome had been altogether right. But at that time the pattern was undisturbed, and all at Nursling were grateful for the way in which he had set these matters before them. Such an eloquent instructor, who embodied so perfectly the spirit of all that he taught, was one whom they were unwilling to lose.

It took months of prayer and persuasion before they were convinced. What arguments he put before them, as he continued to be sure of God's intention for him, we can only guess. He could have reminded them of the interest which he had been led to take down the years in the activities of Wilfrid, Willibrord and others. He may have suggested that, the more settled England became as a Christian land, the more likely it was that the Lord would require some of its citizens to go further afield in the interests of the Gospel. Perhaps he asked Winbert and his fellow monks to consider the challenge which remained after the two Hewalds had been martyred. Was not a replacement needed for Suidbert, who in 713 had died at Kaiserswerth? Of more topical urgency were the additional difficulties facing Willibrord in Frisia since Duke Radbod had successfully rebelled against the Franks (714, after the death of Pippin of Heristal). Many Irishmen had been called abroad – there was a long list of them now, including Kilian, murdered at Würzburg in 689 during Wynfrith's boyhood; Northumbrians had followed. Was there not room for southern Englishmen, 'Saxons' rather than 'Angles', to add their contribution?

Little by little, resistance was worn down. By the spring of 716 the brethren were convinced. The venture was given positive support and generous blessing. Bishop Daniel of Winchester, who at first had been as reluctant as any, joined in the chorus of approval. After due thought and prayer it was arranged that a small number of companions should go with Wynfrith. Western Frisia was the destination in the first instance. It may be surmised from later events and attitudes that if the political situation there proved brighter than was feared, and continued to improve, the party was intended to assist Archbishop Willibrord for a while and then to seek his permission to go further. Eastern Frisia might be tackled next, and after that the Saxon tribes. If the situation in West Frisia deteriorated further, and especially if no effective contact was made with the Archbishop, it would be considered prudent to return to England until a more favourable opportunity might present itself. This was not cowardice, but a matter of orderliness for two different reasons. A mission needed to be undertaken within the framework of the existing life of the Church. Also, as Wynfrith had concluded after much pondering, there was a form of martyrdom which was a senseless waste: rather than be confronted by unfriendly authorities, or leaders too preoccupied to pay attention, it was better to bide one's time. Ideally, in Wynfrith's view, the Church could not exist in its fulness or to the best advantage unless it was constructively related to the 'secular' arm. It was better to wait, if necessary, until those in charge were prepared to help the Christian cause by the provision of land on which to build and farm. In May, 716, no one in England could tell whether the traveller to Europe would find the Frisian Duke Radbod in sole charge of West Frisia, whether the Franks under a younger leader would have regained control, or whether all would be in the melting-pot. The expedition from Nursling might become a mission in collaboration with Willibrord, sponsored by one authority or another (though Radbod was thought to have reverted to heathenism); or it might be no more than a reconnaissance.

There were possible ports of embarkation nearby. 'Hamwih' (and/or 'Hamtun') lay at or near to the place where Southampton later grew, and was already in use. Portchester, in use since Roman times, the point at which St Birinus had entered Wessex, was not much further away. But for those not accustomed to long sea journeys in the conditions which could easily arise in the English Channel, there was much to be said for going overland to London. Moreover that city, famous since Roman times and probably earlier, was the largest trading centre in the whole island. Conceivably Wynfrith had visited it on his way to or from Canterbury in 713. The little party, supplied with ample provisions and supported by much prayer, accordingly set off; and on arrival at 'Lundenwich' (as Wynfrith's biographer calls it) they found a ship of West Frisia waiting to set sail. With a favourable wind they had an uneventful journey. Sailing up the Lower Rhine they disembarked at Dorstett (Wijk-bij-Doorstede), which W. Levison has described as 'the principal place of sea traffic in Friesland before the Vikings'. They quickly found that the prospects were not good, but did not allow themselves to become alarmed. As a small group of men, speaking a language very similar to that of the locality, they did not attract hostile attention. If they were easily recognized as practising Christians because of their monastic 'habit', they were perhaps given a friendly warning by Dorstetters who were inwardly sympathetic. Radbod had control. Christian churches, including that at Utrecht which had served as Willibrord's cathedral, had been destroyed. Pagan cults had been re-instituted. The Archbishop had gone to his retreat at Echternach, 150 miles away, where the Christian Franks were in control. If Wynfrith wished to confront the Duke at Utrecht he would need to take great care.

The story of the four months which followed is a brilliant testimony to the calm, courage and conviction of Wynfrith and those with him. (The biographers mention only two, or possibly three, associates at this time). They proceeded to Utrecht, made certain that the Duke was there or expected shortly, waited 'a few days', no doubt in earnest prayer, and were granted an audience. Wynfrith made no headway with Radbod, but impressed the latter sufficiently to ensure that the party were not actively opposed, arrested or persecuted. They continued to tour the country 'to discover what possibility there might be of preaching the Gospel in the future'. They did not meanwhile forget their brothers at Nursling: the more so as it had become clear that they could not stay long in Frisia. Wynfrith was anxious about a young pupil, Nithard, who was subject to gross temptation and needed more than the usual guidance and support. Finding an opportunity to send a letter back to England, he chose to write to this young man, encouraging him from the Scriptures to avoid the luxury of this world and to 'walk in the light' (Jn. 12.35), and concluding: 'If God allows me to return home, for such is my intention, I promise to remain steadfast at your side.'

Not until late autumn did he return to England. There may have been one or two Frisian men, formerly baptized, possibly monks or 'novices', prevented from practising their faith openly at home, who asked or were easily persuaded to attach themselves to the party. So we might conclude from the wording of the earliest biography: 'taking several companions with him for the journey, he departed to his native land.'

On reflection he did not see the expedition of summer 716 as negative, or as a page to be torn out of his life. It was the beginning of his missionary career. Although he had not made contact with Archbishop Willibrord he had acted in spirit and intention as one who was working in and for the Catholic Church, just as if he had express authority of a kind which the consent of his home bishop and abbot could not by itself provide. Near the end of his life, in the year 752 (before his more serious doubts about an occupant of the papal chair set in), he could put it in writing that he had served the Apostolic See 'for thirty-six years', i.e. from 716. His experiences during his first visit to the Continent, though seemingly discouraging, led him to view the missionary calling more and more clearly as a permanent one, and in some sort of direct relation with the Roman See.

* * *

It is worthwhile to compare the missionary 'drive' of Wynfrith with that of Willibrord and, a century earlier, Columban the Irishman. All three may be said to have been drawn, consciously or unconsciously, along a path which retraced the steps of their ancestors, nearer or more remote.

Columbanus the Celt travelled (*c.* 590 A.D.) across what had been 'Gaul', settling first in the Vosges mountains at Luxeuil. Disturbed, he moved on eastward into further 'Gallic' regions, those we know as northern Switzerland. Disturbed again, and unable to go further east, he turned southward into what the Romans had anciently called 'Cis-Alpine Gaul', and founded the famous Bobbio monastery in Northern Italy, where he ended his days. Although the Celtic populations of all those areas had been long overrun by peoples of Teutonic stock, it can be said that Columban was attracted to that broad belt of the earth's surface within which his distant forbears had moved. Willibrord, a Northumbrian 'Angle', though at first glance concerned with Frisia alone as a mission field, is known to have made excursions further east which reveal an attraction towards 'Old Angel', the southern part of what we call Denmark. Once they tried to evangelise it directly, going by the off-shore islands including Heligoland. On two different occasions, in 704 and 717, he went to preach in Thuringia, whence he might have aimed at 'Old Angel' through Saxon country. For Wynfrith, a 'West Saxon', we may judge that the 'Old Saxons' were his main target, and that the Frisian approach was a part of his strategy. Frisia was the doorway to the Saxon tribes. The Frisians were closely akin to the English, and their dialect was the easiest for an Englishman to understand.

These observations are not to be regarded as integral to an understanding of Wynfrith's career, but as a suggestive comment on the lives of three great men.

Chapter 5

THE POPE'S MAN

Arriving safely back at Nursling before winter the travellers were 'joyfully received'. Wynfrith was struck with the decline that had begun to show itself in Abbot Winbert's health. This gave him deep concern, both on account of the affection and regard in which he held the old man, and also because he feared that if anything happened to the Abbot it would be on himself that the remainder of the community would be inclined to lean.

Little news of events in England or elsewhere had reached the party in Frisia. Now they learnt, with some anxiety for Wessex's neighbour to the North, that the young Ethelbald who had succeeded to the Mercian throne was an open womaniser. While politically Mercia was no friend to Wessex, churchmen cared for the Christian life of communities in a manner which took no account of boundaries. Wynfrith, fond of saying how much the welfare of the church depended on the political leaders, regarded an immoral king in any part of England as a canker in the whole nation in the broadest sense. Mercia did not suffer all at once; but in a long reign Ethelbald did much harm, until he received a stern rebuke, thirty years later, from none other than Wynfrith himself! There was happy news from further north. Iona, the island from which, through Oswald and Aidan, so much of English Christianity had sprung, had at last submitted, basically, to the Roman order. Another talking point was provided by the new occupant of the Roman See, Pope Gregory II. A scholarly man, Roman by birth, but conversant with Greek as well as Latin, Gregory shared with his namesake Pope Gregory I 'the Great' an active interest in the evangelistic task of the Church and in its strengthening where heathenism was creeping back. There were, possibly, vague rumours about his interest in the Germanic peoples. It was in this very year (716) that the Duke of Bavaria asked Gregory to send a legate to reform the Church there; but he died before the scheme could be fulfilled. Any hints of such events as these made Wynfrith listen attentively. Little could he know how closely he was to be involved, and how soon.

The death of Winbert made it impossible for Wynfrith to consider going abroad again in 717, even if political developments on the Continent made such a plan feasible. The monks wished to have him as their abbot, and at a meeting elected him with acclamation. But he steadily refused, agreeing only to act as their father until they and the Bishop could see their way to appoint a suitable man. Not till the year 718 was more than half gone by did Bishop Daniel solve the problem. Having, in spite of all his other duties, taken time and trouble to enter more fully into the life of the monastery for the time being, he had eventually observed a monk called Stephen and had convinced the others that God desired them to make him their abbot in order that Wynfrith might be released. Stephen was a man of sterling character, and Wynfrith was able to relinquish the burden of Nursling with a clear conscience. Twice was Wynfrith's life to be affected by a man called Stephen: in this first instance, with entire happiness. Thirty-five years later he would be profoundly disappointed in a pope of that name.

At this moment, in the late summer or autumn of 718, his confidence in the Roman see was implicit. He had resolved to go to Rome and gain authority from the highest quarter for his missionary endeavours, as Willibrord had done. Bishop Daniel had already given him letters, one (sealed) to the Pope himself and one to 'godly and merciful kings, all dukes, reverend and beloved bishops, presbyters and holy abbots and to all the spiritual sons of Christ', asking them to 'extend to the bearer of this letter, Wynfrith, a holy presbyter and servant of Almighty God, warm welcome such as God loves and enjoins'. It was a journey not only overseas but through several countries that the humble monk-presbyter was now to undertake, in the spirit of pilgrimage. Though his life on earth had yet more than thirty-five years to run, he was leaving his native land never to see it again, except conceivably from a cliff-top on the further side of the Dover Strait.

At the start of the journey it is just 'he' who is mentioned by the biographer, though it seems certain that a few from Nursling again went with him. London was once more the port of departure, and again he was able to embark 'immediately on a small, swift ship'. Soon with a north-westerly breeze they negotiated the Channel, and arrived at the favourite harbour of 'Cuentwick' at the mouth of the river Canche (near Etaples). Here 'they' disembarked: by now the biographer admits to a company. Since he goes on to say that they camped there and 'waited till the remainder of the party came together', it seems likely that Wynfrith collected 'disciples' on both sides of the Channel. On the further side these may have included men who had worked under Willibrord, who had gone 'underground', had met or heard about Wynfrith in 716, and had been waiting for his return to the Continent. For some the pilgrimage to Rome may have been a particular attraction, while others kept the missionary enterprise always uppermost in their minds.

While waiting at Cuentwick the pilgrims had opportunity to consider, and above all to pray. At that very spot was the shrine of Saint Jodoc, a holy man of Celtic origin. To the end of the Middle Ages the shrine was an object of reverence and of pilgrimage. The place was eventually called after the saint in a garbled way: 'St. Josse-sur-mer'. Wynfrith, not too happy with things Celtic, may have had to remind himself that a Celtic *man* could be respected in spite of his defective *customs*. After all, had not Wilfrid (a Romanist indeed!) reported that Willibrord traced his success to relics of Saint Oswald which he possessed; and Oswald, though not a Celt himself, maintained the Celtic order till the day of his death. Indeed, to worry about such differences was out of proportion, now that the whole of Christendom appeared threatened by the 'infidels': Arabs near the Pyrenees, Arabs at the Hellespont; with the Emperor at Constantinople unable to rule his territories in Italy, the Lombards thus encouraged to indulge in aggression and aggrandisement . . . Yes, one could and should pray at St. Jodoc's that a journey to Rome through Lombardy and 'imperial' territory might be safely accomplished. Indeed, throughout France (as we should call it) the party is said to have stopped many times 'to pray that by the help of Almighty God they might cross in safety the snowy peaks of the Alps, find greater kindness at the hands of the Lombards [*i.e.* than might have been expected; or by comparison with Duke Radbod of Frisia?], and escape with impunity from the hands of the undisciplined soldiery', namely the Byzantine troops that guarded the Exarchate of Ravenna!

Of their route from Cuentwick to Rome we are told little or nothing. The shortest way would have been through Amiens, Soissons, Troyes and Dijon to Geneva. From the eastern end of the Lake of Geneva they would surmount the Pennine Alps by way of the pass known later as the 'Great St. Bernard'. They could then follow the valley of the 'Dora Baltea' into the plain of Lombardy. As far as the great pass they were in territory governed by the Franks: as far as Troyes, in the old province of Neustria (the western part of the original Frankish kingdom), and beyond that, in Burgundy, which was practically another province of the kingdom. As passengers they did not seek contact with the authorities. On the other hand they were inevitably interested in the condition of church life under the Franks. Here and there, the unpleasant rumours which had reached England were proved true. Since the time when Agilbert the Frank, bishop of Wessex 640–652, had returned to his home-land to occupy the see of Paris, the Frankish church had declined. The monarchy had also declined. The 'mayors of the palace' of Neustria and Austrasia struggled for power. For these and other reasons discipline and standards were being forgotten. Bishops were known to occupy two sees at once, and grow fat on the revenues. Some spent their time on field sports; a few even fought in the army. Senior and junior clergy kept not only wives, but concubines too. Synods such as had been held to regulate church life had gone into disuse. Indeed, the 'metropolitan' or archbishop who should have convened such meetings in each 'province' was no longer recognized as such. Monasteries were corrupt. Churches and religious houses could 'belong' to local landlords, or to the royal authority, and be quite outside the jurisdiction of the ecclesiastical hierarchy. Wynfrith and his companions saw signs of all this and much more. It was not their purpose nor their place to try to alter such a state of affairs. They could only pray that God would find ways of putting matters right in Frank-land.

Having crossed the Alps successfully in spite of the onset of winter, the party may have had to pick and choose its route to Rome, in view of weather conditions in relation to altitude, and taking into account the attitudes and habits of the Lombards and later the Byzantine soldiery as they went along. It is sufficient to say that they reached Rome, and the tombs of the Apostles, without serious incident. They promptly gave heartfelt thanks to God for their safe arrival. Very soon they visited the great church of St. Peter, founded by the Emperor Constantine four centuries before. (He, too, had journeyed from Britain to Rome, to establish his authority as Roman emperor.) At St. Peter's they offered gifts.

After a few days Wynfrith was granted an audience with Pope Gregory. He handed over to the latter the sealed letter of personal commendation from Bishop Daniel, according to custom, and also the general letter which had been the party's credentials along its route. The Pope, once having met this remarkable monk of Wessex, was not inclined to let him go on his way in a hurry. Here was a man who could be more widely useful than as an additional member of Willibrord's team. There were other jobs waiting for such a vigorous, enterprising and sound churchman to tackle. So, for about five months on end, Wynfrith had the rare privilege of conversing with the Pope every day. Their meeting place was, presumably, the Lateran Palace, which at that period was the regular dwelling of the Roman bishop. The house on the Vatican Hill was in existence (built *c.* 500 A.D.) but was not preferred above the Lateran until many centuries later.

Wynfrith had given a good account of himself at the first meeting with Gregory. This may have something to do with the name by which the Pope wished him henceforward to be known, 'Boni-fatius'. The precise meaning is obscure, but 'an utterer of good' would be one rendering. ('Of good destiny' is a possibility, but less convincing on the whole). It is tempting to suppose that their first meeting took place on 29th December, 718, which was exactly the 300th anniversary of the election of Pope Bonifatius 1st, who in a short reign (418–22) had done much good and was therefore revered as a saint in Rome.

Gregory's purpose, more precisely, in developing his conversation so carefully with 'Boniface' (the English rendering) was to combine the latter's zeal with his own concern for various peoples in the 'German' region. Work under Willibrord was not discouraged; but neither was it the first responsibility (in time) with which 'Boniface' was charged. They came to a good understanding together. On May 15th, 719, the monk of Wessex was commissioned to go north and carry forward the work of Christ over a large area of Europe. May 15th was the day after the festival of another 'Bonifatius', martyred at Tarsus during the early persecutions, whose reputed relics were revered in a church in Rome, on the Aventine Hill.

Armed with detailed instructions relating to Bavaria and Thuringia, and having received more general exhortations in connection with his own chosen aims, Wynfrith-Boniface set out with those who were prepared to continue as his 'disciples'.

Provided with a letter of authority from Gregory, and with Daniel's open letter again in his hands, he set forth to learn the consequences of being 'the Pope's man'.

Chapter 6

FROM ROME TO THE RHINE

'In the company of his fellows', the number of whom is not disclosed, 'he retraced his steps towards the frontiers of Italy'. To what extent they travelled on foot, how far on horseback, our sources do not say. They must have had pack-animals to carry their boxes. There were chests containing relics of the saints. Some of these they had brought to Rome: others they had acquired during their visit. There were larger containers holding books. Clothing and provisions completed their baggage.

Pope Gregory and Boniface (as we shall now call him) had been able to come to a good working agreement although their immediate interests diverged. This was because both had a comprehensive view of the Gospel and the Church. It was also made easier by the fact that the way was not yet open, politically speaking, for Boniface to fulfil his own most cherished aim. There was a third factor which helped, namely that a tour of German areas such as Gregory had requested might result in the discovery of new routes leading to the conversion of the northern tribes. The letter which Boniface carried with him from the Pope declared that his missionary ambitions were much to be commended and supported, and that he was in every way suitable to such tasks. It placed his aspirations squarely within the setting of service to the Church 'under the authority of St. Peter'. The Pope was avowedly seeking 'to make use of your services in spreading the Gospel, which by the grace of God has been committed to our care.' The 'spread of the Gospel' was a concept which could cover everything from preaching to heathens at one end of the scale to the correction of faulty church practices and moral delinquency at the other. The best of the Catholic outlook, and of the Benedictine emphasis within it more particularly, was reflected in Gregory's words concerning the converting of pagans: ' . . . instil into their minds the teaching of the Old and New Testaments, doing this in a spirit of love and moderation'. There may be a deliberate rejection here of the severity of the 'Celtic' approach. A somewhat liberal estimate of who should be admitted to Church membership went along with a strict injunction about the liturgical provisions which Gregory expected to be followed wherever Boniface was able to influence the Church: ' . . . in admitting within the Church those who have some kind of belief in God you will insist upon using the sacramental discipline prescribed in the official ritual formulary of the Holy Apostolic See.' They did not put in writing any precise instruction about reporting back to Rome, except that this should be done when there was some obvious need, and according to opportunity. Yet in view of the various tasks which were laid upon Boniface it must have been assumed that he would send in some report in due course. While it is not impossible that verbal messages could be sent by the hand of reliable persons travelling to Rome, no written account of Boniface's doings was to reach Gregory until 722 so far as we can tell.

The first engagement which he fulfilled in his new role as 'the Pope's man' was at Pavia, the capital city of Lombardy. Pope Gregory and King Liutprand had achieved a fairly friendly relationship. This speaks well for both when it is considered that Rome did not in general favour a Lombard domination of Italy replacing the Byzantine one which was slowly losing its force. Boniface and his companions carried as far as Pavia, in addition to their own things, certain gifts from the Pope to the King. They had been encouraged to spend time there, nominally to refresh themselves before tackling the Alpine passes, but for more subtle underlying reasons. They did so, being well received and entertained by Liutprand. Boniface was showered with gifts and further provisions. (The friendly relationship between Rome and Pavia burgeoned in 727–8, when the Lombards won a great victory over the imperial forces and 'restored' to the Pope's ownership the Castle of Sutri, north of Rome. But the Apostolic See shrank from incorporation into a broader Lombard kingdom, for fear of becoming a mere provincial bishopric. The stronger but more distant Frankish power, with the Alps between, gave less cause for alarm and potentially in the long run more scope for friendship and support. This would become clear in Boniface's lifetime.)

After their break beside the River Ticino, the party of missionary pilgrims had to make its way to the Duchy of Bavaria. Boniface had no doubt received whatever facts could be passed on about the chaotic situation which had arisen there following the death of Duke Theodo and the collapse of the papal envoy's arrangements for reform. Of the three sons of Theodo who were competing for power, Theodebert sub-duke of Salzburg in the south-east appeared to have established himself also at the main capital, Regensburg, in the opposite corner; he was thought to be pushing outwards from the line thus established, to gain ascendancy over Grimoald centred on Freising (SW) and Tassilo at Passau (NE). These were the four cities that Theodo had hoped to form into Catholic bishoprics. While we have no details of the reconnaissance made by Boniface, it is convenient to suppose that he skirted round the sides of the 'square', starting with Salzburg where the strongest of the brothers had his headquarters.

So we envisage the pilgrim party making its way eastward along the Lombard plain and turning northward up the valley of the Etsch (Adige) and so into the Brenner Pass. Just conceivably they had contact on their way with the monastic bishop Corbinian from Freising, with whom Grimoald had quarrelled, and who spent his last years on the Italian side of the border, at Mais-bei-Meran. The pass, by mid-June, presented no special difficulty to stalwart travellers. Boundary disputes between Lombardy and Bavaria were frequent; but possibly the internal situation in Bavaria meant that external and borderland affairs were left to themselves. The party had no trouble in reaching the Inn valley, nor in proceeding down-river and then further eastward to Salzburg. Here they were not far from the eastern limit of the Teutonic tribes, beyond which lay the Slavs and Avars. One or two Christian missionaries (St. Amand for one) had crossed that boundary, with no success. Anglo-Saxons felt no call to speak to peoples so utterly different from themselves, even in the name of Christ and knowing well his command to take the Gospel to all the nations. Nor had the Pope suggested any such thing.

Salzburg, to the ancient Romans 'Juvavum', had provided salt from early times and had been renamed by the Bavarians 'City of Salt'. There were signs of Christian life there. A Frankish bishop, Hrodbert (St. Rupert) of Irish or Celtic style, had done good work over ten or fifteen years, dying in 715. It may have been the gap left by his death which finally decided Duke

Theodo to send to Rome for help in 716. The difficulty with the Celtic system lay partly in its dependence on charismatic figures who were hard to replace. Such had been Hrodbert's charisma that he had exercised an influence over the whole of Bavaria, including Regensburg. Clear boundaries between 'dioceses' were unknown, or at least not characteristic under Celtic customs; although Hrodbert had worked in a diocese earlier, namely at Worms on the Rhine. There is a tradition that 'Saint Rupert' when at Salzburg encouraged the revival of salt-mining.

Twenty years were to elapse before the Roman plan could be fulfilled in Bavaria. During that time at least two further Celtic-type bishops worked at Salzburg, Vitalis and Flobrigis (Latinised forms); and probably a third, Liuti, whom Boniface at a later stage in his career would find it necessary to replace by a more 'catholic-minded' man.

If due opportunity arose to speak with Theodebert, we may be sure that Boniface took advantage of it. There is no positive evidence that he met any of the three brothers, but it would have been characteristic of him to have tried to do so.

We now picture the group moving down the River Salzach ('salt-stream' to the Bavarians: 'Juvavus' to the Romans of old), re-joining the Inn and following it to its confluence with the mighty Danube. They thus kept the Slavic border a safe distance away on their right hand. Under Slav control now, down the Danube, was Lorch, which had known a monastery and perhaps an episcopal see earlier on. Passau, where the Inn joined the Danube, was a city designated (*i.e.* in 716 under Theodo's plan) for a bishopric in that quarter of the Bavarian domain. Passau had many advantages, not least its beautiful situation. Though Boniface may not have known, there was a link here with Frisia and his own visit there. 'Passau' was derived from 'Batava Castra', because the Romans had a force stationed there from the Low Countries. Dorstett, where Boniface had first set foot on continental soil, was in Roman times 'Batavodurum', the chief town of the Batavian tribe. Passau's Christian history is less clear than that of Salzburg. 'Erchanfrid' and 'Otkar' are names which appear and disappear in the seventh century. Boniface may have found little there, but agreed as to its suitability. As things turned out, it was to progress by two stages towards the pattern which Boniface and the Pope approved. Duke Hugobert (725–735) founded a church dedicated to St. Stephen, probably a monastic church including a Celtic-type bishop. His successor returned to the opinions of Theodo, and had a certain Vivilo consecrated at Rome, to serve at and from Passau, shortly before the 716 plan was put into practice in its entirety.

Travelling up the Danube from this delightful spot, with or without having met Tassilo, Boniface found little difficulty in covering the seventy miles or so to Regensburg. (The distances between the four cities were broadly similar). The Slavic boundary was still not far to the right. This capital city of the dukedom was named after the River Regen which joins the Danube there. It may be purely coincidental that the old Latin forms 'Reginum' and 'Regina Castra' savour of royalty! There was a primitive (early Celtic) designation which persisted in competition with 'Regensburg' and has come down to us in the form 'Ratisbon'. The Agilolfing dukes had, by making it their capital, given the city an almost royal status. As the city now most coveted by three competing Agilolfing brothers, it may have been under too much stress for the visitors to gain a balanced impression. There had been a strong Christian presence there in the previous century, when a Gallo-Frankish missionary called Haimhramm ('St. Emmeram') had been taken into service by the duke of the time: it had been his intention to convert the Avars, but he was restrained from leaving Bavaria. 'Celtic-type' monastic bishops such as Rathar and Erhard had been more recently in Regensburg, maybe the latter at this very time of 719. Another, Wikterp, would be there later, eventually to suffer deposition for refusing to submit to reform.

The journey to Freising took Boniface's party south-by-west, a direction directly opposite to that from Salzburg to Passau: but the road was flatter and more direct. Here was Grimoald's provincial centre. Whether Freising had an early history like the other three is not certain. The name is Germanic, and may be connected with a Teutonic deity, Frey. Its Christian history was similar to that of Salzburg or Regensburg, save that the bishop who became 'founder-figure' (cf. St. Rupert, St. Emmeram) was still living, and also, having had Roman consecration, would have fitted into a plan of reform. That was Corbinian, now in exile over the Lombard border. Corbinian had condemned Grimoald for marrying the widow of his deceased brother Theodoald. He died before Grimoald fell from power (725); otherwise he might have returned to Freising.

Dating from before Corbinian's arrival (716) were two Christian places of worship built under Celtic influences: the ducal chapel of St. Mary, and St. Stephen's Church. Corbinian had added St. Martin's oratory, with ducal support, before the quarrel. We must suppose that church life was in confusion when Boniface visited Freising. But in any case, from a geographical and political point of view, and also by virtue of recent history, it was evidently suitable to become the fourth in the ring of 'sees' envisaged under the Roman plan.

Westward from Bavaria lay a great Germanic area, north and south of the upper Danube and straddling also the upper Rhine, known as 'Alamannia', a name reflected in the modern French 'Allemagne' and the middle English 'Almayn'. One puzzling feature of Boniface's career is the lack of really firm evidence that he included this region in his journeys. One of his several biographers does include the word 'Alamannians' at this stage. The earliest biographer has the phrase 'the Bavarians and their German neighbours'. Possibly there were political factors, such as the process by which Alamannia was being brought under Frankish suzerainty, which made it tactless or unprofitable to visit those parts. There were episcopal 'sees' round the border: Augsburg, Chur, Constance, Basel, Strasbourg, Speyer. How far the inner territory had been Christianised is highly questionable. At a later stage we can see a more particular reason for caution, namely the presence of another powerful missionary figure (Pirmin) on the Alamannian scene. But in 719 the omission is not readily explicable. We do not know whether Boniface even turned aside to visit Augsburg, a famous place since Roman times.

In any case, from a personal point of view the pull for Boniface was northward. If he left *via* the Bavarian province of Nordgau, a small district jutting out north-westwards, he is likely to have passed through Eichstätt, a place with which he would later form strong connections more lasting (as it turned out) than his links with Bavaria proper. From Eichstätt he may have proceeded due north to Nuremberg, at that time no more than a village. Following the River Pegnitz downstream to its confluence with the Main, he came to the border of the Thuringian region. Exactly what Pope Gregory had required of him here can only be surmised circumstantially. What he found when he arrived caused him to return later and make it his chief concern, along with areas immediately to the west and south-west.

The Thuringians were an ancient people who had extended their sphere of influence southwards to the Danube in a kind of empire, until heavily defeated by the Franks around 530. That event was stirring enough to inspire the hymn-writer Venantius Fortunatus at Poitiers to write, years later, an elegy entitled 'The Overthrow of Thuringia' (*De Excidio Thuringiae*, *c.* 575). The reduced territory had since been governed by local lords appointed by the Franks and often of Frankish stock. Meanwhile something grand still hung about the name. Christianity had found its way in with the Franks, somewhat haphazardly. Even the bolder missionaries seem not to have worked consistently in the region until the Irishman, Kilian, made Würzburg his headquarters. Active hostility from the Saxon tribes to the north against the Franks, whom they hated, made Thuringia proper and Hesse to the west of it an uncomfortable and uninviting area. Willibrord, as we have already seen, had regarded it as a suitable object of further mission. He had been greatly helped by one of the most powerful local leaders, Heden, who supported the evangelistic campaigns of 704 and 717 with material help. In the two years which had elapsed since 717, however, Heden had lost much of his enthusiasm. Renewed threats from Saxon tribes were tending to give prominence to those leaders who were prepared to compromise with heathenism. It may have been news of backslidings which had led Pope Gregory to ask Boniface to make a careful survey of Thuringia.

The scanty information we possess leads us to suppose that no actual opposition was met by Boniface and his companions in Thuringia. Although they saw much which displeased and shocked them, they found evidence of abundant opportunity for the future development of the Christian cause. There were congregations who were eager to hear Boniface preach. There were 'elders' of these churches who, along with the lay rulers, were ready to be exhorted and reminded of 'the true way'. There was some sort of sacramental ministry here and there; but a fair number of ordained ministers had been 'contaminated and polluted' by heathen standards. The general picture, touchingly painted by Boniface's earliest biographer, describes him as like a 'busy bee' which 'picks its way among a thousand sweet-smelling flowers' and discriminates between 'bitter and poisonous juices' to be ignored, and 'the secret hoards of honey-bearing nectar' to be drawn out.

While in Thuringia he was doubtless constantly aware of its importance in relation to his preferred calling, namely as a missionary to the heathen tribes most akin to his own people; the 'Old Saxons'. He will have seen, however, that until a properly organised church could be brought into being in the border-lands, it was fruitless to tackle those whose pagan obstinacy was hardened by their enmity towards the Franks. There was a strange choice to be faced here: it was only the Franks who were in a position to back the creation of an organised church. From this near-dilemma Boniface was freed by news that West Frisia, where (ironically enough) the Franks had regained control, had reopened the door for Willibrord, and made possible (or at least conceivable) an eastward missionary thrust before long.

His humility, as well as his strong sense of church order, prompted Boniface to join Willibrord at this stage. He had heard and seen enough to feel that there was much to be learnt about the art of church growth, and that Willibrord was one from whom he could and should be learning it. As a mere presbyter without any other bishop (except the Pope) to whom he was responsible, it seemed only right that he should go and join himself to the elderly Northumbrian. Conceivably he wished also to have help in forming an estimate of all that he had seen since leaving Rome in May, in order to prepare an adequate report for the Pope.

Travelling westwards and southwards through Hesse and the Lahngau, he moved out of what could be called 'New Frankland' into the older part of the eastern half-kingdom (Austrasia). Taking his companions with him as always, he went on down the Rhine. The Frisian scene was still chaotic. Willibrord had not re-established himself at Utrecht when Boniface arrived. The Frankish Duke (*i.e.* Mayor) Charles, 'The Hammer' (Martel) as he would later be called, had put himself firmly in charge of the whole Frankish realm, but could not restore order everywhere at once. It was the death of Duke Radbod, not merely the rise of Charles, which had altered things in Frisia. At this moment everything was open and undecided. The boundary down the middle of Frisia had not reappeared. There are signs that, while waiting for Willibrord, Boniface sailed upstream from Utrecht and then conducted a successful campaign northwards in 'districts that had hitherto been untouched by the preaching of the Gospel'. Since Charles did not successfully establish his boundaries beyond those of his father Pippin, there was no follow-up to this campaign. When Willibrord was known to have arrived, the monk of Wessex duly and promptly put himself and the others at his disposal.*

There followed a strenuous period of two years and more, during which the Archbishop, now over sixty years old, was more than glad to have the assistance of such a keen and gifted man still under forty and other younger men. They busied themselves with the total reconstruction of church life in Western Frisia. Boniface had plenty of scope for preaching, since the people had reverted to paganism almost completely. There was everything to do. The report to Rome remained unwritten. It was a good apprenticeship.

* If Willibrord and Boniface were together by October, 719, they could have joined in a commemoration of Wilfrid, whose death had taken place ten years before.

Chapter 7

APOSTOLIC BISHOP

Willibrord (also known as 'Clement'), could clearly see in Boniface of man of similar type and destiny to his own; though he may have suspected that his ideals were a little too tidily conceived and rigidly held. Both were missionary pilgrims who had chosen to seek their authority from Rome. Both had been given a fresh name by a pope, even if there were differences: the younger man had been renamed on his first visit, and it was by this name that he was now widely known, whereas Willibrord had been entitled 'Clement' at a later stage, when Pope Sergius gave him the 'pallium'. (This was the Y-shaped stole applying to the rank of archbishop or 'metropolitan' as recognised at Rome). The name 'Clement' had never been generally accepted however. The two would go down in history as 'Willibrord' and 'Boniface'.

Boniface, for his part, while not (so far as we can tell) lacking in affection and respect for his superior, was silently critical of the general organisation and of Willibrord's policies in certain respects. He was prepared to allow that a missionary leader might, exceptionally, be made a metropolitan bishop in *rank* even before he had other bishops organised as a 'province' who could regularly gather for consultation in 'synod'. It was irregular, but if a pope had arranged it, well and good. More questionable, in his estimation, was the Northumbrian's easy relationship with Frankish leaders civil and ecclesiastical, some of whose standards, both morally and in terms of church life, were deplorable. Willibrord might claim that such compromise had been necessary, for example, in order that he might hold on to his precious monastery at Echternach, which had turned out to be essential to his survival during the period of Frisian revolt. Boniface, who recognised clearly enough the need for co-operation with the lay authorities, hoped that he would never have to stoop to such measures. There was also a suspicion that the archbishop had been 'minimising' his connection with Rome in the same interest, in view of the longstanding habit in Gallo-Frankish circles of practically ignoring the Apostolic See.

Such thoughts did not impair his loyalty. He worked unremittingly under difficult conditions. It would take years for Duke Charles to put things straight. Heathen shrines set up by Radbod had to be eliminated, and it was not always possible immediately to complete the founding and building of Christian places of worship. Although eastern Frisia was beyond his reach, much of the work elsewhere was little different from preaching to those who had never yet heard the Gospel. In letters home he must have spoken in terms of 'converts'. Abbess Eadburga of Thanet (a daughter of King Centwine of Wessex) wrote to him giving thanks that God had inspired the Pope to support him, had 'humbled' Radbod, and had encouraged Boniface in a dream to expect a 'harvest' of souls. Her letter includes, significantly, an apology for having failed as yet to procure him a copy of 'The Sufferings of the Martyrs', and mentions gifts which she is sending, namely an altar cloth and fifty gold or silver coins (*solidi*: 'shillings'). He may well have 'reaped' in abundance, and not only in those places which are particularly linked with his name. These lay westwards and north-westwards from Utrecht: Woerden, Achtienhoven and Velsen. (Amsterdam was then no more than a small fishing village.)

A crisis came when Willibrord asked Boniface, now aged forty-one, to accept episcopal orders. Perhaps because of considerations already mentioned, he declined. It is somewhat fascinating that his first rejoinder to Willibrord's suggestion was to the effect that he was not yet fifty years old. Some have doubted the truth of this detail, since those early church 'canons' which reserved the episcopate normally to men over fifty had long been suspended. Willibrord himself had been consecrated at the age of thirty seven. We may choose to take Boniface's remark as a quaint expression of that humility which was characteristic of him. Conceivably he had a *private opinion* that the Church would benefit if the early canons had been adhered to: if so, this incident witnesses to a Boniface who was 'his own man' (or more simply God's) alongside the one who was 'Willibrord's man' and the one who was 'the Pope's man'. The balancing of loyalties was a more subtle matter than he had hitherto realised. The second reason which he gave for refusing the archbishop's offer reflected, in fact, a conflict at that moment between two loyalties. He pleaded that the Pope had given him a wider field than Frisia alone, and that his duties elsewhere now needed attention. His earliest biographer envisages him saying that he had come to serve under Willibrord 'without the knowledge of' the Pope. The Pope had not *directed* him to the Frisian scene; but there had been this period of two years during which service to Willibrord had been the proper expression of loyalty to the Apostolic See. Boniface is also supposed to have said that, because of his direct connection with the Pope, he could not agree to be raised to the episcopate without an express command from the latter. He then asked to be released to go back to an area where Pope Gregory had specifically asked him to operate, as though he had a solemn promise yet to fulfil by so doing. On this last ground the archbishop 'gave him his blessing and granted him his permission to depart'. We may be inclined to suspect that, at the level of the subconscious, his independent self was at least as active as 'the Pope's man' or more so, in seeking this freedom. But he worked within the constitution, trying to hold all his loyalties together in one: as witness the fact that he did not feel at liberty to leave the Frisian field until his superior had been persuaded that it was right.

What amount of time, if any, had been spent by Boniface at the Echternach monastery it is impossible to say. A 'planning session' at the beginning of the period under Willibrord can well be imagined. A diversion once or twice from pastoral and missionary work in order that Boniface's teaching gifts and experience might benefit the community at Echternach, while he himself benefited from the change; such speculations are not entirely hypothetical. There is an anecdote about his journey back to the German territories, which shows that it was at Echternach that he took leave of Willibrord, rather than at Utrecht. It reveals that he had contacts with at least one other monastery at the southern end of Willibrord's sphere of interest, or just outside it. It is related that he called at the monastery of Pfalzel, beyond Trier, and observed a young monk failing to translate into his own Frankish tongue a passage from the Scriptures (*i.e.* the Latin Bible). At once Boniface gave the lad the correct rendering. It thus appears that, amid a host of urgent duties, he had in a few years perfected his knowledge of the speech used by the Franks. Clearly he expected the Frankish domination to grow rather than lessen. In later years his linguistic achievement proved to be of even greater service than he could have envisaged at this time.

The conclusion of the anecdote is touching. This young monk of noble birth, Gregory by name and no more than fifteen years old, a nephew of the foundress of Pfalzel, rose promptly from his desk, declaring that he would be Boniface's disciple from then onward. As suddenly as some of the Apostles had gone after Jesus, he 'followed him in the way', joining the party forthwith. Other men had been impressed, such as Gemberht or 'Gebbo' at Achtienhaven. We do not know that any apart from young Gregory the Frank accompanied Boniface out of Willibrord's sphere of action; but there is a tradition that some Frisians came to visit him later in his German mission-field. Just possibly Bynna (see below) was a Northumbrian who had started with Willibrord but now joined up with Boniface. (cf. the place-name element BIN- in the north of England and north Midlands).

Boniface again felt drawn towards the Saxon border. He was once more a free agent responsible only to God and the Pope. Perhaps because of his final words with Willibrord about priorities, he was conscious in a fresh way that he owed a report to Pope Gregory. But for the purposes of such a report he would wish to offer a plan of church extension in the Saxon marches, to put alongside what he had to say about Bavaria and Frisia. His sense of order being by this time stronger than ever, he could envisage two possibilities. The Frankish bishop of Mainz might be asked to oversee a missionary extension of his diocesan responsibilities north-eastward: indeed, this may have been the theoretical position already in regard to the Lahn valley and beyond, or if not, Boniface, as a mere presbyter but also a monk (and in 717–8 an acting abbot), would have to initiate a movement of Christian advance based on one or more monastic centres. The prospects of co-operation from Mainz may have looked poor in any case. For, if Boniface's experiences of Trier had led him to see Bishop Liutwin as altogether too easy-going, Mainz was developing a still more unsatisfactory reputation from a strict churchman's point of view. If Bishop Gerold was already in office in Mainz in 722, he promised to be more interested in military adventure than missionary endeavours. If Boniface on this occasion travelled via Mainz, his worst opinions were confirmed. If he already knew that it was not worth calling there, he could with greater advantage proceed down the Moselle, then up the Lahn; for these rivers joined the Rhine only a few miles apart, at or near Coblenz ('the confluences'), an ancient strategic and commercial centre.

We assume that the worst of winter was over. As Boniface's party travelled towards the regions of the German winter, that hard season was giving place to spring. Their object, now, was to find the right place for their first monastic house. They doubtless desired a beautiful spot; but other considerations had to come first. The headquarters of their mission must be near enough to the Rhineland to be under the effective surveillance of the Frankish administration, but far enough to avoid an obvious clash with the ecclesiastical authorities at Mainz. It could be built only where either local or Frankish overseers, or both together, were prepared to provide a site and endow the place with lands or other means for subsistence. These conditions were quite soon fulfilled, but only after a dramatic prelude. Arriving at a point seventy-five miles up the Lahn valley, on the little River Ohm, the missionary pilgrims found an example of heathenism being practised by nominal Christians. The pressure of Saxon influence, which was affecting Hesse seriously, had been felt on the near side of the Hesse boundary, here at the north-east corner of the 'Lahngau'. Two brothers, Dittich and Deurolf, both baptized, were leading the people astray. Experience over the last two years in Frisia enabled Boniface to convince these two of the error of their ways. Brought round to his side, they quickly gave him what he wanted. There and then, at the place called Amöneburg, they began to build a small monastery, on the scale that Boniface had known in his youth at Exeter. From Amöneburg he and his companions could go out and preach and restore Christian practice wherever it had lapsed, in the whole area. At Amöneburg a place of worship was built which served both monks and people. Round about in the countryside, after the pattern of his earliest memories, Boniface had 'preaching crosses' set up until churches could be built.

Before long there was an encouraging response. Baptisms, along with recantations from backsliders, rose into the thousands over a wide area of Hesse. But nothing was easy. He could foresee the heathen tribes to the north reacting, possibly by raids and incursions; while at the end of the Lahngau where his base lay, the Frankish presence was none too strong (it was even weaker in Hesse and Thuringia). In spite of the likely adverse effect on evangelism among the Saxons, he needed a stronger backing from the Frankish authorities, a degree of support such as no merely local leader could provide.

It may have been this thought, among others, which led him at last to write to Rome. His messenger was Bynna (see p. 58). The letter, the text of which has not been preserved, is said to have summarized 'all the matters which by God's grace had been accomplished', and to have sought 'guidance on certain questions concerning the day-to-day needs of the Church and the progress of the people'. The Pope detained Bynna for 'some days' and no longer. He very much wanted to hear more about the Bavarian reconnaissance than had appeared in the letter. He desired to know the reasons for Boniface's having left the 'German' areas for Frisia and for his returning again into eastern Austrasia. He could see that the time had come to put the latter on to a better basis in terms of church order. He knew that this in its turn would require the active sympathy of the Frankish administration at the highest level. For all these reasons he sent Bynna back quickly to his master, summoning the latter to Rome without delay.

Nothing is said of the route taken by Bynna in either direction. Boniface, on receipt of the Pope's message, prepared at once to travel to Rome by a westerly route. It was late summer. He had seen Duke Charles' army marching eastward to Thuringia on an expedition against the 'Ostphalians' or eastern Saxon tribes, and the troops had not yet returned. He took with him 'a number of his brethren' and also 'a large retinue'. His courage was by now tempered with prudence on behalf of his colleagues. Perhaps he had seen for himself that Englishmen were not popular elsewhere in the Frankish domains. Through Frank-land and Burgundy they went. The way up the Moselle was familiar. Did they then join Boniface's original route over the Great Saint Bernard Pass, or did they, out of interest, or perhaps to avoid Pavia where Liutprand might wish to entertain them and cause delay, go southward up the Saône and make for Turin across the passes of the Savoy? In either case they 'descended through the marches of Italy (*sc* Lombardy) and the territory held by the soldiers (*sc* Byzantine Exarchate)'. Experience, again, may have taught Boniface that there was strength in numbers when travelling through those unpredictable areas, whether or not they carried arms (and it is unlikely that any of them did so, on his orders).

In Rome they went straight to St. Peter's, where thanksgiving was followed by lengthy and earnest prayer on the part of Boniface himself. A message was sent to the Pope, who arranged for them to be 'welcomed with great kindness and conducted to the pilgrims' lodge'. Gregory appointed a meeting between the two of them alone, in the precincts of St. Peter's. Somewhat to his surprise, Boniface found himself questioned not so much on his doings over three and a half years, as over the teaching which he was accustomed to give, his understanding of the creed and of Christian tradition in general. The significance of the interview was not hard to perceive. He who had refused the episcopate at Willibrord's hands was now being examined in preparation for that very office, and that by one from whom alone (as he had said to Willibrord) he would consent to receive it. Knowing that it was usual for a candidate to give a written statement of faith, he made excuse to be allowed time to put his thoughts in order and submit them in writing. It has been suggested that there was some slight difficulty in conversation, if the pronunciation of Latin differed as between England and Italy. (We do not hear of such an impediment at other times.)

A few days later he delivered his statement. After a period of waiting he was summoned to the Lateran palace. It was immediately evident that his affirmations had been accepted. He followed custom by prostrating himself before the Pope. But it was not merely protocol. The heart of this essentially modest monk was overwhelmed. At Gregory's feet he implored a blessing; for he would need all the grace that he could find. The Pope raised him from the ground, handed back the document, commended it as containing 'pure and uncontaminated truth', and invited him to sit at his side. They spent almost the whole day in conversation. After duly exhorting Boniface to maintain and uphold that which he had so clearly expressed, Gregory entered upon a general exchange of views. At the end of it all, when Boniface had gone over the whole position as far as the time allowed, the Pope formally declared his intention to raise him to the rank of bishop, for the sake of that 'vast number' of newly baptized and restored Christians who otherwise 'were, in the words of our Lord, languishing as sheep without a shepherd'. It seems likely that further discussion was contemplated, and that time was left for this before the date fixed for Boniface's consecration, namely, November 30th. St. Andrew's Day was an ideal occasion for the making of a 'missionary bishop'.

The man of Wessex, so deeply attached from an early age to the Roman allegiance, could look forward to becoming an 'apostolic bishop' in more senses than one. 'Apostolic' meant 'missionary': but also under God he would have his authority as an overseer of churches direct from the Apostolic See.

Chapter 8

HEATHENDOM IN RETREAT

'Bishop Boniface' he was to become. His more recent personal name would be doubly official after his consecration. 'Wynfrith' thereafter would be written only occasionally in his letters to England: 'Boniface, who is also Wynfrith'. He was now indeed to be entitled 'bishop', yet not quite an ordinary bishop. A bishop should have a clearly defined diocese, but he would not have one. A diocesan bishop should be answerable (among others like himself in a 'province') to an archbishop, who in turn should be responsible to the Pope. He, Boniface, would be answerable direct to the Pope, belonging to no 'province'. Frankish bishops no longer had any provinces; but they declined to be responsible to Rome. The only other style of bishop was the 'country-bishop', rarely found in the West. This 'chor-episcopus' (from the Greek word) was like a suffragan-bishop in the modern Anglican sense, assisting the diocesan bishop and under his authority. (Willibrord is said to have had one before or after Boniface worked with him; and Boniface would have been in that position, had he consented.) The humble man of Wessex certainly did not think of himself as competing with Augustine of Canterbury, who had been raised from abbot to archbishop all at once and told to carve himself a province and appoint bishops to dioceses within it. Nor did he expect to be treated like Willibrord, who also had been exalted from presbyter-monk direct to archiepiscopal rank: but Willibrord, whether as bishop or archbishop, had been allotted a fairly well-defined geographical area of ministration. Boniface, with all his tidy ideals of church order, was now about to receive a unique roving commission as a 'bishop without boundaries', one whose territory was only delimited where other recognized dioceses impinged upon it. In the case of Mainz, virtually the only neighbour with whom the issue arose, that limit had probably never been defined. He had to accept that affairs in this life were not as tidy as could be desired. He must treasure the privilege and exercise the unusual responsibility that was being thrust upon him, losing his questionings in the confidence that Pope Gregory knew what he was doing in appointing him thus.

Gregory for his part treated the case as one in parallel with those bishoprics which existed around Rome itself. The wording of the oath which was prepared, which Boniface wrote out (Ep. 16) and swore at his consecration, was much like that of a 'suburbicarian' bishop. Its wording is of interest for several reasons:–

> 'In the name of God and our Saviour Jesus Christ. In the 6th year of Leo, by the grace of God crowned Emperor . . . I, Boniface, by the grace of God promise to you, blessed Peter, chief of the Apostles, and to your Vicar the blessed Pope Gregory, and to his successors, in the name of the indivisible Trinity, Father, Son and Holy Spirit, and on your most sacred body, that I will uphold the faith and purity of holy Catholic teaching and will perservere in the unity of that same faith. . . .
>
> I will not agree to anything which is opposed to the unity of the Universal Church, no matter who may try to persuade me, but in all things I will show . . . complete loyalty to you and to the welfare of your Church on which, in the person of your Vicar and his successors, the power to bind and loose has been conferred.
>
> Should it come to my notice that some bishops deviate . . . I will have no part nor lot with them, but so far as in me lies, will correct them, or . . . report the matter to the Holy See.
>
> And if (which God forbid) I should be led astray . . . may I be found guilty at the last Judgement. . . .
>
> This text I, Boniface, a lowly Bishop, have written with my own hand and placed over your sacred body. I have taken this oath, as prescribed, in the presence of God, my witness and my judge: I pledge myself to keep it.'

First, the document was dated, as customary from the days of Constantine the Great, by reference to the Emperor's reign: yet the equally customary words of loyalty to the Emperor were omitted. Pope Gregory had passed a milestone in the history of relations between the Western Church and Constantinople. The Emperor was by 722 too remote a figure to command loyalty from Western bishops. Boniface was in due course to help to fill the gap thus left.

Secondly, and quite usually for that period, the oath was addressed in the first instance to St. Peter, and its solemnity was emphasized by its being laid over the tomb of that apostle. Whatever our views may be about that in general, in the study of Boniface's life and outlook its significance lies in his strong sense of the *localisation* of the Papacy at the place of St. Peter's tomb. Later it appears that, even if Boniface could have envisaged a Pope leaving Rome for some universal synod (as one was to do in a later generation, before the end of the eighth century), he had doubts about the propriety of one going to another country for lesser reasons, for example the temporal and material security of the Roman See.

Thirdly, as a matter of purely general interest, it is noteworthy that the Pope was seen as Vicar of St. Peter but not yet precisely as Vicar of Christ. (This does link with the former point.)

Fourthly, Boniface took very seriously indeed his promise not to associate with bishops who wandered away from right teaching and conduct. He was to have much heart-searching on this account in later years.

On the great day itself the Pope presented Boniface with a copy of a book which summed up the ecclesiastical laws or 'canons' as his necessary aid in putting his consecration oath into practice. Afterwards he armed him with several letters of commendation. The most important was to Duke Charles (Ep. 20), as effectually governor of the whole Frankish realm. Gregory addressed him (surely with inward reservations) as 'beloved son in Christ', 'a man of deeply religious feeling'. Charles was informed of Boniface's new dignity, and given official cognizance of his mission 'to preach the faith to the peoples of Germany who dwell on the east bank of the Rhine'. The Duke was exhorted to 'help him in all his needs and to grant him your constant protection'.

The second commendatory letter was to civil and religious leaders (Ep. 17), namely dukes and counts, bishops, and other lower dignitaries along with 'all Christians of Germany'. (The Pope was hoping, it seems, that such *bishops* as were serving in 'Germany', none of whom had been the kind of men to care much for the See of Rome, might be persuaded to a better point of view.*) Leaders and people were to 'support' Boniface,

* According to another opinion, Willibrord may have appointed 'country bishops' on his visits to Thuringia.

'receive him in the name of Jesus Christ' and to 'see that he has all that he requires.' They were to 'give him companions', too.

Thirdly, Gregory had written to five particular (named) leaders of the Thuringian area (Ep. 19), whom he addressed as his 'distinguished sons'. These were a few, out of all the local lords of that region, whom Boniface (in 719, presumably) had observed as having 'loyalty to Christ' while others had tended to revert to paganism. The Pope's requests to them were, to look to the Apostolic See for guidance and encouragement, and to co-operate with Boniface as representative of that See.

The fourth and last letter was addressed to 'the clergy and people' (Ep. 18), presumably of Thuringia and of other areas without effective episcopal oversight. It gave some particulars of the manner in which Boniface was to carry out his functions, and told those concerned to obey him implicitly in all things approved by Roman standards. The letter contains an interesting list of qualifications for the ordained ministry. Some of the prohibited categories are reasonable: criminals, men seriously in debt, those who suffer from a physical disability (such as to impair their ministry or offend others), those who are lacking in education and knowledge. Other prohibitions sound narrow to modern ears. Granted that in any case a man could not be ordained (in the Roman view) while living in the married state, it may be thought severe that beyond that, no man might be considered for ordination if he had been twice married, or if his one wife had been a widow when she married him. Still more strange at first sight is the injunction that no African was to be allowed to enter the ranks of the clergy. We have to remember, however, that the African churches were in disgrace for having been so weak and confused in their Christianity that Islam had conquered all the way from Alexandria to the Atlas Mountains. We have to suppose that a considerable number of Africans had wandered into Europe, or come by sea, as refugees. There was no suggestion of a 'colour bar' as such, at least not overtly. Pope Gregory regarded them somewhat indiscriminately as heretics, and gave two examples of their aberrations: some were dualists, despising the human body and the material world (Manicheans); others had so little grasp of what it meant to become Christian that they had been baptized over and over again.

Armed with the four papal letters, and bearing all these cautions in mind, Boniface started on his return journey. Winter was even nearer than it had been when he had first travelled over the Alps just over four years earlier. His first duty was to deliver the Pope's letter to Duke Charles, at whichever of the Frankish royal palaces he was to be found. We do not know where in fact their meeting took place. The pilgrim party under their newly-made bishop may have had to try several places in the older parts of Neustria and Austrasia (western and eastern Frankland) before catching up with the Duke. As to their route, the biographers give rather vague information: Boniface 'passed by devious ways through the densely populated territories of the Franks'. Assuming that they had decided not to attempt the passes of the Alps, those words may mean that Boniface took his companions round the coast nearly as far as the Rhone delta, namely to Marseilles. Then, bearing in mind the Arab occupation of 'Septimania' immediately west of the delta, they turned northwards through Arles and Avignon to Valence; across to Le Puy; via Clermont and Bourges to Tours; to the right and through Orleans to Paris. Either at Paris, St. Denis, Soissons or Rheims Duke Charles might have been found; these Neustrian centres being more likely than any in Austrasia. In any case, it is certain that they succeeded in finding the great man; and also that Boniface made a deep impression upon him at the time.

Charles, in consequence of their meeting, gave the bishop a clear letter of authority (Ep. 22). For political reasons he did not refer to the Roman See as such. He described the subject of the letter as 'apostolic father': but this is of no great significance, as he mentioned other 'apostolic fathers' among various lay and ecclesiastical categories to whom the letter was addressed.

> '. . . the apostolic father Boniface has come into our presence, and begged us to take him under our protection. Know then that it has been our pleasure to do this . . . wheresoever he goes . . . he shall with our love and protection remain unmolested and undisturbed, on the understanding that he shall maintain justice and receive justice in like manner. And if any question or eventuality shall arise which is not covered by our law, he shall remain unmolested and undisturbed until he reach our presence, both he and those who put their trust in him, so that as long as he remains under our protection no man shall oppose or do him harm. And in order to give greater authority to this our command, we have signed it with our own hand and sealed it below with our ring.'

In a general sense it was a highly satisfactory document. But it had its limitations. It did not bind Charles to a programme of aid to Boniface's mission 'on the ground'. If this was not apparent at the time, it became clear enough later on. The Duke may have been willing enough, but could not foresee himself necessarily being able to provide the actual needs of the Christian people, the churches and ministries, the religious houses and charitable work which Boniface would wish to establish. This question of patronage would often have to be left to the local leader concerned. If Charles assumed that this would be adequate, he was too optimistic.

Even though the Apostolic See was not mentioned in Charles' letter, the fact that he gave recognition to Boniface, and over a wider field than had been accorded to Willibrord, was a definite step towards the close relation which was eventually established under Charlemagne between the Papacy and the Frankish 'Empire'.

Returning to Amöneburg and the Hessian field, Boniface as bishop was able to take those whom he had baptized one stage further in their Christian commitment. After more adequate preparation and testing than had been received before baptism, hundreds if not thousands were now 'confirmed' by the laying on of hands. Others were solemnly reconciled and reinstated into the communicant life of the Church, in a manner which had not been possible while Boniface had only the rank of presbyter. There was great joy among the people of Hesse. We may assume that churches were now being built and suitable men were being prepared for ordination as presbyters to serve them.

The boundary question was quickly provoked by Bishop Gerold of Mainz, so that Boniface wrote to the Pope. A reply came early in 724 (Ep.24): 'As for the bishop who was too lazy to preach the Word of God and now claims a part of your territory, we have written to our son Duke Charles asking him to restrain him.' The Pope, evidently pleased with the progress that was being made, explained in the same letter that he had also written to the local landlords of the Thuringian region asking them to be ready (*i.e.* whenever Boniface could extend his activity eastwards) to build churches and, looking forward further still, to endow bishoprics.

But 724 was not an appropriate year for Boniface to promote the Christian enterprise in Thuringia, for two reasons. Duke

Charles intended to repeat the harrying of the Saxon tribes which he had carried out in 720 and 722, supposedly again by the Thuringian route. Also, Boniface had to deal with the difficult border tribe of the Borthari, north of Hesse, who although not strictly 'Saxons', were tenaciously maintaining and propagating the worship of the old gods. There was a notorious cult of Woden at a place whose modern name is Gudensberg (Woden's Hill); while some miles to the west was an ancient oak tree sacred to Thor, at Geismar. These were on the border between the Bortharian and Hessian territories.

It was about this time that Boniface wrote to his beloved former bishop, Daniel of Winchester, and described the excesses of heathenism which he was encountering in Germany. He admitted that converting those who clung to the old gods was a real problem. Later in the year he had a reply. It was a carefully set-out essay, but disappointing, since Daniel seemed to take an over-academic and 'uninvolved' view. Discussions about the relative merits of the true God and false gods, suggestions as to the inferior character of 'divine' beings who procreated other divine beings, a doubtful argument about Christians having been blessed by Providence with the most fertile lands: all this had little to say to people emotionally bound to pagan cults and morality. What was needed, in Boniface's estimation, was some dramatic event, some sort of 'mass exorcism' which would prove the superiority of the Christian faith. Proper teaching and the building up of Church life would follow after that.

Without much hope of support from Duke Charles, whose writ ran rarely, if ever, north of the River Eder, and least of all in matters of religion, Boniface slowly secured his ground in northern Hesse, managing to allay any opposition as far as Büraburg, paving the way for a decisive blow at the strongholds of heathenism beyond.

In 725 it became urgently necessary to deal with those strongholds in order to leave Boniface free to go further east. The Saxons beyond Thuringia were temporarily quelled. Duke Charles and his nobles at their 'March Assembly', 725, decided that it was Bavaria's turn to receive military punishment (perhaps because there was now the challenge of one single Duke over all that country). Thuringia should be ready for Boniface's attention as soon as the danger north of Hesse could be removed.

At length he decided on a plan. The sacred oak at Geismar must be felled. We may guess that it was a dead or dying tree, one which had been struck by lightning years before, and had for that very reason been thought to be a habitation of Thor, the god of thunder. Boniface, as his earliest biographer relates, went to the place with his companions and 'took his courage in his hands'. In front of a crowd of cursing heathen he wielded an axe and made an incision in the side of the trunk. According to the story, a great wind arose at that moment. Without further human effort the tree fell to the ground. The populace, amazed to see it lying there in four large pieces and many small fragments, 'ceased to revile' Boniface as 'enemy of the gods'. They 'began on the contrary to bless the Lord'. Afterwards the pieces of the tree, which may have formed very roughly a cross on the ground (why else bother to mentioned four pieces?), were picked up and used in the building of a chapel on the spot.

The Bortharians as a tribe were not converted to Christ until about 770, forty-five years after this. But the northern limits of Hesse now adhered to the true faith. Boniface completed the operation just in time, in that the Thuringians were rapidly falling under evil influences. The powerful leader Heden, who had supported Willibrord's missions, had come under the influence of a certain Theobald. These two had won over several former missionaries left behind by Willibrord in 717: Trudwin, Berechtar, Eanberht and Hunraed (Conrad). These names, alas, may well have belonged to Englishmen. The five faithful leaders to whom the Pope had written were presumably trying to maintain the cause of Christianity, though under increasing difficulty. The problem in Thuringia was in some ways more difficult than that which had been solved in northern Hesse, for here was not an example of rank paganism, but a Christian deviation not unlike one known to St. Paul, involving 'free love'. Even the Saxons, whom Theobald in some sort regarded as his overlords, did not descend to that. Licentiousness gave rise to more than one kind of passion. Violence began to be used against the faithful. Pope Gregory, possibly knowing nothing and believing Boniface to have begun to develop his work in Thuringia, had written another letter to 'all the Thuringians' (Ep. 25). They were to avoid being hoodwinked by heathenism, they were to receive and honour Christian baptism, they were to welcome Boniface as 'father and bishop' and 'build him a house'.

About that very time Boniface did in fact move in. Quiet perseverance and courage, along with the definite support of faithful Christians who had 'gone underground', sustained him in a year of gradual progress. It was a hard and testing time. Some of his colleagues fell by the wayside, spiritually. During the winter of 725–6 even survival was not easy. The theoretical backing of the Frankish Duke was of little service when the Franks could not maintain a consistent hold over the region.

In all this, however, Boniface succeeded in writing and sending letters to England. It was a kind of life-line to him. He wrote to Abbess Eadburga, '. . . pray for me, because for my sins I am wearied with many trials and vexed in mind and body.' Patience was rewarded. The life-style of Boniface and his remaining companions could not fail to impress the people of Thuringia. They practised what they preached. Their lives demonstrated the beauty of holiness about which they sang in their psalms. Their bearing in face of threatened violence was eloquent testimony to the rightness of their beliefs. The people themselves began to assist in arraigning their misguided leaders, who confessed their errors before courts of justice and accepted banishment. This sudden access of 'order' may have been helped on in the latter part of the year 726, when the campaigning season was over: Duke Charles, as one may conclude from circumstances, began to encourage the movement towards reform in a Christian sense. Enough real support was given to enable Boniface to found his first monastic house in Thuringia, at Ohrdruf. As the atmosphere cleared, problems crystallized. There were monasteries of a different style, and churches too, surviving or needing to be revived, with traditions arising from earlier Christian endeavours, not in accordance with Boniface's standards. He wrote to Rome, sending a letter to Pope Gregory by the hand of a certain presbyter Denewald, filled with questions. By the end of the year, or soon after, Denewald had returned with the Pope's reply. Gregory rejoices at 'the welcome news that you are well and . . . making progress', and is deeply satisfied that the field which had been 'sown with the tares of paganism' had now been ploughed and 'sown with the truth' and even produced 'an abundant harvest'. Boniface had given the first evidence of extreme sensitivity about his consecration oath in relation to clergy of poor standards, moral rather than doctrinal. The Pope recommends that 'provided they are not heretics . . . admonish and correct them with our apostolic authority.... Do not refuse to eat and speak with them.... Where correction fails ... the comfort and gentle persuasion of their table-companions leads them back to the paths of goodness.'

Boniface's correspondence with English friends over the years ensured that a flame of interest was kept alight beyond the Channel. From time to time, with or without prompting and prayers from the man of Wessex himself, churchmen from his native land were inspired to come and join him. Of these a fair proportion were of a calibre such as would enable them to play important roles in the churches and monasteries which he founded. A certain Burghard, if not an original member of the team, joined it about now (726). He was not young. A still older one bore the name Wigbert. The former was to become a stalwart bishop; the latter would soon be a much beloved abbot. The stream of new members, not all known by name to us, flowed intermittently for another twenty years and more. Like Boniface himself, they yearned to share the advantages of Christian England with peoples less fortunate than themselves. This stream did not until later include a significant number of women, although the balance was to be restored at the end of the period. The Continent was not a good place for women to visit except under close protection and care. Boniface had to tell his friend the Abbess Eadburga, in reply to one of her letters (about 725), to postpone a projected pilgrimage to Rome until 'the threats of the Saracens' had died down.*

On a later occasion he had to advise against nuns being allowed abroad, as the pilgrim ways were strewn with English women who had lost their virtue. It needs to be said, however, that the German peoples, among whom Boniface was working, almost certainly showed less sign of moral degeneration than those of the older, nominally Christian countries further south.

* See Chapter 9.

Chapter 9

ACHIEVEMENT IN ISOLATION

The sense of isolation which could come over the missionaries in Hesse and Thuringia is hard to imagine in all its starkness. Added to all the obvious difficulties and dangers was the slowness of communication with the outside world. Over and above all this, the German winter could bring everything to a halt, under conditions of extreme deprivation. No doubt those working in the monastic tradition knew how to organize and discipline themselves even at such times and to bring relief to others. By such means, in the long run, the Christian message was commended and its adversaries put to silence. Nevertheless the missionaries, too, were human. Boniface himself had the additional burden of being without what a bishop badly needed, the opportunity of consulting others in a like position of authority and responsibility. The book of 'canons' which he had received at his consecration was useful, even indispensable as an encyclopaedia of such order. Yet, in the absence of anyone of sufficient seniority with whom to talk things over, it could be very difficult to decide where an exception might be made to a rule, or under what range of conditions a particular regulation could reasonably be supposed to operate. Things which were normally obvious did not seem so under the pressure of circumstances and the demands of humanity from moment to moment. He, too, was human and could come to the point of wishing that a certain rule was different, or that another did not exist at all.

Only thus can we explain some of the issues dealt with in the correspondence with Rome (726), already mentioned. Concerning the monastic life, Boniface had to be assured on the highest authority of two points well known to him: that a child devoted to God by parents could not opt out on arrival at years of discretion; and that monks or nuns were not to flee from their house when it was visited by plague or other contagious disease. The Pope, giving instructions about the due trial and defence of a clergyman accused by the pople, found it advisable to add a reminder of the familiar fact that a man could not be deprived of holy orders as such, but must be considered to retain his rank even if (because of proven offences) he might have to be restrained from exercising his ministry. These matters reflect the development of the monastic life at Amöneburg and Ohrdruf, and the pain of adjustment in pastoral matters where clergy (sometimes lapsed or corrupt) had remained from former periods of Christian endeavour, before Boniface's arrival.

In matters of elementary baptismal discipline also, Boniface had evidently wavered. Unsettled conditions of one sort and another are seen as the background to his questions to the Pope. Must one *always* baptize a child who, having been separated from his original environment, says, 'I think I was baptized, but I don't know for sure'! (*Answer*: Yes, you must, of course, 'conditionally'.) If people come and say, 'The minister who baptized us was, as we now see, a disreputable man. Some people say he was unsound, or that he was not properly ordained'; and they go on to say that they feel really deprived, as if they had not had real baptism at all; is one never allowed to baptise them afresh? (*Answer*: Never, because 'the condition of the minister does not hinder the effect of the sacrament', *provided* that he has used water in the proper Threefold Name.)

On marriage discipline there was more excuse for his questions, as opinions had not been so firmly agreed, and extenuating circumstances could easily arise. In this matter Boniface received one generous reply and one severe one. A man whose wife through illness was unable to grant him sexual intercourse might eventually be allowed to marry again, but must maintain his first wife unless she had contracted her illness through sexual misconduct. On the other hand (in this Pope's interpretation) marriage between cousins was to be forbidden as far as the fourth degree of consanguinity (i.e. 'third cousins'). Another understandable question, in view of the heathenism all round, had to do with food which had been offered to idols. No doubt strong pressures and various opinions around him had led Boniface to open a question which (as Pope Gregory was quick to point out) had been once and for all settled by St. Paul. Two interesting points involved the Holy Communion. The Pope insisted on a single chalice only, even at a large gathering, because Jesus had said 'Drink of *this, all* of you'. He also declared that lepers could receive the Communion, but not at a public service.

All these matters illustrate clearly the life and task to which Boniface and his fellow-workers had committed themselves. It is necessary to bear such things in mind as we speculate about the next four or five years, during which there was no exchange of correspondence with Rome and less help than ever from Duke Charles. Only so can a just estimate be formed of the progress that was made in the face of every sort of hardship.

Those bleak years can be largely explained by the 'crisis of Europe' which was coming to a head. Both directly and indirectly, the Moslem threat overshadowed everything else. One could, to be sure, believe that the call to convert the Germans was an important part of the Christian answer to that threat. But the threat itself meant that that vocation had to be carried out with almost every normal advantage and encouragement removed. The Kingdom of the Franks was increasingly threatened by invasion from the south. The Arabs from Spain and Septimania (N.E. of the Pyrenees) carried their cavalry raids further and further until, on one occasion in the 720's, they passed the 48th degree of latitude and harried the city of Sens. (Sens, as it happened, had been a 'metropolitan see' in the earlier Gallo-Frankish church). Duke Charles, having already enough problems with the Saxons, the Bavarians, the Alamannians and sometimes the Duchy of Aquitaine, now had this additional and grievous burden. It was impossible for him to supervise every corner of the kingdom. He had to be mainly in the south. As for the churches, so far from adding to their benefactions, he had for some time been allowing his nobles to bleed them to pay for 'defence' measures. (That phrase has a familiar ring in the modern world, where 'defence' has also often involved large-scale aggressive campaigning, as in Duke Charles' time.) This process was now carried a stage further. No relief from the state of emergency was felt until 732, when Charles earned his title 'Martel', the Hammer, by a decisive victory against the Arabs between Tours and Poitiers.

Rome was affected too, and doubly so, though less directly. There was the obvious fear that the successes of the Arabs in France (as we should call it) might lead to their invading Italy, perhaps in a two-fold drive by land and sea. But there was also the unforeseeable effect of Arab culture upon the remains of the Byzantine Empire, in which (as usual) Church and State were inextricably intertwined. Some eastern Christians had been impressed by the refusal of Moslems to use any formal representations (pictures, carved images) in their worship, and had reacted against the long-standing habit of using 'icons' at prayer, a practice in which reverence was paid to the icons themselves. This party, although bitterly opposed by the monastic communities in general, gained the upper hand and the support of the Emperor, Leo III 'The Isaurian' (717–741). In 726 (after which year Boniface did not exchange letters with a Pope again until 731–2) the Emperor issued an edict of 'iconoclasm', forbidding images of all kinds and ordering their destruction. Opposition in the Empire was silenced, or confined within the high walls of monastic houses. Although in practice the whole issue was of less importance in the West, a Roman synod of 727 declared against the edict, and the Emperor was officially discountenanced. The quarrel was destined to go on for years, and to absorb much time and energy at Rome. In 730 Leo deposed the Patriarch of Constantinople and installed another who was more whole-heartedly in favour of inonoclasm. The issue was further embittered. Two further synods at Rome, in 731, pronounced iconoclasm to be 'anathema' and its adherents 'excommunicate': but by that time Pope Gregory II had died.

A man of Syrian origin now ruled the Church, Gregory III; Conceivably the appointment of an easterner had to do with the handling of the iconoclastic issue. His decade in office has been described as one of the most difficult in the history of the Papacy. All things considered, he fulfilled his office well.

Boniface took an early opportunity to send a letter of greeting, good wishes and loyalty to the new Pope. The two may well have met and have come to respect one another, on the assumption that this Gregory had served in Rome through the period of Boniface's visits in 719 and 722. It is interesting to note, in parenthesis, that he (and his predecessor) must have been reminded of Boniface five years earlier not only by the exchange of correspondence, but because King Ine of Wessex resigned in 726 and ended his years in Rome, in a monastery. Now, from this fresh letter from Thuringia which had arrived after so long. Gregory III gained the impression of a vast achievement under adversity of all kinds. Again there was an array of questions, not dissimiliar in some items from that of

726; but the difficulties of the work only served to throw into relief the magnitude of Boniface's success.

After due consideration, early in 732, Pope Gregory III drafted his reply. What he had decided went further than words. His letter is much more than a list of detailed answers to queries received. He addresses his 'most reverend and holy brother bishop, Boniface, sent by the apostolic Church of God for the enlightenment of the German people who live in the shadow of death, steeped in error'; and after congratulating him, because quite evidently 'many heathens have turned away from error and embraced the truth', he goes straight to the practical point: 'Hence we have sent you the sacred pallium as a gift, desiring that with the authority of the Holy See you accept it and wear it; and it is our wish that you be recognised as one of the archbishops divinely appointed.' He goes on: 'Wear it . . . during the celebration of Mass, and when . . . you consecrate . . . a bishop'. He immediately makes the last point doubly clear. 'Since, as you say, you are unable to deal with all the matters involved in imparting the means of salvation to the multitudes . . . we command you . . . to consecrate bishops . . . in accordance with the sacred canons, choosing men of tried worth.' The object is to create proper dioceses, each with its proper episcopal see, which ought to be at a place of some note, 'in order that the dignity of the episcopal office may not be cheapened'. In the midst of many perplexing responsibilities devolving upon the Pope at this juncture in history it is remarkable that he was able to give as much careful attention to the German mission as he evidently did. With all that was on his mind, it is hardly surprising that he did not realise all the circumstances of those so distant and so different peoples in the north. The strictest canonist would have difficulty in finding a ring of cities in Hesse-Thuringia such as had formed 'worthy sees' for bishops in the old Roman empire. Likewise, Gregory had failed to apprehend the difficulty of consecrating new bishops 'according to the canons' when that required three existing bishops, or at least two, to co-operate with the archbishop. The prevailing situation in Frank-land, as also that in Bavaria and other neighbouring countries, was not at all promising in that respect.

Chapter 10

FRUSTRATIONS OF AN ARCHBISHOP

The former Wynfrith was by now over fifty years of age. Today a man approaching his fiftieth birthday may well find himself being warned by an older friend to look after himself during the next five years. If the health hazards associated with men between the ages of fifty and fifty-five are not merely due to the conditions of life in the twentieth century, but have a necessary relation to his progress through the 'seven ages of man', something similar may have applied in earlier centuries. It is attractive to link with this the Church's change from 'bishops at fifty' to 'bishops at thirty-plus' in the period between, roughly, the third century and the sixth century. Boniface had been made a bishop at forty-two, and since that time had spent nine years toiling under conditions far more taxing than those of a settled episcopate in a secure diocese. Only after that had he written to the newly-elected Pope stating that he could not manage without some better provision. Now, about six months short of the tenth anniversary of his consecration, he received Gregory III's letter and with it the pallium. As an archbishop, at the age of about fifty-two he still saw around him the opposition and frustration which had almost overwhelmed him, and little chance of using his newly acquired authority in a manner which would bring relief. What he needed, ideally, were endowments sufficient to found at least three episcopal sees, and two or three bishops of the right calibre to fill them.

It was not that he had no men with him who could have become worthy 'diocesans' there and then. Certainly Burghard, and perhaps (if they were already with him and senior enough) Witta and Dada could fulfil this kind of role, as they, in fact, were to do later on. But he was hampered by lack of material resources, Duke Charles and many other leading Franks being far away, preoccupied with the Arab problem. Quite apart from this, he was not prepared to risk using other bishops of dubious status to assist in the consecration of new ones. Since the Council of Nicaea in A.D. 325 it had been universally agreed that not fewer than three bishops should consecrate. Where the system of 'provinces' with metropolitan archbishops prevailed (as Rome preferred) it was considered normal to have three beside the archbishop at a consecration ceremony, though two would suffice. In the letter he had now received along with the papal token of authority, this last point had been underlined: 'As often as you consecrate a bishop, let two or three other bishops join you, so that what you do may be pleasing to God', in that everything will have been 'done with their assistance and sanctioned by their presence.'

Boniface was faced with a problem. If there were 'country bishops' in Hesse-Thuringia left there as a result of Willibrord's visits, he was not clear (in view of the uncertainties of canon law on the subject) that these would be reckoned at Rome as proper for such a purpose – most likely not. Having no dioceses of their own, they could not be said to represent the Universal Church in relation to the diocese to which a new bishop was being consecrated. Insofar as there were, within reach, 'monastic bishops' of the 'Celtic' type, he had even more hesitation about their propriety: Bavaria could have provided these, and maybe Alamannia too. His chances of gaining co-operation from the older parts of the Frankish kingdom were not good. Gerold of Mainz was very unsympathetic, and was probably at this moment going off to fight the Arabs in southern Gaul. At Trier, twelve years ago, Liutwin had looked upon Boniface with condescension and suspicion as 'far too strict a young man'. He had died about that time and matters had become worse. It was typical of the degenerating state of the Frankish Church that Liutwin's son Milo had secured the bishopric of Trier and along with it that of Rheims and was now living on the proceeds, hunting with the nobility and neglecting his pastoral duties with total impunity. No soldier he, but a huntsman. Owing to the Saxon salient which at times could come uncomfortably near to the Rhine between Cologne and Coblenz, the whole of the remainder of Frank-land, and with it the diocese of Utrecht and Willibrord himself, were inaccessible to Boniface behind the barrier created by Gerold and Milo. He suspected that he, whatever the Pope hoped or supposed, would remain the only fully-qualified bishop in Hesse-Thuringia for years to come. His fears were well grounded.

The whole position was anomalous. A 'wandering' archbishop was an even rarer, indeed a still more unimaginable concept than a bishop fully qualified but without a see (which was what he *had* been). If he was supposed to be constructing a 'province', its boundaries were undefined, at least toward the south. How far was he supposed to have responsibility in that direction? The region which later became known as 'Lower Franconia' was at that time somewhat amorphous, lying between the Hessians and Thuringians on the one hand and the Alamannians on the other. There was a Christian element in Würzburg which leaned heavily on the memory of the Irish 'St. Kilian' (d. 689). In the same area, traditions of the 'Gallo-Irish' sort had been given further expression in recent years, these being brought up from southern Alamannia. The strongly Celtic tendencies of the monastery of St. Gall had coloured Alamannian church activity for over a century. Now, in the 720s, a not altogether dissimilar movement had arisen under the influence of Pirmin.

Pirmin's work was an embarrassment to Boniface, who was puzzled as to what attitude he should adopt toward a figure comparable (and contemporary) with himself. This undeniably great Christian came from the area of the Pyrenees. Like Boniface he had been brought up as a monk in the moderate tradition, and could be styled a Benedictine. Overtaken by the Arab thrust northwards in 711, he had then or later moved through Aquitaine into Neustria, where he had an opportunity to view Frankish affairs from a vantage point on the River Marne. At Meaux he received episcopal orders, but not under conditions of which Boniface could approve: he became a monastic bishop, not responsible to the bishop of a diocese, able to ordain men to the sacred ministry in competition with the normal arrangements, and to found monasteries (with lay help) unrelated to church life as a whole. This was a kind of disorder which Boniface, perhaps even more strongly than the Pope at times, regarded with abhorrence. It had disadvantages beyond even what might have been foreseen. For example, it left too much room for the notion that pastoral help was to be sought from the 'best' presbyter, abbot or bishop who was within reach or could be brought in. This could have serious abuses; and in any case it was clean contrary to the strict and Catholic doctrine, viz. that the important qualities of ministry depended upon the grace vouchsafed through ordination, and that the 'charismatic' differences between (for example) one presbyter and another were secondary, even if useful and enriching.

It was a pity that for such reasons Pirmin was regarded with disfavour by Boniface. It was distressing, not only because their fields of activity or influence were beginning to overlap, but because Pirmin was a genuine Benedictine bent on moderating the gauntness of the tradition of Columban and Gall, and more fundamentally, a first-class teacher of sound basic doctrine. He used a form of the 'Apostles' Creed', presumably as known in Spain, which later became standard (and has remained so), but of which we have no other example from so early a date. It is ironical that whatever form or forms of the shorter creed were known to Boniface and the Popes of his day, those would be ousted by Pirmin's. (Historically, Rome was to receive many influences from further west during the period of its political weakness, especially in the tenth century.) The encroachment of Pirmin's circle upon that of Boniface began about 730, or soon after. Pirmin's first great enterprise, when he left Neustria as a sort of missionary-cum-reformer in 724, was the foundation of the monastery of Reichenau on the Bodensee, the Lake of Constance. This was done specifically with the cooperation and patronage of Charles Martel as ultimate overlord, and of Lantfried Duke of Alamannia. (Reichenau, later on, was joined canonically to the diocese of Constance, a combination which helped Constance to become one of the most powerful sees in mediaeval Europe.) When the two lords quarrelled a few years later, Pirmin moved into Alsace, regarded by the Franks as within the Alamannian administrative region, but a separate dukedom. In 728 he founded Murbach, in the Strasbourg area. The disciple who had followed him as Abbot of Reichenau, Heddo, soon traced a similar path, but became diocesan bishop of Strasbourg and eventually showed sympathy towards Boniface's ideals. Other disciples of Pirmin fanned out over Alamannia from the west and south. A small convent was founded at Kitzingen on the River Main under their influence, in the early 730's, with the nun Hadeloga as abbess, reinforcing for the time being the atmosphere that was uncongenial from Boniface's point of view around Würzburg. (Later, the same movement was to penetrate Bavaria and disturb the effects of work which Boniface had meanwhile done there.)

So, with Pirmin's disciples to the south, disputes with Mainz in the south-west, and varying boundaries with the Saxons and

Slavs all round the northern parts of his region, Boniface's only fixed limit was a stretch of sixty miles of border with Bavaria. A fluid situation indeed! Yet a further factor removed him far from the ideal pattern of things contemplated at Rome: apart from Würzburg, which was hardly within his reach as yet, he had no prospective 'city' in his whole great area recognisable as such by those who thought in terms of ancient Greece and Rome, and of the early centuries of church history.

It was thus a matter of soldiering on, relying on the spiritual armour to which St. Paul had referred in the sixth chapter of his Epistle to the Ephesians, and relying heavily also on the conviction that if the Bishop of Rome, Vicar of St. Peter, had put him where he was, there must be good purpose to it. Two years of hard work, similar to that which he had known in the previous decade, bore its own fruit. The expected support from Charles Martel, after his famous victory in the south, failed to materialize: but with his colleagues or 'disciples' there was mutual encouragement and inspiration. Contacts with England continued to uplift and sustain this brave contingent of Anglo-Saxons far from home. Conversions and recantations from false religion continued. Tens of thousands by now owed their Christian allegiance directly or indirectly to Boniface. With recruits to the monastic way of life and potential clergy appearing 'on the field', and a trickle of men joining from England, further focal mission centres could be planned where local lay leadership was both powerful and sympathetic. Northern Hesse saw the building of a monastery at Fritzlar, not far from Geismar where the Oak of Thor had been felled. The houses at Amöneburg and Ohrdruf were strengthened.

By 734 Boniface felt free to accept an invitation from the Duke of Bavaria to conduct a preaching mission. Hugobert, a nephew of Theodo, had obtained the dukedom in 725 under the good pleasure of Charles (Martel) who had defeated the sons of Theodo. (It was Grimoald, actually, who had obtained the upper hand and was killed.) Either the memory of Boniface's tour fifteen years earlier (719) or the report of his work in neighbouring lands, made such an invitation possible. Hugobert, after nine years of rule, had also accepted the widsom of his uncle's plan of church reform, and hoped that Boniface might bring it a stage nearer by means of a thorough visitation. Such details as we have of that event make it clear that a spirit of canonical discipline was already in the air. A heretic called Eremwulf was dealt with, and was banished or went voluntarily into exile, while his followers were turned from their misguided path. After Boniface had returned northward the Duke sent the presbyter Vivilo to be consecrated Bishop at Rome, and gave him the see of Passau with a sort of jurisdiction over the whole of Bavaria. Thus an important positive step towards an overall reform was taken before Hugobert died in 735 or 736.

For the missionary Archbishop himself this Bavarian episode was at once demanding and bracing. It required of him more than those gifts which he regularly exercised; for he had also to show great patience with the kind of church order (or lack of order, as he might describe it) still prevailing. But he gained refreshment not merely from the change of scene, and not only from the manifest response to his preaching in general, but also because a number of stalwart Christian men offered themselves as willing disciples of Boniface himself. The impression created by the whole affair is best gauged by the fact that many of the Bavarian nobility declared themselves more than content that their sons should attach themselves to him, some actually encouraging them to do so. Among these was one who would later play an important role in the Bonifatian scene, a young man by the name of Sturm. Despite his name, Sturm was of a gentle disposition, though severe with himself, and possessed of a humility equal to that which all recognised in Boniface.

In spite of all this the Archbishop, after returning to Hesse-Thuringia with his new found followers, suffered a reaction, and for three years was liable to depression. It may be that he was affected by his time of life. Very likely he became more aware of the opposition to his cause which was tending to grow in the older parts of Frankland. The fact that Charles Martel still kept his distance (partly because of the need to avoid dividing the loyalties of his subjects) was a heavy grief and caused almost insuperable difficulties. The continuing impossibility of fulfilling the wishes of the Pope by developing a proper episcopal oversight in the region gave Boniface a sense of disappointment that was hard to bear. Perhaps at times, maybe always 'in public', he could envisage the positive side and count the blessings: progress in converting and reclaiming souls did not slacken, monasteries and local churches were shining like beacons, the Archbishop and his colleagues were held in as high regard as ever. But the troubles which weighed on Boniface's mind were real enough, and there were definitely opponents and evil-minded persons near at hand as well as further away. Although these were only a part of the picture, in moments of depression they could seem almost overwhelming.

Correspondence with friends in England was a safety-valve. A charming letter (Ep. 29) arrived from his cousin Leoba, now at Minster-in-Thanet under Eadburga, and in her mid-thirties. She sends him Latin verses to criticize, being disarmingly modest about her own abilities. She wishes him 'long life here and a happier life to come'. These words show that she had some appreciation of his sufferings. Two letters addressed to Eadburga herself (Epp. 30, 35) date from the period 735–6, in which Boniface speaks of being 'tossed about by the storms of this dangerous sea'; but he is able to thank her for sending books on spiritual subjects, and sends her a little gold (gold-leaf?) with which she may adorn a copy of the Epistles of St. Peter 'in gold lettering' and send it to him. (One may note that it is *St. Peter* who is thus honoured.) To a former pupil, Duddo, now an abbot, he opens up (Ep. 34) and begs him, 'Take pity on an old man worn out by troubles', and, 'Remember your father now failing in health and going the way of all flesh.' Abbot Sigebald of Chertsey writes (Ep. 36), asking to be allowed to name Boniface in prayer as 'his' bishop alongside Bishop Daniel of Winchester and the Bishop of London; and says that he would like permission to continue under Boniface's spiritual patronage after the latter's death, supposing that he (Sigebald) should outlive him. He too was aware, presumably, that Boniface had begun to describe himself as 'old' and 'worn out'.

Pastoral problems continued to worry the Archbishop, particularly in the field of marriage relationships. The problem of degrees of consanguinity became more acute. Gregory III, not approving marriage at a degree nearer than the fifth*, had instructed him in 732 to ask all baptized persons to keep a record of their cousins as far as the seventh degree. His English contacts had confirmed a suspicion in his mind, that there was some evidence of Augustine having allowed marriage within the third degree, supposedly on a canonical basis and with

* The fifth degree of consanguinity is that between 'fourth cousins' as we would call them.

papal backing. The difference was alarming. Boniface wrote (735) direct to Canterbury, to Archbishop Nothelm, over this (Ep. 33). We do not know what answer was given. Historically the canons were on the stricter side. But we gain the impression that Boniface would much rather have taken the more lenient view. This impression is favoured by his evident dissatisfaction with another marriage restriction, one which was so unreasonable that any knowledge of it from former years had been 'rejected' by his mind and departed from his memory. He mentions this also to Archbishop Nothelm, after having acted in such a way as to contravene the 'canon'. His very words reveal the issue: 'Further, I would like your advice as regards a sin which I have committed by allowing a certain man to marry. The man, like many others, had stood as godfather to the child of another man and then on the father's death married the mother. The people in Rome say that this is a sin, even a mortal sin, and state that in such a case a divorce is necessary. They maintain that under the Christian emperors such a marriage was punishable by death or by exile for life . . . I cannot understand how spiritual relationship in marriage can be so great a sin, when we know that through baptism we *all* become sons and daughters, brothers and sisters in Christ.' The phrase 'the people in Rome' is an unusually roundabout reference to the Pope. The depth of his anxiety is revealed by his mention of the same subject in two other letters, among a group which were taken to England by presbyter Eoba (whom we meet again at the end of Boniface's life). To Abbot Duddo he gives a very brief reference, saying that Eoba will tell him the story in full, and asking why 'this is held to be a capital crime in Rome'. To a Northumbrian bishop who came from Wessex, Pecthelm of Whithorn, he made a similar plea (Ep. 32). Perhaps Boniface remembered Pecthelm as one not so firm on the papal allegiance as himself, and therefore wrote: 'The whole episcopate of Frank-land and Gaul affirm' that persons thus involved are guilty 'of a crime of the first order'. Significantly in this letter he not only says that he was not aware of any such 'canon' nor papal decree from the past, but adds: 'Nor have I observed that the Apostles anywhere included (this offence) in a list of sins'. While we suppose that he eventually had to bow to what was indeed a canonical rule, we can discern here a side to Boniface which many have ignored or desired to conceal. This correspondence belies the typical remark that Boniface 'was not an original thinker'. We may well conclude that he kept it as a private (and thoroughly theological) opinion to the end of his life, that such a regulation did not make sense.

Shortage of books was a continual concern: references to it in the correspondence of 735, as at other periods, bear witness to the expansion of the work at this time when Boniface was finding it hard to 'count his blessings'. Not only from Abbess Eadburga does he expect a succession of volumes: Duddo is begged to procure further sections of a commentary on St. Paul, of which only Romans and 1 Corinthians are to hand. Also, 'if you have anything in your monastic library which you think would be useful to me . . . pray let me know about it.' Touchingly he adds: 'Help me as a loving son might an ignorant father, and send me any notes of your own.' It is the old humility again, transparently sincere. No doubt Boniface would use many of the books which came his way, not only for his own personal and headquarters study and worship, but to be copied out at Amöneburg, Fritzlar or Ohrdruf, as members of those houses promoted the skill of copying and bookbinding after the fashion of the English monastic tradition.

Had he but known it, a new day of opportunity was about to dawn for the Anglo-Saxon mission, in that Charles Martel had resolved on the defeat of the Saxons, and was going to need Boniface and his colleagues in the work of Christianizing which should follow. Inwardly, and aside from political expediency, Charles believed that the Roman system of church life would be best for Frankland. He made a more than merely symbolical gesture, about 737, by bringing the calculation of Easter throughout his domains into line with that of Boniface and Rome. The prevailing method was out of date by Roman standards, though less antiquated than that which had persisted in Celtic Britain until not long before. Probably before he knew of this, Boniface felt that his difficulties could be cleared up only by a face-to-face meeting with the Pope. Five years as an archbishop, without any provincial or diocesan structure having been created in his region—that was more than enough! Conscious that he was growing old he feared to postpone a Roman journey any longer. In spite of the illness which had overtaken his friend, the elderly Wigbert, Abbot of Fritzlar, sometime in 737 Boniface departed for Rome.

Chapter 11

ROME AND RECOVERY

It was from Fritzlar, almost certainly, that Boniface's third journey Romewards began. This, the latest of the three communities which acted as focal and radiating points for his whole enterprise, was now his favourite, virtually his home. Its nearness to that place where heathenism had suffered its biggest blow endeared it to him. Amöneburg was thirty miles away, Ohrdruf twice as far. Yet a living link between Ohrdruf and Fritzlar had been provided in the person of the presbyter from Dorset, the elderly Wigbert, whose experience and power of discipline were renowned, and who was abbot of both places. With a good prior and teachers under him in both houses, he had managed well in spite of his age, having been renowned for his energy. Now he was on a sick bed. The archbishop, to whom Wigbert was extremely valuable and a firm friend, sincerely hoped that the illness would not prove fatal. Either with or without the abbot's knowledge, some rearrangements were proposed in case he died while Boniface was away.

There is general agreement that the route taken to Rome on this occasion was through Bavaria: everything points to that. Conceivably some parts of the journey may have been by river. In any case, river valleys were followed for easy travel. Perhaps he called at Amöneburg first and spent a day or two before going due south to the river Main: up the Main, up the Tauber, across to the Altmühl and so down to Eichstätt: thence to Freising by the road he had taken in 719 in the opposite direction, up the Isar, and over to Innsbruck by the Seefelder Sattel; or else by Achensee and down the steep, twisty road to the Inn valley from there.* So to Rome over the Brenner, but taking a more direct way than in 719, when the Pavia visit took him further west.

* It may be irrelevant, but there is a place on the Achensee named after St. Scholastica, sister of St. Benedict of Nursia.

It is likely that he had not gone further than Amöneburg when a messenger from Fritzlar caught up with him: 'Abbot Wigbert is dead'. He had resolved not to turn back on any account. After due prayer with the brothers of Amöneburg, commending Wigbert's soul to God's safe keeping, he wrote immediately to Fritzlar (Ep. 40) confirming the arrangements already discussed there. It seems that a certain Tatwin had been already 'acting abbot'; so that Boniface's instructions are as follows (with the final one at the beginning for clarity's sake):

> 'On all matters, seek the advice of Abbot Tatwin as occasion arises, and follow out his suggestions . . . . Let the presbyter Wigbert (*viz.* a younger man of the same name) and the deacon Meningaud expound the Rule . . . observe the canonical hours and . . . offices . . . administer correction and preach the word of God to the brethren.
>
> Let Hiedde be prior and keep the servants in order, and let him have the assistance of Hunfrid if necessary.
>
> Sturm should take charge of the kitchen (*an interesting detail*!).
>
> Let Bernard do the manual labour and build us small houses as they are needed.'

Boniface's exceptional humanity, already reflected in his pre-dispositions over marriage rules, appears in what seems an astonishingly lenient word to all the brothers together: 'Let each one of you, according to his strength and character, try to preserve his chastity', as well as (obviously) 'to assist the others in the common life'. Confessed unchastity was not rare, it seems, among monks.

Boniface was going to face the Pope feeling that he had had enough of tribulation and would be glad to be released from responsibilities which he had not been able to fulfil. We see the other side of him, however, in the concluding words of the letter to Fritzlar: 'So you may abide in brotherly love until, God willing, I return to you once more. Then, together, we shall all praise God and give thanks to him for all his benefits. Farewell in Christ.' There was before him (as his first biographer describes) a 'long and painful journey'. Very likely the more pessimistic mood overtook him again before he reached his destination.

If we have to guess at the time of year when he left for Rome, a reasonable conjecture would make it a while after the week of Pentecost, during which (as perhaps also at Easter and during the seven weeks between) he as bishop would regularly conduct confirmation services, either in conjunction with baptism or as a follow-up to baptism administered by his presbyters. His arrival in Rome may be put in August (737 was the year). His tiredness may well have slowed the journey. Political troubles, and therefore possible military skirmishes may have caused delay on the border between Bavaria and Alamannia, west of Freising, and again in the Ravenna-Bologna region. Here the 'undisciplined soldiery' were in a highly nervous state: Ravenna had been occupied by the Lombards for two years (733–5) and had been recovered with difficulty. Both inwardly and outwardly, the journey was therefore without doubt a 'long and painful' one. He felt the benefit more than ever of being 'accompanied as usual by a group of disciples'.

The Pope gave him a welcome beyond all that he could have imagined. Gregory perceived at once that he was in need of considerable rest and refreshment, more than he was likely to get if he attempted to return before winter. He was treated with a respect amounting almost to reverence. Little by little he was given opportunity to preach, and, as on the previous occasions, was able to meet a wide variety of people. Rome's cosmopolitan character was not much affected by the political turmoil which prevailed in Italy, although now and again this impinged directly upon the 'duchy' of Rome. (Technically, the Pope is thought to have been seen as 'regent' of the duchy under the Emperor. Whenever the Lombards were displeased with Rome, they started to threaten. Liutprand had once been friendly, but his attitude had changed.) Boniface's preaching began to attract attention from a wide audience. Franks, Bavarians, Anglo-Saxons and others flocked to hear him, and 'followed his teaching with the closest attention'. He soon recovered his self-confidence.

Whatever he had said to the Pope on arrival, the question of his future was left open for the time being, not because Gregory had any doubt about it, but for the sake of Boniface himself. In time, Boniface was told that he was required eventually to return and continue what he had so nobly begun and had carried through for a decade and a half. But he was not expected to return without receiving further instructions. These would take time to work out, and the Pope needed to consult with others beside the Archbishop. It could not happen all at once. The Apostolic See had on its hands a vast number of vital concerns, including the political tensions in Italy and the doctrinal issue with the East.

Boniface took the opportunity to write to some of his principal colleagues (Ep. 41), probably sending back as messenger one of those who had come to Rome with him. In view of his prolonged absence, the letter was intended to reach as many of his scattered flock as possible. We may therefore assume that the names at the head of it are representative of the three monastic houses. There are actually four names, 'Geppa, Eoba, Tatwin and Wigbert', whom he addresses as his 'beloved sons'. 'Geppa' is conceivably Gemberht, who could have followed him from Frisia. Eoba we have already met, carrying letters to England in 735. Tatwin and Wigbert both belonged to Fritzlar, as the new abbot and principal teacher. Geppa and Eoba, whose names appear *before* this pair, must surely have been abbots, or acting abbots, of the two houses founded earlier, Amöneburg and Ohrdruf; although we have no other evidence of this.

After describing the welcome which he had received, Boniface went on to give the gist of the 'satisfactory reply' which the Pope had given 'to the matters for which we came'. In fact 'he counselled and commanded us to return once more to you and to persevere in the work which we have undertaken'. But that could not be at once. 'At the moment we are waiting for the opening of a council of bishops, and we do not know when the apostolic Pontiff will order it to sit. As soon as it is over we will hasten back to you, if God so wills and our health is spared.' He concluded: 'In this knowledge, await our coming with fraternal love and in the unity of faith, 'bearing one another's burdens'. So doing, you will 'fulfil the law of Christ' and will renew your joy. Fare ye well and pray for us.' It is because of this letter that we strongly suspect that Boniface had offered his resignation to the Pope.

The proposal to hold a Roman synod gives us, incidentally, an insight into the constitutional working of the Papacy. The Pope wished thus to add weight to the encouragement which he presumably offered to Boniface, and to maximise the delegated authority which the latter held from the Apostolic See.

Meanwhile during the waiting period, while the estimate and appreciation of Boniface's true worth rose steadily and reached the highest limits, there was time for discussion during which plans could evolve. Between the Pope and Boniface, there was a tension of interests similar to that which had had to be resolved between the earlier Gregory and the Anglo-Saxon missionary in 718–9. The priorities in Boniface's mind in 737–8, almost twenty years later, had not basically changed, in that the conversion of the 'Old Saxons', along with the tribes of eastern Frisia, came first. A close second, after all these years, came Hesse-Thuringia. Bavaria followed in third place. Over Alamannia he could not raise positive enthusiasm because of his doubts and difficulties over Pirmin, who was being promoted and supported without reservation by Duke Charles. Pirmin's adherence to Benedictine ways could not compensate for his other defects, not least his independence of Rome. To Pope Gregory III the order of interest was almost the reverse, at least from the standpoint of urgency and awareness. Alamannia and Bavaria were only just beyond the Alps. Alamannia could provide a key to unlock the Gallo-Frankish door for the admission of papal and canonical influence. It had bishops who were of a Catholic order in most respects, and less deficient ethically and pastorally than many in Frank-land itself; but their aloofness from Rome was no less serious. The partly beneficial influence of Pirmin needed to be carried a stage further by someone allied to Rome and also supported by Duke Charles. As regards Bavaria, only one major effort was now needed to secure the fulfilment of the 716 plan for a Catholic diocesan system. Duke Odilo, who had succeeded Hugobert, was known to be in favour, although possibly he valued chiefly the tidy administrative division involved in the plan, and was not so deeply convinced about all the details of episcopal authority as the Pope (and Boniface) understood these. From the Roman point of view the Hesse-Thuringia region was further off. Had it not been for the success of Boniface's pioneering work, and the report that those who owed their Christian allegiance to his labours now numbered nearly 100,000, those lands would not naturally have seemed important to the Pope. The same consideration applied to the Saxon and Frisian districts, to a still greater degree. No doubt the peoples of such remote districts might receive mention in their turn amongst other nations yet to be brought into the light of Christ; but only the fire in the heart of a Boniface could kindle a genuine warmth of interest in them, on the banks of the Tiber.

The meeting of minds, so differently oriented, in prayer and charity, issued in a result which gave a place and proportion to all their interests. Gregory brought into vivid focus, as well as he could, the concerns of Boniface among the more northerly peoples. Boniface had to learn to understand and comply with the wishes of the Pope, not only in relation to Bavaria in which his interest was already engaged but also to Alamannia which otherwise he would have left on one side.

In working towards a set of proposals, attention was presumably given to the need to find or provide enough Catholic diocesan bishops to assist Boniface in episcopal consecrations as and where these would be needed. The proposals which emerged were intrinsically impressive and also widely comprehensive, if somewhat optimistic.

Chapter 12

THE GRAND DESIGN

Although Germany as a political entity did not take shape until many centuries later, an inhabitant of the Italian peninsula in the eighth century A.D. readily thought of 'the German peoples' as an identifiable group. The curve of the Alps could act as a sort of concave lens, so that an enormous area of land, which stretched from Basel to the Baltic and from Salzburg to the Zuyder Zee, could be envisaged as it were in one glimpse. If the river Rhine flowed just within that vast tract on its southern and western sides, the great Danube appeared to bisect it between the northern and southern 'halves'. The effect, from the Italian standpoint, was the opposite of that given (in our day) by the telephoto lens. From the Danube to the Danish border might seem little further than from Innsbrück to Ingoldstadt, although in reality the distance was three times as great.*

To reduce thus the dimensions of 'the parts of Germany' was no slight to Boniface, whom Pope Gregory III saw as fit to organise the Catholic Church of Christ over the whole region. But the above consideration helps us still more clearly to understand the proportions of Gregory's thinking and that of his colleagues in the Roman synod. We may indeed be glad that their vision extended as far as it did, and that their concern for distant peoples was as deep as it was. This is the more true because of the danger that the hazards of Italian politics at the time would lead to a short-sighted viewpoint. Preoccupation with the balance of power between the Lombards and the Byzantines could, but for the grace of God, have rendered all more distant causes invisible. The question whether or when to call in the Franks to put things right in Italy was a further insistent issue. For although 'Frank-land' was as far away as Germany and could have been almost as indistinct, the heirs of

* This effect is not really incompatible with the considerations mentioned on p. 91 (lines 28ff.) though it may seem so superficially.

the old Roman Empire felt much more familiar with it. The Franks were, in the long memory of Roman churchmen, friendly because of the Catholicism which Clovis had adopted at a time when the Lombards were still anathematized as 'Arian' heretics (*i.e.* denying that the Son is equal to the Father in his Godhead). Gregory III, like his predecessor in the Apostolic See, had taken care to be on good terms with Charles Martel, whatever the latter's faults might be: so much so, that in preparing to send Boniface back to the Germans, he did not suppose it necessary to write again to Charles as Gregory II had written in 719. Charles must, of course, come into the picture here, as much as in Italian politics, because the Franks were steadily bringing the German peoples under their sway. Boundaries such as that between Bavaria and Alamannia were irrelevant in the long run, even if Bavaria could sustain independence more fully for the time being. The Saxon peoples had to be distinguished for some purposes, since they were still unevangelized. But the drift of events was such that they too would come under Frankish influence before long; and it was in their interest and that of the Catholic Church that they should be thus absorbed, for otherwise the Church would not have the means to flourish on their soil.

With the complexities and perils of home politics, the continuing rift with Constantinople over religious issues, and many other urgent necessities facing Rome, it was determined that Boniface should become little less than 'vice-pope' among the Germans. He was still to be mobile, even more than before, in spite of his advancing years and recent ill-health. After the Roman Synod of Spring 738 four letters were prepared for him to take on his journey. These reveal the overall plan and also certain particular developments within it.*

The first letter (Ep. 42) bears the address:

> 'Bishop Gregory, servant of the servants of God, to all the bishops, venerable presbyters and religious abbots of all provinces, beloved of us'.

The term 'all provinces' is defined early in the letter by the use of the phrase 'the parts of Germany', which really makes no closer boundary than all lands under German settlement. Occurring in a passage referring to the original mission of

* The evidence has been given another interpretation. *See* Appendix A.

Boniface in 719, this phrase indicates, if anything, a broader field, since Gregory II had specified the peoples on the right bank of the Rhine. The whole of Alsace and what we call German Switzerland could now be considered as included: 'Alamannia' in the wider sense. The letter is tactful, as intended for some whose adherence to the Roman primacy was purely nominal. Sent simply from 'bishop' Gregory, it commends Boniface as a prophet and a preacher 'sent' to the 'parts of Germany', without defining precisely the kind of authority which his presence among the Germans is intended to involve. Rather, the senior clergy are asked to be ready to allow those working under them to join Boniface, in order that the Church amongst the German peoples may rise to its evangelistic task. At Rome this task was considered to include the reformation of defective and backsliding churches; but this also is not brought out in the letter. Those addressed are exhorted, in the Lord's words, to 'receive a prophet in the name of a prophet', and to help him in every way they can. In this connection certain words reveal the colossal respect in which Boniface was held, as well as the extreme dignity of the status which was being accorded him: 'The angel of God goes before him.'

By contrast with this general approach to German clergy who might anywhere and everywhere strengthen the drive of mission (and reform) in the hands of Boniface, we have the letter (Ep. 44) in which the Pope envisaged a 'canonical' Church structure to be developed in the same overall region. It is here that the viewpoint described early in this chapter determines the approach, in part at least. The Danube is taken as a kind of axis, and indeed, if there is a more precise centre of gravity it is south of the Danube, at Augsburg. The plan is to set up a Church 'province' of six bishops who are accounted by Rome (in prospect) as having proper consecration and suitable loyalty. Precise dioceses are not yet in view throughout Germany as a whole, though it is implied that these will be appropriately marked out when a larger number of bishops is available. The six bishops will meet twice a year in the first instance, in order that such matters may be attended to, and the whole detail of church order worked out. Their meetings will take place 'either beside the Danube or in the city of Augsburg', according to Boniface's discretion.

It was what in today's colloquial language would be called a 'long shot'. The letter was written quite explicitly as from

'Pope Gregory', and addressed to 'bishops beloved of us in the region of Bavaria and Alamannia, (namely) Wigo, Liudo, Rudolf and Vivilo, also Adda.' The first name, which might stand for Wig*bert*, Wig*hard* or Wig*mund*, is taken as meaning the bishop of Augsburg, where the synods might be held. Luido is traditionally held to have been the bishop of Speyer, a see which could be called Alamannian or Austrasian according to the point of view. Rudolf is said to have been bishop of Constance. 'Adda' is taken as a mis-spelling of the name of Heddo of Strasbourg. Both of these were Alamannian sees. Vivilo of Passau is the only name from Bavaria proper; as already noted, he had a general oversight of the dukedom from the standpoint of Catholic order. Wigo of Augsburg was in both camps, so to speak, since the population of his diocese was Alamannian, but at this moment in history that area had been annexed to Bavaria politically. Boniface himself would be the sole representative of the northern regions, until such time as diocesan bishops were appointed in Hesse-Thuringia. (Vivilo could likewise be joined later by other duly constituted bishops in Bavaria proper.)

If a synod after this pattern had ever been held, and had taken place at Augsburg, the distances involved would have been roughly as follows: from Passau, 120 miles; Constance, 100 miles; Strasbourg, 150 miles; Speyer, 130 miles; and for Boniface (if starting from Fritzlar), over 200 miles. Such an arrangement would have made colossal physical demands upon Boniface if meetings were to be held at six-monthly intervals. A site on the Danube would have eased the situation by no more than twenty-five miles in Boniface's favour. Possibly in connection with this disproportion in distance, but also for more general reasons, Boniface needed to know how far his own 'mission' area was considered to extend southwards. There was the question of Pirmin's influence spreading northwards and eastwards, as well as that of boundaries with established bishoprics, not only Mainz but also Worms and Speyer.

This matter which, if resolved in Boniface's favour, would bring him so much nearer to Augsburg or the River Danube, is reflected in the third letter which he was given to carry north (Ep. 43). Addressed to various peoples in and around the Hesse-Thuringia region, it suggests by implication that 'Lower Franconia' (a later designation) is included in Boniface's episcopal area of interest. Possibly the Pope had already been in touch with Duke Charles over this, and had had some assurance that

Boniface would be given full support as far as a point south of Würzburg. (The alteration of the calculation of Easter in Frankland in favour of Rome's newer method provided an excuse for Gregory to write to Charles; as also did a victory over the Saxons, assuming that took place in 737). In any case it became clear during the next four years that the Würzburg area was as much Boniface's immediate charge as Hesse and Thuringia, and that the Frankish authority was behind this.

In detail, this letter was addressed to 'all those who are established in the eastern tract', that is to say, the newer and further part of the half-kingdom called 'Austrasia'; but specifically to eight districts or divisions.*

To 'all the nobility and people' of these eight districts the Pope commends 'the bearer of this letter' whom his predecessor had appointed 'to the perfecting of the people of God' and had sent to them. He tells them all how Boniface had benefited from his sojourn in Rome, not in reference to his feelings when he had gone there, but in terms of the additional 'training' he had received. He asks that this great servant of God be now welcomed back in such fashion that his preaching is given fresh attention. And he goes on: 'You are to welcome in the ministry of your church the bishops and presbyters whom he will himself appoint'. There follows a lengthy exhortation to accept discipline and punishment for error, to avoid heathen cults of all kinds, and to turn wholeheartedly to the one true God, who has promised such great things to those who seek the good.

In this letter Boniface had a clear authority to set forward the proper organization of the Church between the Saxon bor-

* Four of these had been undoubtedly Boniface's responsibility from earlier years: in name the Thuringians, the Hessians, the Niftarians (a small tribe on the Upper Eder) and the Lahn valley people. These together formed an arc of a circle from the river Saale where Jena later stood to a point on the Lahn around Limburg. With these were included the more northerly Bortharians or Bortrini, most of whom were obstinately heathen and remained so till after 770, but whose southerly extremity may have become Christian after the felling of the Oak of Thor at Geismar. Within (and to the south of) the arc were the people of the 'Grabfeld' between the Thuringian forest and the Rhön mountains, and those of the 'Wetterau' bounded by the river Kinzig, the Vogelsberg and the Taunus range. Further south still, and most relevant to the question of the limits of the 'mission' area, were the 'Suduodi' or southern woodland dwellers. 'Suduodi' we may take as the word used by the people further north (*e.g.* around Amöneburg and Fritzlar) for the 'Waldsassengau' or 'district of the wood settlers'. This district, on a very slightly generous interpretation, included the city of Würzburg, the convent of Kitzingen (already existing, perhaps one of Pirmin's) and two sites where convents would one day be founded under Boniface, namely Ochsenfurt and Tauberbischofsheim.

ders and the Main basin, always assuming that effective support such as had been lacking in the years 732–7, was now available from the Frankish authorities. Such a well established church, preferably forming a constituent part of the wider German church envisaged in the previous letter, was to be the base of operations for a consistent spiritual attack on the heathenism of the Saxons further north.

The fourth letter which Boniface carried on his return was addressed to 'the people of the region of the Old-Saxons' (Ep. 21). The term 'Old-Saxons' was purely *Anglo*-Saxon in origin. Gregory can have taken it only from Boniface. The letter takes it for granted that there are 'Old-Saxons' who have accepted Christ, and among them those who have maintained the faith long enough to be congratulated on their perseverance. A considerable number of converts may have been recently added, assuming a successful campaign by Charles Martel in 737, suitably followed up by evangelism on the part of Boniface's colleagues. The attractions of the old religion, however, were insidious and had to be guarded against. The description of idolatry, and the warning against its dangers, are more pungently expressed in this letter than in the one addressed to the Thuringian region.*

A feature common to the two last letters is the expectation that some will wish to put obstacles in the way of Boniface's success. The Thuringians and their neighbours 'are not to hinder him when he finds people who have wandered from the right path and disciplines them'. The Saxons are warned that 'whenever anyone among you wishes to turn to Christ, you are not to prevent him, nor are you to put pressure upon him to worship things fashioned by human hands.' In the first and most general letter the expected 'hindrance' had been in the matter of men wishing to join the work. There is, naturally, no such suggestion in the letter to the bishops of Bavaria and Alamannia, the object of which is different. What has to be avoided by them, in the Pope's estimation, is more particularly the 'Celtic' type of aberration in church order (which easily, in the Roman view, paved the way for other abuses). An intriguing detail is the word used in this one instance for Celts, namely 'Britons'. ('Scots' was the more usual word for Irish mission-

* It is interesting that Gregory did not succeed in penetrating to the heart of the old Teutonic outlook, but condemned its expressions and symbols without appreciating the character of its deities. Daniel of Winchester had understood better.

aries.) Had there been a rash of Christian workers from Brittany working in Central Europe? Or was it just that Boniface used the word as of early habit as a West-Saxon, thinking of the Cornish 'Britons' as the Celts of whom he disapproved?

Further attention to that same letter (to the five bishops) will help to elucidate the events which followed. Wigo of Augsburg is not otherwise known to us, but may have had the reputation of one who valued the Roman allegiance. His see was also in a strategic position having links both eastward and westward. Liudo of Speyer is likewise unknown, but presumably was cast in a better mould than the Frankish episcopate as a whole, as was also Heddo of Strasbourg, who appears to have been put in as an afterthought, and who as a disciple of Pirmin might have been suspected of views differing from those of his master in some respects. He certainly showed himself unexpectedly sympathetic to Boniface some years later. Rudolf of Constance, another shadowy figure, must also have been close to Pirmin in the previous decade when Reichenau was founded: conceivably, if he were known to have sided with his duke against Pirmin in 728 he may have been thought to be susceptible to influence in a 'canonical' direction. Boniface would surely need 'the angel of God going before him' if he was to sweep all these into the same net with himself and Vivilo, and bring them to a fruitful conference 'at Augsburg or on the banks of the Danube'.

Chapter 13

APATHY IN ALAMMANIA

Along with his restoration to health and the privilege of planning with the Pope, Boniface gained a number of new disciples from his third sojourn in Rome. As before, these consisted mainly of Anglo-Saxon churchmen who were on pilgrimage to Rome, or who after so coming had stayed on.

Two whose names we know were Wessex men. Lull, a deacon in his late twenties, had been educated at Malmesbury. He was to become Boniface's constant companion and aide and finally to succeed him as bishop of Mainz. It is interesting to compare him with the Bavarian, Sturm. After what has already been remarked about the latter, it is a curious coincidence that Lull, though not exactly 'stormy' in character, was easily roused and did not readily yield. The 'storm' and the 'lull' were almost reversed in their personalities. This was to become apparent many years later, after Boniface's death; although Sturm would then show that he too could be tenacious. Another contrast between them stands out clearly: Lull was a scholar, Sturm (although also of gentle, even noble birth) was an ascetic.

Asceticism was a strong feature also in Wynnebald, the other Wessex recruit of 738. Wynnebald was a first cousin to Leoba, as Boniface was on the other side of her family. His home was in the eastern part of Wessex, and he had grown up in a monastery called by a German writer 'Waldheim'. (This was probably at Bishop's Waltham, in Hampshire; but we have no other evidence of its existence.) His family contributed three members altogether to Boniface's mission. Their story is of interest in itself.

The father of the family, Richard, was a man of great charm and radiant Christian goodness. In 724 he went on pilgrimage to Rome with two of his sons, Willibald and Wynnebald. He died at Lucca after being taken ill on the way to Rome. (The people of that town revered him posthumously as a saint.) His two sons completed their pilgrimage. Willibald went further, and made a round trip to the Holy Land, of which an account has been preserved. Wynnebald chose to remain in Rome, presumably attaching himself to some strict monastic house. He was in Rome when King Ine of Wessex, following the example of his predecessor, resigned in 726 and went to live out the last months of his life beside the tombs of the Apostles. In 728 Wynnebald made the journey back to England in order to gain the approval of the remainder of his family for his decision to stay abroad indefinitely. Another brother is said to have returned with him to Rome; but we hear no more of this brother. Their sister, Waldburga, a nun of Wimborne, came to the Continent years afterwards and became as prominent in Boniface's circle as her two brothers already were by the time she arrived.

Willibald, who returned from the East in 730, went to Monte Cassino rather than Rome. Less ascetic than Wynnebald, he was nevertheless 'a good monk', having been marked out for the service of God from infancy. We have no evidence that Boniface made the journey to Monte Cassino in 737–8 (or on either of his earlier visits to Rome), although its interest for him as the original Benedictine house would have been great. Nor do we know whether Willibald came to Rome during Boniface's stay. But it is a fact that the Pope later sent for him and despatched him northwards to make his contribution to the work of which Boniface was in charge.

Having had nine months in which to prepare himself for the next strenuous phase of his work, Boniface and is enlarged party left Rome about May 738. He was now 'Boniface, by the grace of God archbishop, legate of the Apostolic See', and was apt to style himself 'one sent by St. Peter' (*missus Sancti Petri*). If our interpretation is right, he had the unenviable responsibility of trying to draw together the Church, as it existed throughout the German lands, into one ecclesiastical structure and fellowship.

Not for the first time, his journey to those lands was interrupted by an interview on behalf of Italian politics. As in 719, but much more surprisingly, it was Liutprand King of Lombardy with whom he had to deal. This time there is no mention of the Pope designating any gifts for Liutprand in particular. This visit was not one confirming a friendship already existing. The Pope was taking advantage of the impression made upon Liutprand by Boniface almost twenty years before. He was hoping that if the king consented to receive Boniface, their meeting might appease the vexation felt on the Lombard side since Rome had returned to its acknowledgement of the Emperor Leo as nominal overlord.

There is a question as to where the two were expected to meet. In the earliest biography of Boniface we read: 'After travelling Italy, he came to the walls of the city of *Picena* and, as his limbs were weary with old age, he rested awhile with Liutprand, king of the Lombards'. Leaving aside the writer's naive approach, and his ignorance of the political circumstances, and concentrating on geography, we might summise that *Pavia* was intended. That city, the Lombard capital, was where the meeting had taken place in 719, and its early name had been *Ticino*, like the river: 'Picena' could be a confusion (Pavia/Ticino). But in a modern gazetteer we find the name '*Piceno*', with note 'see *Ascoli*'. North-eastwards from Rome at a distance of a hundred miles was this ancient stronghold, once *Asculum* the capital of the district *Picenum*: now *Ascoli-Piceno*. To reach it from Rome, Boniface would literally have 'traversed' or crossed the leg of Italy, almost to the Adriatic shore. A plausible reconstruction of Lombard manoeuvres between 735 and 739 could give Liutprand a long salient south eastwards down the Apennines by 738. From that salient he could divide and menace the Pope in one direction, the Byzantine Exarch of Ravenna northwards, the Duke of Spoleto nearby and the Duke of Benevento not far to the south. We may suspect that it was at *Ascoli* that Boniface and his party were received by the Lombard king. The courtesy and welcome which were given bear testimony to the great impression which had been made by Boniface nineteen years before.

Whatever the details of the Lombard encounter, Boniface's journey could continue into the Alpine passes without leaving Lombard territory. If we are not content to believe that he went straight to the Duchy of Bavaria to begin the fulfilment of the 716 plan, we may suppose that he travelled through the borders of Alamannia, beginning to test reactions to the synod ordered by the Pope. One place on his route would be Augsburg, politically Bavarian but ethnically Alamannian, a possible location for the synod, and the see whose bishop, Wigo, was the first of the five addressed by the Pope.*

* cf. Appendix A

Augsburg could, of course, be reached by the road over the Brenner, now familiar to Boniface. More could be learned about the Alamannian situation *en route*, however, if he and his companions took a little extra time and trouble to go round by the Bernina Pass and the city of Chur (Coire). Chur was the seat of an ancient bishopric. It was Alamannian from an administrative point of view but populated largely by a Romano-Helvetic population. The Pope had apparently not regarded it as 'German' in relation to the proposed synod. It was a place, however, from which much might be learnt of the state of affairs in Alamannia proper, particularly Constance.

Any reactions which Boniface in fact received on his journey are not likely to have been favourable to the synod proposal. At Augsburg he may have received personal support from the bishop, but little more. Wigo very likely agreed to participate in the consecration of further bishops, either in an all-German synodical arrangement or, failing that, in Bavaria itself.

The party probably proceeded northward from Augsburg and crossed the Danube at the confluence of the Wörnitz, where later the town of Donauwörth grew up. It is intriguing to ask whether there was an inhabited place there at that time. It would have been more central than any other point 'on the banks of the Danube' for a gathering of representatives from Alamannia, Bavaria and the Würzburg area. As he crossed the river Boniface might well have considered the words in the Pope's letter to the five bishops concerning the synod proposal.

The intention to hasten back to his northern territories had, we may guess, the Pope's blessing and approval. Boniface probably either rejoined the River Altmühl at Solnhofen* and returned by the road he had taken on his way south, or chose to explore fresh Alamannian territory by keeping further west, to enter his own enlarged field of work somewhere along the River Tauber.

From then on he was kept busy over a period of months. He needed to make a visitation of all his earlier monastic foundations and churches, confirming those who had been baptized during his year of absence. Especially urgent was a visit to any Saxon areas which had been opened up by Frankish conquest. In this, not for the first nor for the last time, he was doomed to disappointment. The fruits of victory were shortlived. There

* A place taking its name from the Anglo-Saxon hermit, Sola.

may have been few to benefit from the Pope's letter to the 'Old Saxons'. If it had become clear that the Würzburg region was now to be administered by his disciples rather than Pirmin's, with the full approval and backing of Duke Charles, then there was much to be done amongst the peoples around the middle Main basin.

Though well recovered, he had enough to exhaust him again in these territories alone. To this period we may ascribe a letter which seems to indicate that on his return Boniface had learned of losses by death more recent than that of Abbot Wigbert of Fritzlar. Boniface writes to a certain Abbot Aldhere in England, concluding his letter with the following:–

> 'We ask also that you may be studious in prayer for those Germans who are given over to the worship of idols . . . (1. Timothy 2.4) . . . Likewise we would pray for the souls of our brothers who have fallen asleep, men who were working with us in the Lord, that you may arrange to hold services of prayer for their assistance and to celebrate solemn masses on their behalf: the bearer of this letter will give you their names in detail.'

The shock of bereavement, the disappointment over the hope of fresh converts among the Saxons, added to his uncertainity over the Pope's grand design and brought back to Boniface some of his feelings of a few years earlier. Indeed, he was prepared to face death if that should be his lot at any time. He begins this same letter with strongly worded requests for prayer 'that the good Lord, who is the cause of our pilgrimage, may protect and guide our fragile "ship" so that it may not be submerged beneath the waves of Germanic tempests; and that he may bring it through to the tranquil shore of the heavenly Jerusalem.' He says further: 'We commend ourselves to your prayers, that whether in life or death we may be associated in the communion of your love.' (This prayer fellowship across all boundaries including death was characteristic of the religious tradition to which Boniface belonged.)

Through the latter part of 738 and into the following year there was opportunity to begin to plan a diocesan structure for the enlarged mission-field, although the consecration of bishops would have to wait. At least three dioceses would be needed. The acquisition of Würzburg made things easier. An ancient city of such proportions could not fail to gain approval at

Rome as an episcopal see. Hesse and Thuringia presented problems in that respect. Risks would have to be taken. It would have to be explained to Rome (or had Gregory already been warned?) that there were no large towns. Büraburg, near to Fritzlar and Geismar, was the best that could be provided for Hesse, and Erfurt, north-eastwards from Ohrdruf, for Thuringia. As for the consecration of bishops by canonical process, if Alamannia proved uncooperative it would be necessary to tackle the Bavarian situation first and work from there.

Following the scheme by which we are interpreting the available evidence, we may assume that Boniface set out early in 739 to convey the Pope's message to the bishops of Speyer, Strasbourg and Constance, without much hope of response. There is no evidence that Liudo of Speyer and Rudolf of Constance agreed to support his cause or the Pope's plan, either officially or unofficially. Heddo of Strasbourg was privately impressed but unable to make his interest public or official at this stage. None of them has left any record of a visit from Boniface. The whole matter, seen in retrospect by Boniface's followers many years after, appeared so disappointing that it was omitted from his biography altogether.

But the Bavarian reaction was entirely different.

Chapter 14

ARCHBISHOP IN ACTION

As he had planned, Boniface went again to Augsburg after the final frustration at Constance. Bishop Wigo probably went with him to help to carry out the reform of the Bavarian Church. (Wigo would be a second assistant, alongside Vivilo, in episcopal consecrations.) Their first object must have been to discuss the whole enterprise with Duke Odilo, who had declared himself in favour of a plan similar to that of 716. For that purpose they presumably went to Regensburg, the capital. They worked out with Odilo the division of the dukedom (Augsburg apart) into four dioceses with clearly defined boundaries. They discussed ways and means of endowing four cathedral foundations, the conversion of Celtic-style monastic establishments into houses of a Benedictine type, and the question of candidates for the office of bishop where Celtic monastic bishops might not consent to be re-consecrated or were deemed unsuitable to become diocesans. (This may in part have been a continuation of what Boniface and Duke Hugobert had thought out together in 734.)

Wikterp, monastic-bishop in Regensburg, was known to be hesitant. It was arranged that the capital should be left until last of the four cities involved. Odilo, seeing that matters would take time, allotted about four months to the reform, and made it the occasion of a deliberate 'progress' round his domain. Clearly his authority would be much better exercised directly in such an important and delicate task.

Vivilo may have come from Passau to Regensburg to take part in the discussion. But in any case it was obvious that Passau was the first city to be approached. The ducal party therefore travelled down the Danube or along its banks. Inevitably the subject of the Pope's larger plan came up for consideration at some point. Alamannia having been eliminated, as it were, a second-best might be achieved through Bavarian reform and subsequent consecrations in Boniface's regions to the north-west: synods at Regensburg or Passau, as well as at Augsburg, could be held according to the 'letter' of the Pope's intention although on a smaller geographical basis.

At Passau the diocesan boundaries were proclaimed. Vivilo was henceforward to confine his ministrations to that part of the dukedom. The Church and monastery of St. Stephen were re-ordered to form a cathedral foundation with a Benedictine community serving it. Its endowments were accordingly transferred, and so far as appeared necessary, increased by ducal gift. Odilo and Boniface remained at Passau with their combined party long enough for matters to settle down, in view of the fact that Vivilo was needed to go further with them.

Proceeding to Salzburg, they had greater obstacles to overcome at that furthest point of German ethnic concentration. The entrenched 'Celtic' tradition proved adamant against change, and could only be removed by more radical methods. A new nominee was needed for the post of diocesan bishop. A certain presbyter John was agreed upon. (As he did not live many years, he could conceivably have been an older man, already noted by Boniface on his 734 visit.) Since Hrodbert (St. Rupert) had died in 715, Vitalis, Flobrigis and Liuti had each been 'bishop', but under the direction of the abbot of St. Peter's monastery. John was duly consecrated bishop under the Roman rite, and also named as abbot of the (reformed) monastery. Boniface was assisted by Wigo and Vivilo at the consecration ceremony. The monastic endowments were, again in this instance, reapplied: they were ample for the new foundation. Diocesan limits were again carefully defined and proclaimed. The duke and Boniface remained until John's authority was assured. (What happened to Luiti and the former abbot we do not know.) John may have been asked to take part in the next stage of the tour. Faithfulness to canonical provisions would require that three bishops, when available, should assist an archbishop at a consecration. Vivilo and Wigo would therefore also remain in the party.

At Freising there were fewer problems. Since the time of Corbinian, the Rome-oriented bishop who had been exiled under Grimoald, and who died before he could return, there had not been a 'monastic bishop', although one or two monasteries existed which needed to be brought under the Benedictine rule. A brother of Corbinian, the presbyter Erembert, was available as a suitable candidate for the bishopric, into which he was duly consecrated. The larger of the two places of worship, St. Mary's, was converted into a cathedral. Excess endowments belonging to the monastery of St. Stephen with St. Martin were allocated to the bishop and the cathedral foundation. The monastery, remodelled, was left with sufficient means of subsistence. Once again, diocesan boundaries were defined.

Wigo could conveniently return to Augsburg from Freising, and would have been glad to return to his own charge. Erembert, once the situation had been accepted at Freising, could accompany the main party on its way to Regensburg, and act as one of the co-consecrators in the establishment of a see there. If Wikterp *could* ever be persuaded, the sight of the three bishops Vivilo, John and Erembert and the thought of all that they signified must surely be sufficient. But he proved to be unwilling. A certain Gaubald was therefore consecrated bishop of Regensburg. The religious house of St. Emmeram (Haimhramm) was used as the basis of the reformed arrangement. Its church became the cathedral. The community became Benedictine and served the cathedral, as at Passau. Endowments were suitably modified.

So, the great ducal tour being completed, we see Vivilo returning to Passau, John to Salzburg, Erembert to Freising. It is possible that Erembert took with him Boniface's report to the Pope, since from Freising such a document could be conveniently taken by messenger over the Brenner. We have no copy of such a report, but can gauge its matter and its manner from the reply which was sent from Rome, dated October 29th 739, and presumably reached Boniface at Fritzlar some while after his return northward. Pope Gregory first congratulates Boniface on having attained a total of over 100,000 converts 'through your efforts and those of Prince Charles (*sic*)'. The successful months in Bavaria had evidently made it easier to count the blessings that had been received over the years; and because Charles Martel had lately been able to co-operate more, Boniface had written in a manner which caused the Pope to overlook the comparative neglect shown earlier by the Frankish leader.

Gregory next approves what has been done in Bavaria, and trusts that the follow-up will be thorough. 'In carrying out our commands . . . you have acted wisely and well.' It is clear, from a later passage, that the 'commands' in respect of Bavaria had been irrespective of the German Synod plan. Part of the follow-up concerned the status of clergy in Bavaria who had received ordination from bishops whose own 'orders' was in doubt: 'Let them be ordained by a bishop and fulfil their sacred charge, provided they are Catholics of blameless life, trained to the service of God, well versed in the teachings of the Church and fitted to hold office.' Even closer scrutiny had had to be made, of course, in the case of the bishops whom Boniface had consecrated. Evidently the period of contact with Vivilo had given rise to some doubt about the latter's own standards of doctrine: 'If . . . he has deviated . . . correct and instruct him according to the traditions of the Church of Rome as you have received them from us.'

The extent to which latinity had developed throughout the Western Church, with strong encouragement from Rome, is shown by implication in some other words of Gregory, answering a point in Boniface's report: 'Those who were baptized with a formula expressed in a heathen (i.e. German) tongue, provided their baptism was performed in the name of the Trinity, should be confirmed with the sacred chrism and the laying on of hands.' (As at other times and places in Church history, it is not clear how far 'confirmation' had to do with checking up on the condition of those baptized, and how far it was concerned with the conferring of some gift over and above the baptismal gift.)

Two points of special interest are made toward the conclusion of Gregory's letter. First, whatever Boniface had included in his report about the 'larger plan', the Pope writes firmly as though he has been working separately to ensure that it comes about, and is unrealistically confident: 'We command you to attend the council which is to be held on the banks of the Danube and, vested with apostolic authority, to act as our representative.' (This is all very mysterious, in view of the total lack of any evidence that such a meeting ever took place, or came near to taking place.)

The second point has to do with Boniface's own activities, concerning which the Pope will allow no relaxation, even if the former in his sixtieth year might be thought to have a right to a more settled, less roving existence. He may have complained that the Pope's instructions had given him impossible tasks to fulfil all at once: a full-blown mission to unconverted heathen had to be conducted alongside a wholesale scheme of church organisation and reform, with himself as a sort of runner between all the German provinces. Add to that the fact that an archbishop normally had a settled centre or 'metropolitan see' from which to work, and that his own present roving commission could appear almost 'Celtic' rather than 'Catholic' from one point of view. . . . Gregory, doubtless because of his enormous appreciation of Boniface's unusual qualities, and regarding him as able to achieve (even in his sixties, as long as he might be spared) what no one after him would be able to achieve, wrote back in terms which sound relentless enough: 'As far as God shall grant you strength, continue to preach . . . so that the Christian faith may increase. . . . You have no permission to remain in one district when your work there is completed. . . . Continue to preach and consecrate bishops. Do not shrink from journeys.'

If our account of the year 738 and 739 is correct, Boniface had travelled 1,500 miles in two years: too far, in all justice. Obedience to the Pope alone led him to accept the burdens laid upon him. Mercifully, during the next three years he was able to spend a large part of his time in the northern territories with which he had been chiefly associated, and which had now been extended somewhat towards the south. He was thus able to fulfil his responsibilities as archbishop in the stricter sense throughout those territories, creating as in Bavaria a full Catholic church organisation, and doing so without the obstacles which had needed to be overcome in Duke Odilo's domain.

The local leaders who had been addressed, along with their peoples, in the Pope's letter (Ep. 43) of 738 had accepted their responsibilities, and were prepared to co-operate with higher (Frankish) authority in creating the material and moral conditions for the episcopal system which was to be set up. Duke Charles' own favourable attitude had received freer expression since the death of Bishop Gerold of Mainz, who had gone on active service in the recent Frankish expedition against the Saxons and had been killed at the river Weser. Gerold's son Gewilib, possibly a bastard, had succeeded in filling the post left vacant by his father's death, presumably by popular wish (such was the state of things). Gewilib appears to have interfered little in church affairs, and was chiefly concerned to avenge his father's death.

Würzburg, although only recently put under Boniface's tutelage, was the first bishopric to be set up* in the whole region, as had presumably been contemplated. Burghard, a close disciple and of the archbishop's own age-group, was chosen to fill the see. We have to suppose that Wigo of Augsburg, Erembert of Freising and Gaubald of Regensburg, or any two of these, assisted Boniface at the rite of consecration. While Regensburg honoured the memory of the Irish missionary Kilian, and thought of him as 'founder', we do not hear that it was necessary for Boniface to reform any institutions which had persisted after Kilian's death in 689. Burghard, its new bishop, was a strong character, and could be relied upon to look after the diocese which was defined around Würzburg, thus leaving Boniface free of anxiety when he was concerned with Hesse-Thuringia and the Saxon borderlands.

To Büraburg (Hesse) and Erfurt (Thuringia), when their turn came, the archbishop consecrated two less well known Anglo-Saxon colleagues. A certain Witta, of whom we know little else, was elevated to the Hessian see, which included in the Lahn valley area along with Hesse proper. Only by roundabout deduction can we allot the name Dada to the more easterly area, by virtue of the attendance of 'Dada' at a synod later on.

In view of the Pope's request that the Bavarian situation be carefully fostered, Boniface paid a visit there in the first part of 741, and toured the dukedom once again to see that all was in order. His visit was timely in another sense, or possibly owed its timing to news reaching Boniface early in the year. Pope Gregory, whose life had only a few months to run, had acted in the spirit of his own instructions to Boniface by drawing Willibald out of Monte Cassino and despatching him northwards, presumably as a likely candidate for a bishopric, though still only in deacon's orders. (The stamina of the man had been revealed by his journey to Jerusalem: his other qualities could be vouched for by the Abbot of Cassino.) Willibald arrived in Bavaria when Duke Odilo had been discussing church arrangements for the 'Nordgau', a territory out to the north-west, with its local lord, Suidger. The area was somewhat isolated, and not readily covered by either Gaubald or Erembert. After consultations all round, Boniface during his Bavarian tour allowed Willibald to be shown round the Nordgau, particularly its chief

* Schieffer believes that it did not precede the two which followed, but that all these coincided, in Spring 742.

town Eichstätt, and later raised him to the presbyterate with a living at Eichstätt provided by Suidger. This was a temporary arrangement, preparatory to greater things. A year later, 742, Willibald was called to Thuringia. After a joyful reunion with his brother Wynnebald at Sülzenbrücken, where the latter was resident presbyter at the time, he was consecrated bishop at that very place. Boniface had as his assistants Burghard and Witta, along with one whom we may be fairly sure was Dada, even if his name does not remain attached to the occasion in tradition.

So was created the seventh episcopal see, or eighth if we include Passau, which Boniface brought into being. It was the last one that was needed. After two years the Nordgau slipped out of Odilo's hand, and was joined more closely with Würzburg and the others. That development belongs to a later phase of the history of those times, which opened in consequence of three deaths in 741. The whole turn of affairs was to affect profoundly the 'Legate of the Apostolic See'.

Chapter 15

BONIFACE AND THE ANGLO-SAXON MISSION

It is helpful at this stage to try to gain an overall picture of Boniface's flock, and to take a look at various aspects of its life. This requires a forward glance, to bring into view those who had not yet joined him until after the early 740s and also some whose names do not appear earlier but who came into focus later. Bavaria can be left out of account for this purpose. So, for the most part, can the Frankish scene which Boniface was to enter during the 740s. In both these cases he was a reformer from without, so to speak, rather than a chief shepherd with a flock and a band of assistant shepherds around him. It is his mission area, as enlarged to include 'Lower Franconia', with which we are mainly concerned. A few of his 'assistant shepherds' also worked in West Frisia from the time of Willibrord's death in 739, or soon after, and beyond the date of Boniface's martyrdom fifteen years later.

The number of the 'flock' could be reckoned in six figures, as we have already seen. To give pastoral care to this large family, and at the same time to continue an evangelistic initiative, must have made necessary a band of assistant 'shepherds' running into hundreds. These were involved in differing kinds of work. There was a sort of task-force (to change the metaphor) of those who went out from the monastic centres as ministers of God. From Fritzlar, for example, there might be considerably more than the seven office-holders appointed after Abbot Wigbert's death; perhaps most of those monks who had been ordained to the diaconate and all who were presbyters. (We have little idea how many were thus involved.) To Fritzlar, Ohrdruf and Amöneburg we may add the later foundations of Fulda and Heidenheim, at least five male houses in all. Those nuns, too, who were deaconesses or were regarded in a similar light, ministered to women in a variety of ways: even in the liturgical sphere, a female assistant minister was needed at baptism whenever women candidates were coming forward.

So, if we add to the convent at Kitzingen (which came under Boniface around 740) his own foundations at Ochsenfurt and Tauberbischofsheim (where his dear cousin Leoba was abbess), not forgetting also the women's house in the double monastery at Heidenheim, we have four convents in view. Out of not fewer than nine monastic institutions we may reckon that the 'task-force' numbered above a hundred.

While some of these were drawn from the continent of Europe, such as Sturm from Bavaria, Gregory the Frank and possibly Gemberht the Frisian, perhaps three quarters were English, and most of them from Wessex. Thirty English nuns came in one contingent with Leoba, but not all to the same convent. There may have been twice that number of men altogether from England in the monasteries, though their arrival was spread over the years. The total population of monastic inmates under Boniface's general oversight was of the order of two or three thousand, mainly natives of the region, if it is true that there were 400 at Fulda alone at the time of his death.

Added to the 'task-force' were the individual clergy looking after separate churches, mostly in small and scattered communities, often in conditions of loneliness and hardship. The more fortunate presbyter might have a deacon, a sub-deacon and perhaps one or two other helpers. Most would be working alone. We may put the total number of such churches at between one and two hundred, though even so broad a guess is hazardous. When the Saxons burned down thirty churches in a single raid, it was a serious but not a catastrophic event. No doubt Boniface, and the bishops whom he eventually consecrated for the area, ordained many presbyters and junior ministers from the local population, as was envisaged in the course of his dealings with Rome. But quite certainly some of his fellow-countrymen also held local pastoral charge. Wynnebald, although technically a monk, spent several years as resident pastor of Sülzenbrücken, being in presbyteral orders. A touching example of the lonely shepherd is provided by Boniface's namesake, Wynfrith son of Ward* related to Boniface on his father's side but a Thuringian on his mother's side. He is mentioned (though in a late source only) as 'the only presbyter beyond the Weser', at a time when it might be thought that all ground beyond that river was securely held by heathen

* Or possibly, son of *Ullard*

tribes. It is fascinating to speculate concerning 'Ward', as possibly a distant cousin who accompanied Boniface to Rome and Germany in 718–9, and fell in love with a local girl in Thuringia, married her, and about 721 became the proud father of a boy, who was named 'Wynfrith'. That was while the older Wynfrith was with Willibrord. Twenty-five years later, if the need for presbyters was regarded as sufficiently urgent, he would be old enough to be ordained presbyter, i.e. in 746, well within the period we are now considering.

An overall estimate of the size of the 'ordained ministry' in the north German territories, not including West Frisia, would give a number greater than 300, inside and outside the monastic houses, male and female. If the total number of Christians in the same area was approaching 200,000 at the end of Boniface's life, the proportion seems reasonable, bearing in mind that constant pressure from heathenism on one side and abuses in the Frankish Church on the other. Persons of English origin in the ministry were perhaps about one-third of the total.

Relations with the neighbouring heathen Saxons varied, and could occasionally be friendly. The fact that friendship was easier when the Frankish army was furthest away was presumably an embarrassment to Boniface. Such fraternising as took place did not result in any great willingness to accept Christianity on the Saxon side: the awesome prospect was that it would take a Frankish conquest, an enduring one, to create the opportunity for consistent preaching, while psychologically defeat did not give rise to receptivity. There was an insoluble dilemma. The 'Old-Saxons' evidently recognized Boniface as his fellow-countrymen as 'cousins', quite apart from the Christian issue. Boniface was always hoping that this would eventually help them to turn to the true God. He wrote a letter to the English clergy sometime after 738, asking for prayers for the conversion of the Saxons, whose 'repeated cry is, we are of the same blood and bone.' (Ep. 46*) It is interesting to note that in the same general period he could write to a leading Frank, asking him to 'protect the Christians from the hostility of the heathen.'

Life in the monasteries, which were the power-houses of the whole enterprise, reflected the traditions in which Boniface had been trained in England. Preaching, teaching and study went

* cf. also Ep. 47 to Bp Torthelm of Leicester.

along with the regular prayer, the 'daily office' and the sacramental life. Each religious house had its school, from which others beside those aspiring to the monastic life could benefit. The Benedictine daily round of eight offices of corporate prayer and psalmody was faithfully followed. Such physical labour as was needed to maintain the community, and to leave a margin for hospitality and care of the sick, was carried out by the monks and a number of servants. The use of servants left the senior presbyteral members free for preaching, teaching, study and mission. In most monastic communities of any size, some of the monks or nuns were engaged in the various arts and crafts connected with books. Rarely there might be those who composed or compiled fresh works, but regularly the work of making copies of standard books was carried out: scriptural, doctrinal, liturgical, disciplinary, and occasionally more general volumes.

In the local churches and the monasteries alike the sacraments of baptism and eucharist were celebrated according to the usage at Rome, broadly speaking, but with a certain variety which also prevailed in England. Once a diocesan structure had been set up, baptism was not customarily held in monastery chapels, since Boniface was anxious to avoid the danger of allowing monasteries to become 'para-churches' interfering with the canonical arrangement of authority. (This was one of the sharp differences between Boniface and Pirmin.) The Roman-style rites were shorter than those of the Gallo-Frankish churches. The latter shared with the Celtic world a considerable variety of much longer services, going back to eastern influence in early times. As regards service-books, there were separate volumes for various ministers who, in a well-staffed church, shared the conduct of the service: a volume of Epistle passages, a volume of Gospel passages, a book of selected Psalms in order of use, as well as the celebrant's own 'sacramentary'. In a full service the carrying out of the rite took on the quality of a drama performed by the several ministers and the congregation.

Returning to the subject of books, churches and monasteries varied widely in the number and range of volumes possessed. Books which had come with Boniface from England or Rome, and others which were sent to him at his request from English communities, were doubtless in many cases used as examples for copy after copy as the mission work developed. During the earlier years, as already noted, letters home had to do with

New Testament portions that had as yet not been available to Boniface. In the early 740s we have an instance of his requesting an Old Testament portion, when in a letter to the aged Bishop Daniel of Winchester he asks that 'Winbert's volume of the Prophets' may be sent.

Boniface's own collection of books became famous, especially as he was apt to carry around with him quite a number at any one time. A post-script to one of the biographies of the great man gives a vivid picture: 'Wherever he went, he carried his books with him. They were his "treasure", his "estate". In the intervals of a journey' (or even '*during* a journey', perhaps) 'he would either read the Scriptures or sing psalms and hymns, when he was not giving alms to the poor.' The story of his martyrdom was to add further fame to his travelling library.

The scope of his collection as a whole covered books of the Bible and commentaries upon them; writings of the early Fathers; volumes of conciliar 'canons' and papal decrees, such as those given to him at Rome; and a few more general works, particularly in the classics. Amongst those belonging to him or his circle which have survived are a volume of the second century Father, Hegesippus; a collection of theological treatises in a damaged condition, thought to have been the book in his hands at his death (see p. 203); an assortment of writings of various dates from St. Jerome (fourth century) to St. Aldhelm of Wessex (d. 709), written in various West Saxon hands but finished off in a French style of script; and a commentary on Virgil's Aeneid by Servius (400 A.D.). A fragment of Boniface's own Latin grammar has also come down to us, through its having been used in binding a later book.

Some of the above-mentioned have signs of Boniface's own handwriting upon them. This applies remarkably to a New Testament volume in which the Epistle of James has been heavily 'glossed' in the margin by two hands, thought to be those of Boniface and Lull. The earlier glosses are simple and trenchant, disclosing those features which might be expected of Boniface: a strong moral and sacramental emphasis, and a stress on apostolicity both in the evangelical sense and in connection with succession and order. Continuity in and through the Roman See figures prominently; although, also, high value is placed on the apostolic ministry of James, the Lord's brother (and reputed author of the Epistle) as having been received from Jesus himself.

Apart from the fragment of the Grammar, there are very few Anglo-Saxon words to be found on the pages of surviving books, even in the margin. Latin was the language of the Western Church. This leads us to pay tribute to Boniface and his colleagues, in that their mission had lasting success amongst peoples untutored in the Latin tongue. This language problem made it all the more necessary that the truth of the Christian message should shine out from the life-style of its preachers. Boniface stresses the importance of this in some of his letters in a general way, without specific reference to language problems. The passage quoted at the end of this chapter shows how far he illustrated that principle in his own ministry, in the estimation of one who lived a century later, Radbod of Utrecht.

Our picture can be filled out with some brief reference to the detail of worship and to music, arts and crafts in association with it. Christians of to-day are at one with Boniface's 'family' in virtue of many elements of liturgy which we share with them, as well as the basic Gospel message itself. Those who still use 'Gregorian' chant are closer still to the practice of Boniface's people. With or without any particular type of music, the Psalms form an important part of the wealth of our common heritage. Hymns are mentioned a number of times in the correspondence and biographies of Boniface, but not under specific titles. Those of the great St. Ambrose of Milan (fourth century) he may well have known and used: such as (in our version) 'O strength and stay', or 'The eternal gifts of Christ the King'. Likewise, of additional interest because of the poem on 'The destruction of Thuringia' by the same writer, there are one or two from Venantius Fortunatus (sixth century) which we also use: 'The royal banners forward go', and 'Sing, my tongue, the glorious battle'. In Boniface's later years, when there had been contact and overlapping with Frankish churches and even with Pirmin's circle (he was from the Pyrenees), there were the Spaniard Prudentius' hymns (late fourth century), such as 'Earth has many a noble city'. Hymns and psalms were widely known by heart, and were brought forth spontaneously at times of deep emotion, for example when the death of a Willibrord or a Boniface was first made known to those who revered them.

Pictorial art was used in the adornment of books. In such matters, as distinct from traditions of doctrine, discipline and forms of service, Boniface could be glad of the Celtic skills, which had also influenced England through Northumbria. The

'Cadmug Gospels', preserved at Fulda, give a good example of Irish illumination work: the volume is thought to have belonged to Boniface himself. The gold-decorated book of 'Epistles of St.Peter', for which he sent gold to England, has not come down to us; but we can see the brilliant use of gold in a tome of not much later date, of Frankish style, The 'Golden Volume' (Codex Aureus) of St. Emmeram, Regensburg. Other crafts, equally sophisticated, were used in the manufacture of liturgical vessels and reliquaries. We do not know for certain of an such article surviving from the Bonifatian circle. The nearest is the 'Tassilo Chalice' at Kremsmünster convent in Austria, east of Passau. This is a large communion vessel, copper gilt, with an extraordinary profusion of decoration and figurative work. A gift of Duke Tassilo of Bavaria (successor to Odilo) and his wife, it is judged to have originated in Northumbria. The fact is especially interesting, in that the Anglo-Saxon influence in Bavaria waned even during Boniface's last ten years.*

Such material beauty is helpful when it encourages and represents the inward beauty of holy lives; but it can become a snare if it begins to take the place of genuine Christian devotion and service. A parallel thought was in the mind of Radbod of Utrecht when, writing the preface to a life of Boniface, he contrasted him with the builders of ornate churches in his day (ninth century), when corruption abounded:

'But indeed, not long before our own time there was sent from God a most wise "architect", Boniface . . . In place of *stones* and *mortar* he arranged that *faith* should be built with *hope*. For *gold*, he declared that the mysteries of *Holy Scripture* were to be understood. For *silver*, he affirmed that the *Name of God* was to be preached to those who would believe. Instead of *painted ceilings* overhead, he taught people to lift their minds to *heaven*, which is *adorned* with that "variety" with which the Psalmist says that the Queen of Heaven is clothed about.

For *shining jewels* he gave to understand that the *lives of those with teaching authority* were to be bright and *crystal-pure*. By this means their hearers would be able to examine themselves as in a mirror . . . They would not then be seduced by vainglory . . .

Above all things, moreover, he "put on *charity*" as an

* Coloured illustrations of these items are found in 'Art from the Dark Ages', by Backes and Dölling, transl. Garvie (Abrams, New York, *c.* 1970).

ingredient in his building instructions; with utter good sense, as it is of the heavenly order and unequalled in the scale of virtues.

In this manner did that man build; and he persuaded those who were with him to build likewise.'

Chapter 16

THE DOOR OPENS TO FRANKISH CHURCH REFORM

We may judge that the death of Willibrord in 739 affected Boniface in more than one way. Personally, and despite the circumstances of their parting, he is likely to have felt the loss of one under whom he had worked, from whom he had learnt, and whose career had in some sense paved the way for his own. It was a bereavement, although the two had seen little of one another for a long time, even if we have to regard as apocryphal the story that Boniface went to Utrecht to 'weep with those who weep'. But what is more, Boniface was concerned for the churches in the West Frisian region, to which his missionary vocation had first taken him. Now they were without a chief shepherd. They had no bishop, much less an archbishop. It seems likely that Charles Martel, though ready to support Boniface's work at the eastern end of his domains, did not in the last two years of his life show the initiative to tackle a new situation further west. The Gallo-Frankish Church took little interest, being itself riddled with corruption and abuse. Boniface might well cry out to God in prayer, and trust that somehow responsible churchmen in Utrecht and the places hitherto subject to its oversight might be enabled to hold the position until such time as a constructive solution could be found. We can imagine that he might have applied to have West Frisia included within the scope of his own general oversight, had not a wedge of 'Old-Frankish' episcopal sees stood in between, indifferent or hostile to his aims.

The year 741 was a turning point in this and in much wider fields. Charles Martel's death in October of that year was preceded by that of the Emperor Leo at Constantinople in June, and followed by that of Pope Gregory in December. The Papacy was in process of seeking closer relations with the Franks, directly because of the unbounded ambitions of the Lombards in Italy, and therefore indirectly because of the condition of the old 'Empire' in both political and ecclesiastical terms. Pope Gregory had sent an urgent message to Charles in 739, and the latter had been willing and able to secure Liutprand's co-operation. The time was ripe for developments in various directions. After Charles' death his sons divided the realm for administrative purposes, Carloman taking Austrasia or the 'German' part and Pippin Neustria, the 'French' portion. Grifo, their half-brother, was left with no lands. There had been no official king since the death of Thierry V in 737. The two new 'Mayors of the Palace', though regarding the kingdom still as one entity in principle, did not immediately appoint a king; but the following year (742), in order to prevent trouble from a royalist faction, they installed Childeric III on the throne.

The papal chair was taken by Zacharias, a man of Greek origin, born and brought up near the southern tip of Italy in territory belonging to the 'Empire'. His background did not make him other than a fairly strict Roman ecclesiastically, though he showed himself in the course of time to be tolerant in some respects. He had met Boniface in Rome, and had gained a real affection for him, while suspecting that his tremendous drive and firm convictions might lead occasionally to an over-zealous move. Boniface returned the affection, but was to find Zacharias by no means always in agreement with every detail of his activities.

Zacharias took office hoping that under the new Emperor Constantine V relations with the Byzantine authority might be restored. He was reluctant to envisage an end to the traditional pattern of a 'Roman' world with New Rome as its civil centre and Old Rome as its ecclesiastical focus. He was to be disappointed. Constantine took up the banner of 'iconoclasm', and after being temporarily subdued by his brother-in-law Artabasdos who opposed him in this, returned to power as one whom the Pope could not respect. His treatment of his foes earned him the nickname 'Copronymus' ('his name is dung'), a title which was transmitted down the centuries. His main interest was in extending or defending his borders eastward and northward against Arab peoples. He paid little heed to the Byzantine possessions in Italy. From the Roman standpoint the old Empire was receding further and further from view. Such independence as the Papacy could maintain would depend in the coming years on the Lombards and the Franks, and on the balance of power between them; as had already been made fairly clear by 739.

The Kingdom of the Franks, united in the sense that the two brother 'Mayors' worked well together, required the maximum inner coherence in face of a number of actual and potential foes. The traditional 'March Assembly' might be held separately in Austrasia and Neustria, or a joint meeting might be arranged; but in either case Carloman and Pippin were in touch with one another, and with their nobles planned each year's campaigns in an orderly and efficient way. The range of their needs in terms of national defence may be shown by the following examples. In 742 Pippin fought against the difficult duke of Aquitaine, Hunoald. In 743 the two brothers dealt with Bavaria, after a dynastic quarrel with Odilo who had married their sister. In 744 Carloman made one of the periodic incursions into the Saxon region with a view, if possible, to permanent occupation and out of revenge for Saxon raids into Austrasia. (In this campaign Bishop Gewilib of Mainz avenged the death of his father, Bishop Gerold, killed at the River Weser in 737 or 738.) In the same year Pippin occupied himself in squashing the phoenix-like dukedom of Alamannia, after buying off Odilo of Bavaria who had become its ally. In 745 Carloman joined his younger brother in tackling Aquitaine again more successfully. After the suppression of an Alamannian revolt in 746 conditions became more stable, except that the Saxon problem remained for Charlemagne (768–814) to settle. In 747 Carloman, the more spiritually minded of the two brothers through Boniface's influence, gave up his position and retired to a monastery, although he was not by any means a weak ruler. Pippin ('the Short', as he was known) thereafter governed the whole kingdom, gaining in 751 the actual kingship, as we shall see.

It was with a view to restoring and strengthening the 'soul' of the Frankish nation that the brothers favoured church reform from the early years of their reign; though Carloman who led the way had more specifically Christian motives from the very start. They needed to stiffen the moral fibre of their people. For this they were prepared to face opposition. At the same time, as politicians they were ready to temper their policies in order that the overall unity might not be too severely strained. In this, Pippin was by nature more prudent and farsighted than his brother; but Carloman too would compromise when he saw the necessity. To bring in Boniface and the Roman connexion in the interests of reform was a bold step. A more distant goal may have added to their courage and determination: a double goal, possibly, namely the attainment of 'imperial' status for the Frankish régime and domain, and (more distant still, it may well have seemed) of royal status for the Carolingian house to which they themselves belonged. In the achievement of both these ends the Papacy could give indispensable assistance. If a Pope agreed, Frankland could replace Byzantium, and the Carolings their impotent 'masters' of the Merovingian dynasty. How far these thoughts were in the minds of the two brothers when they came to power, it is hard to say; but such hopes could have given them additional motivation, patience and steadiness in the tasks which lay before them. To all this, as well as to reformation of religion and morals, Boniface was the providentially-afforded key of opportunity.

Boniface himself, being over sixty by the time of Charles's death, had had opportunity for more than twenty of those years to observe the poor state, spiritually and morally as well as from the point of view of organisation, of the older churches within the Frankish realm. His journeys through France (as we should call it) had revealed much. The period spent with Willibrord had brought him close to the corrupt condition of things especially when Bishop Liutwin of Trier was succeeded by his son Milo, the sportsman who also secured the see of Rheims in plurality.* More recently Boniface had suffered from the situation at Mainz. He thus knew of at least two cases in which sons had succeeded their fathers as bishops, both of them highly unsuitable characters; and one being actually illegitimate.

But the matter went deeper even than such crude examples of 'nepotism'. For a long while the chief offices of the Church, being linked with property and revenues, had been used by political leaders as counters in the game of securing allegiance; notably by Charles Martel himself. Episcopal sees, abbacies and other posts had thus come into the hands of 'owners' who could treat them in almost any way they might choose. Those who occupied the positions so impropriated might or might not receive suitable ordination. Revenues in particular instances might be divided between two persons, one ordained and one

* Of these two important sees one (Trier) had been of metropolitan status at an earlier and healthier period.

lay (occasionally, both ordained), each bearing the title. Or a man might heap together several offices to himself.

The life-style of such people, whether technically 'clergy' or not, was no different from that of careless folk scarcely affected by Christian standards or habits. If in 738 a Gerold could die in battle beyond the boundaries of the realm and more than a hundred miles distant from his see, nearly twenty years later (757) in spite of reforms a Milo could meet his end in a boar-hunt, still in office as a bishop. One of the most glaring instances reported to Rome by Boniface in the early 740s showed that a man with several concubines (with or without a wife in addition!) could rise not only to the diaconate but right through the ranks of the clergy without correction.

It is not surprising to find that the main pillars of the structure and discipline of the Church had been allowed to crumble. Presbyters were not properly responsible to the bishop of their diocese, and conversely bishops did not regularly visit and inspect the clergy and parishes. (Monasteries were in a very varied state: some [for example those under Pirmin's influence] might be healthy enough, but the other extreme was all too common.) Bishops did not look to a 'metropolitan' or arch-bishop nor expect to meet regularly for the true and spiritual advantage of the whole church.

The consequences were manifold. It was easy for religious charlatans, men who were sometimes merely misguided, sometimes wicked also, not necessarily holding any regular office, to gain a hearing. The people generally had no firm guidance, and were prone to immorality and vice. Princes and nobles, pleading (sometimes seriously enough) the needs of 'defence', diverted church financial resources on a vast scale to the use of the state; a less heinous but no less disastrous business than the transfer of church assets to private hands.

We cannot tell how far Boniface was aware, at the time of Duke Charles's death, that he was destined to be involved in church reform under his sons and successors. Any reluctance which he felt about such a matter may have been tempered by the desire to clear a path between the Hesse-Thuringia mission field and that which had been Willibrord's. Carloman is unlikely to have disclosed his hand until after his first annual Assembly in the opening days of March, 742. Boniface was busy setting forward the diocesan organisation of the churches he had founded, a task for which he had the undoubted support of Carloman. Meanwhile, eager as he was to send greetings to the new Pope, he held back until his group of three bishoprics was fully formed. It was convenient to be able to ask for confirmation of all three sees at the same time; and possibly he hoped to 'carry' the two smaller ones more easily along with Würzburg.

In March, after Carloman's Assembly of nobles, a formal invitation was probably given to the archbishop to assist the Mayor in leading a programme of reform, and to spend time during the coming months in preparing the way for a synod of churchmen and nobles in a year's time, either at or after the March Assembly of 743. By the time he was ready to report to Pope Zacharias concerning the episcopate in the eastern provinces he had also sorted out the major issues which were due to be dealt with in Austrasia as a whole. It would be wise to ask Zacharias' opinion about some of these, and to make sure that he would have the full authority of Rome behind him when insisting on measures which many would be reluctant to accept.

The long letter which Presbyter Denehard eventually took to Zacharias on Boniface's behalf reveals the affection and respect which already existed between them. Humility is still clearly a characteristic of the now elderly soldier of Christ; yet at the same time the letter breathes an underlying awareness that in experience (as well as in age, presumably) its writer can for the first time rival his Father-in-God.

His personal appreciation of Zacharias is evident from greetings and remarks at the beginning and end, and in a poem which he composed as a postscript. 'Nothing', he writes, 'gave us greater pleasure than the knowledge that God had appointed your Holiness to enforce the canonical decrees and govern the Apostolic See.' As a token of his 'affection and obedience' he sends gifts, 'a warm rug, and a little silver and gold.' The six lines of Latin which he composed in Zacharias' honour (in hexameter verse) are quoted on p. 30.

There is, however, a slightly sharp note in the opening greetings when the writer makes request that 'as with your predecessors, . . . we may . . . be counted obedient servants, *under canon law*, of your Holiness'. The Pope as well as his 'servants' is 'under canon law', as has already once been implied in his predecessor's charge to Boniface 'to enforce the canonical decrees'. The Bishop of Rome is trustee of what the Church has decided under God's guidance, and is to see that the Church abides by its own decisions: he is not an isolated or independent oracle whose word alone, as such, is to be unquestionably obeyed as God's.

Of the main burdens of his letter, Boniface delivers himself first of the report on his three episcopal foundations, Würzburg, Büraburg and Erfurt, and asks the Pope for formal ratification of these. But the larger part of what he writes has to do with Carloman's invitation and with issues that will inevitably arise at the synod. He describes in general terms the situation in the Gallo-Frankish churches, giving instances of the various kinds of corruption among bishops and clergy; and he stresses the importance of ensuring that decisions he will make, or instruct others to make, will be in conformity with the Pope's judgements. He cites two cases of people who have tried to take advantage of the change of Pope by claiming that they had permission for this or that from Gregory III, each claim involving a flagrant breach of the Church's standards. One was a marriage issue involving lay people, including a woman who had actually been a nun: the other concerned adulterous bishops of the Frankish church who claimed that they had been confirmed in office in their present way of life. This last wus a particularly good instance of what Boniface would have to oppose.

He did not include all the possible subjects in his letter. He omitted, for example, all references to the expropriation of church assets, the reform of monasteries, and even the restoration of diocesan and 'metropolitan' order; but in such matters, so far as they were already in view, he presumably knew what Rome regarded as proper and desirable, and could count on the support of the Mayor without a positive and precise written statement from the Apostolic See. Two further matters he did, however, raise. One rested upon his own experience of the city of Rome, confirmed by reports from other travellers. The work of reform in outlying parts of the Church, he said, was made much harder by the prevalence of immorality and pagan customs in Rome itself. He begged the Pope to put a stop to all this. The other matter arose out of his own sense of old age. In a controversial way (though seemingly he did not see it as such) he made a claim for himself in which (fascinatingly!) he said he had had authority from Gregory III to nominate the man who would succeed him after his death. He even maintained that Gregory had bidden him to do so, and implied that Duke Charles had been party to the arrangement. Now, the presbyter whom he had had in mind had been disqualified in the eyes of Carloman, since the brother of the said presbyter had 'murdered the duke's uncle'.* Boniface was now seeking Zacharias' goodwill in the matter of a new nomination.

Zacharias considered these questions over the winter of 742–3 and replied on 1st April 743, the second Monday before Easter. His reply begins by emphasising the friendly relations between them, in thankfulness for Boniface's good state of health, and in 'great joy' at hearing again about the salvation of souls and the conversion of new peoples '. . . to our Holy Mother the Church' (echoing the conclusion of Boniface's poem with consummate tact). They share, therefore, the evangelical ideal, a basic Christian concern. Near the conclusion of his letter Zacharias re-affirms his fellow-feeling and friendship unmistakably: 'It would give us great pleasure to have you always by our side as a minister of God in charge of the Churches of Christ'. High praise indeed!

The three new bishoprics Zacharias is content to endorse 'in response to your earnest appeal' and in spite of hesitations over the two smaller towns. He stresses that 'the sacred canons decree' (again reflecting Boniface's own words!) 'that bishops should not be attached to villages and small cities lest the dignity of the episcopate be lowered'. That may be true, but 'the canons' were drawn up in a very different world from that of the sparsely populated regions of northern Europe. In one sense the familiar comment that Zacharias was unsympathetic to Boniface's problems is not unjust; but he never descended to personal animosity.

Clergy, including bishops, who live 'in flagrant contradiction to the decrees and laws of the Fathers', Zacharias continues, are to be suspended from priestly duties 'on apostolic authority'. Sexual sins and military service are mentioned explicity; bloodsports are included, presumably, under the phrase 'in any other way contrary to ecclesiastical law'. He does not specify penalties, but remarks that such men 'are guilty of sins worse than those of laymen'. This is a consideration to be borne in mind when they are sentenced; or so we are led to infer.

* Some have supposed the nominee to have been Gregory the Frank, and that this was why he never became a bishop even when in charge of Utrecht diocese years later.

As an illustration of the difficulty of interpreting 'canon law', and as possible evidence of the effect of the Pope's Greek background, it is discernible that he can say flatly of the clergy that 'their state precludes taking even one [wife]' when he has let slip earlier the more lenient words '. . . bishops, presbyters and deacons living in adultery or having more than one wife . . .'. We can, today, imagine Zacharias having written inadvertently (out of his sub-conscious mind) a phrase which was more appropriate to the Greek-speaking churches than to the Latin (since 400 A.D., about), viz. one permitting lawful marriage to the clergy, including bishops.*

The particular marriage question which Boniface raised is given separate attention, and the situation is regarded as serious not so much as involving a woman who had taken a vow of celibacy, nor because she married a man and then left him and married again, but on the grounds that the man she now wishes to marry is the nephew of her second husband who has died. Zacharias calls it an 'incestuous' desire on the part of the nephew and his intended bride, and it is clear that no permission can possibly have been given by his predecessor. The couple are to be told that as persons 'redeemed by the blood of Christ . . . they must not wittingly hand themselves over to the devil'. The arbitrary relativity of values placed by the Pope on the various aspects of the case, including, *e.g.* the fact that he does not mention bigamy, are of interest to Christians of a later age in which the whole field of divorce and remarriage is a burning issue. We cannot tell whether the case in question was from Boniface's normal sphere of operations or whether he had met it among his newer Frankish contacts.

On the subject of Boniface's nomination of a successor to his office Zacharias' reply show, to those who regard it objectively, a yet more glaring instance of the uncertainties surrounding the law of the church. Boniface's assumptions are also those of his earliest biographer; indeed the latter goes rather too far by saying that the appointment of a successor during his lifetime was 'as ecclesiastical law *demands*'. Zacharias writes with some asperity (for the moment) giving a quite opposite judgement. 'You say that you are entitled to name your successor and to

* The subject is a complex one. After 692, in Zacharias' childhood, *bishops* in the east were supposed to live only as brother-and-sister with their wives. On the other hand, the Latin church of Milan in Lombardy permitted its bishops to be married and have children openly until 1058, despite successive Roman decrees.

choose a bishop to take your place during your lifetime: this we cannot allow . . . It would . . . be quite wrong . . .' This and the words which follow, namely, 'But we will allow you to have an assistant' make it appear at first that the question is only whether Boniface can resign during his lifetime. But this is far from being the case. An assistant can be appointed, but *not* as a designated successor. The most that Boniface can do in the latter interest is to pray continually in the hope that on his death-bed ('as soon as you become aware that your death is not far off') he may designate his successor 'in the presence of others and send him to me to be consecrated'. And although we might suppose that Zacharias is made the more cautious and strict by the fact of Boniface's unusual, even unique position, he is plainly including his case within the wider category of episcopal or archiepiscopal appointments when he goes on: 'This is a privilege which we grant you out of our affection: we cannot allow it to be conferred on any other person.' The uniqueness of Boniface's position and character together have allowed this Pope to give him an exceptional favour. In the rules, as Zacharias sees them, even a death-bed nomination is out of order.

In receiving this news, Boniface must have been struck with a number of conflicting thoughts, happy and unhappy, including that of the possibility of successive popes giving opposite judgements (though not quite opposite recommendations in practice), and the fact that Zacharias had made no suggestion as to how his predecessor could have thought and acted differently. Only by a sheer act of faith, at times, could Boniface maintain his integral picture of the Church's faith, life and unity. . . .

On the abuses at Rome, Boniface is told that these have already been stringently dealt with. It may be significant, however, that in the same year (743) a synod was held in Rome, at which certain heathen tendencies were deplored and measures taken for their suppression.

With Zacharias' personal and official letter, which gave the great Anglo-Saxon most if not all of the authority and the directions for which he had asked, Denehard carried northwards three letters of confirmation, one to each of the episcopal sees which had been founded. Two of these, with virtually identical texts, are known to us today. That of Erfurt, not transmitted down the generations, doubtless followed the same

pattern, which was similar to most documents of its kind in that era.

From Rome to Würzburg the distance is almost eight hundred miles by road. Starting on Tuesday, April 2nd, the day following the sealing of the four letters, and aiming to arrive by the evening of Friday, April 19th, Denehard had only eighteen days' travelling time. If he was to arrive in advance of Carloman's projected synod, he needed to average forty-five miles per day all the way, including the crossing of the Alps. He could afford no rest periods. (Had Pope Zacharias deliberately left things until the last moment because politically it was inexpedient, or hazardous, for the presbyter to loiter in Lombardy?) The shortest way, avoiding the main provinces of Bavaria in view of Odilo's disfavour with the Frankish Mayors, was through Chur, Boniface's route of a few years before. It was a challenge, and much depended on the state of the snows in the high passes.

Chapter 17

PROGRESS ON TWO FRONTS

As winter gave way to spring in the year 743, Boniface could discern the hand of God at work in different ways, in relation to his own calling and destiny. An intuition had led him to regard the vacant see of Utrecht, in the light of all that was happening in Austrasia under Carloman, as a signpost, pointing towards the conversion of the Saxons, those kinsfolk who from a standpoint in Hesse-Thuringia so often appeared as enemies. The increasing tendency of Pippin to follow Carloman's lead in the direction of reform suggested to the great Anglo-Saxon that the desire of Pope Gregory III might be nearing fulfilment in a roundabout way: political and military developments, now in the course of unfolding, would help to draw Alamannia into the orbit of the other German churches before long. Sturm, at present living with two other monks of similar persuasion somewhere up the Fulda river in rough wooded country, could provide Boniface with a much needed sense of vicarious purification. As the latter became increasingly involved with court life, first in Austrasia and before long in Neustria also, he found it more and more difficult to live in a manner consistent with his oath. The aim to set up a model monastery with Sturm's assistance, which was something he had in mind, enabled him to feel that, in spite of the compromising situations in which he personally found himself, he could still set the seal on the whole work of the past twenty years and more. We may envisage that with such thoughts the archbishop prepared expectantly for the synod which Carloman had planned, and for the return of Denehard from Rome (God willing) in time for that event.

It was Carloman's intention, and Pippin's after him, to concentrate the decision-making towards church reform at the assembly of optimates or nobles held each year at the beginning of March. Thus much is made clear by the events of 744 and 745. There is little doubt that originally, after the Austrasian assembly of March 742, and at the time when Boniface wrote to Pope Zacharias a few months later, the same was intended for 743, provided that the Pope's reply arrived well in advance of March 1st that year. In view of the possibility of delay, however, at some stage it was agreed that a separate 'synod' might be held later, failing any word from Rome in time for the regular March assembly: and this was how it turned out. April 21st, the Sunday after Easter, was the latest date which could be arranged without seriously affecting plans for the summer campaigning season. At the beginning of April, even if Zacharias' letter had not been received, the synod of nobles and bishops would have to be summoned; and if necessary, it would be carried through at the prescribed date without the actual evidence of papal approval. It was not that there was any doubt of the Pope's attitude; but documentary proof of it would encourage those who were in favour of a thorough-going reform, turn the waverers and isolate the opposition.

Carloman summoned the lay and ecclesiastical members of the synod while still waiting for Boniface to receive word from Rome. We may suppose that Würzburg was the place of meeting, since that city was the first which Denehard would reach on his return journey. Wherever the March assembly had been held, and it was probably at Les Estinnes far to the west, a rendezvous well to the east seems most probable for the re-summoning of the optimates and the convoking of the bishops and representative presbyters. One effect of this was to give recalcitrant Old-Frankish bishops a further excuse to stay away. Some would have a distance of more than two hundred miles to travel. Doubtless Carloman expected difficulty, and had prepared to meet the problem of abstentions as best he could. He secured the attendance of Reginfrid of Cologne. Whether this was by special inducement or not, we cannot tell. Also and perhaps with an eye to developments in the longer term, he invited Heddo of Strasbourg, who consented to come. In this way the movement of monastic reform which had been led by Pirmin in the southern and western parts of Alamannia was for the first time brought into relation to Boniface's work. In the event it was only these two who came from the Rhine basin and beyond. Others from the west copied Milo of Trier and Gewilib of Mainz in having nothing to do with the synod. From the eastern region, beside Boniface himself, there were his three Hesse-Thuringian bishops (if we count Burghard under this head) and Willibald of Eichstätt, consecrated since Boniface wrote to Zacharias.*

The nickname 'German Council' (*Concilium Germanicum*) by which in later ages the event was described, was justified by the preponderance of eastern sees represented in spite of the Bavarian exclusions. The Germans were five to two; or six to one if Strasbourg (Alsace/Alamannia) is included. The location of the meeting doubtless also favoured the appellation 'German'. Had they deigned to come, the old-Frankish bishops could have outweighed the 'Germans' in number. This could have been the case even if Boniface's disciple Wera was consecrated to Utrecht before rather than after the synod. In the Rhine valley – Cologne, Mainz, Worms and Speyer; on the Moselle – Trier, Metz and Toul; in the valley of the Meuse – Maestricht, Tongres and Verdun; at least ten sees of 'Old-Frankish' provenance could be reckoned. As things turned out, it was going to be comparatively easy to pass reforms provided that the nobles in attendance were agreeable; but it would be less easy afterwards to carry them into effect over a large area of the part-kingdom.

Cologne is 150 miles from Würzburg as the crow flies, Strasbourg 130 miles. Reginfrid and Heddo could each celebrate Easter in their own cathedrals and hope to travel to their destination within the week. The available sources provide no evidence on such matters. Nor do we know in what place or manner Boniface himself kept the great Feast on April 14th. Was he at Würzburg already? Was he at Fritzlar in the monastery which was virtually his home, or at Büraburg nearby? He would have had a long journey during the week from either of these two, going south and then east to avoid the hard forests of Buchonia (modern 'Buchenwald') where Sturm and his companions preferred to be. Wherever he was on Easter Day, he certainly could not guess that in 754, exactly eleven years later, when the Feast would chance to fall on the same date, April 14th, he would celebrate his last Easter and go forth to be martyred in the week of Pentecost. He may well have thought that a natural death would come his way before that; or conceivably, death at the hands of some recalcitrant Frank, nominally Christian: but at this present juncture, saving only

* The four bishops from 'Bavaria proper' were excluded by the political *impasse* between Odilo and the Frankish leaders.

perhaps the recurring thought about Utrecht and West Frisia as the gateway to the Saxons, he must have felt as far away from martyrdom as at any period since 719.

At Easter, 743, his prayers both private and public will have included earnest intercession for friends and enemies, lay and clerical, among the Franks, and petition for the divine guidance at the forthcoming synod. Thanksgiving, too, for the divine response to past prayers on behalf of Duke Charles and his sons. God's answer was to be seen in the present break-through, involving both vision and daring on the part of Carloman.

There were limitations. It was clear that neither of the two 'Mayors' intended to create a purely Rome-orientated church. Carloman had not suggested that the synod should be under Boniface's chairmanship, or that any decrees it might ordain should be signed and sealed by anyone but himself. This had to be accepted. It was enough that the leader of the eastern Franks, wielding the power of a king in all but name, desired a church in which ministry and monasticism were properly ordered and disciplined, in which teaching was sound, and in which the Christian moral code was generally observed.

It is tantalising that we are not told whether Denehard arrived in time. There is no record concerning this. We may well think that he managed it. Judgement on such matters, indeed the whole picture of the manner in which the synod progressed, has to be inferred from the contents of the document which was put out afterwards on Carloman's authority.* The tone of this is confident. The intention is fairly plain, to make a sweeping reform such as Rome would desire and strongly approve. The 'duke and prince of the Franks' has sought the advice of those present, clerical and lay, 'by what means the law of God and the Christian religion may be restored' in view of their rapid 'dissipation during the time of the princes who have gone before.' The object has been to make it possible for 'the Christian people to arrive at the salvation (*or* health, *salutem*) of the soul and not to perish through the deceit of false priests'. (The last word, *sacerdotes*, implies bishops without mentioning them distinctly.) The first step has been to ensure that the whole of Austrasia is divided into bishoprics. Now, henceforward, Boniface is constituted archbishop over

* So called Epistle 56, or at least the first six paragraphs of it.

all of them. The Roman connection is, for reasons of politics and tact, mentioned only indirectly in that Boniface is described as 'he who is sent from St. Peter'. The bishops are to gather annually in synod with their archbishop (the Rome-approved pattern) but definitely 'in our presence' (i.e. Carloman's); and by such gatherings 'canons' will be decreed which will 'restore the laws of the church' and 'repair the Christian religion'.

This document of April 21st, 743, goes on to state without qualification that 'we restore and return the moneys of which the churches have been defrauded'.

Perhaps in a moment of prudence, as recommended by some of the nobles and Bishop Reginfrid of Cologne, the decree which follows comes short of necessitating the deposition of any existing bishops: 'We deprive and degrade false presbyters and adulterous or fornicating deacons and clerks, and compel them to do penance.' However, certain bishops (as well as other clergy) will have to beware for other reasons; 'We prohibit ordained ministers (*servos Dei*)* from bearing arms, fighting in an army or proceeding against an enemy', except a strictly limited number of duly appointed chaplains of episcopal and presbyteral rank. All forms of hunting, hawking and falconry are entirely forbidden to clergy of all ranks and other 'servants of God'.

Next comes the ordering of church life within each diocese. Every presbyter is to be subject to the bishop of the diocese in which he lives, and is to give an annual account of his ministry to the bishop, in terms of teaching and practice, at the beginning of Lent. He is to prepare those who have been baptised to receive Confirmation from the Bishop. He is to obtain fresh 'chrism' (for baptismal use) from the bishop every Maundy Thursday. In all these ways the bishop becomes 'a witness to the purity of his (the presbyter's) life, faith and doctrine'. (The fact that all is spelt out in this way reveals the extent of indiscipline and ignorance prevailing hitherto.) Every bishop, on his part, is to have one diocese in which he resides in a settled fashion, and is to exercise due care and concern over it constantly, with active support and defence from his local lord (the 'Graf' or count). In these ways all forms of pagan superstition and practice are to be eliminated, of which some have been disguised by being performed 'in church in the name of holy

* The term also includes monks and nuns.

martyrs or confessors', their perpetrators 'provoking God and his saints to anger'. By a final decree, monastic foundations are made to conform to the Benedictine order.

It was a good beginning, on paper, and it set a standard. The realities of the situation were such that it would take a long time to implement. The patience of those who had the cause of reform at heart was to be sorely tried in the years which followed. Yet the influence already exerted by the Anglo-Saxon missionaries over Frankish affairs was real enough. A token of this, at least, is the manner of the dating of the document issued by this first synod. This is no longer according to the year of an emperor's reign, but by the year of our Lord's incarnation; a method recommended and used by the learned Northumbrian, Bede. Because of the novelty of this practice, a mistake might be made. It appears that this actually happened; so that the figure 742 (or Roman numerals representing it, DCCXLII) was used. All other evidence points to 743; for example, the relation of the event to the foundation of Boniface's bishoprics and to his first exchange of letters with Pope Zacharias, already discussed.

It is hard to believe that the proposed reforms could be given serious attention by Carloman (and those supporting him) during the summer season of military campaigning. On the other hand, Carloman and Pippin were closely in touch, if not actually campaigning together, in view of the alliance between Odilo of Bavaria and Theutbald, unrecognized duke of Alamannia. They may have begun to concert plans for their March assemblies of 744 in such a manner that Boniface could attend at least part of each. Pippin was to hold his a few days after Carloman's; and the two meetings were to be near enough for the archbishop to travel between them.

Their current commitments drew them away from the Saxon border, where it is likely that raids and perhaps settlements were being made by the heathen tribes across the less well defended parts of the frontier. This southward pressure was felt between 'Austrasia proper' and Hesse, where the Frankish army would eventually strike back. But it also affected the border land between Hesse and Thuringia, a fact which takes us straight into the story of Sturm the hermit and Boniface's dealings with him.

Chapter 18

FULFILMENT EASTWARD: CHALLENGE WESTWARD

Perhaps it was soon after the 'German Council' that Boniface received a visit from Sturm, who had been living austerely for nearly two years at Hersfeld in 'Buchonia' with two companions. Boniface warned him that his present location was too near the Saxons for safety, and advised him to 'look for a spot deeper in the woods'. (The normal distance of the Saxon boundary from Hersfeld was fifty miles!) Later in the year he sent a messenger from Fritzlar to find and bring Sturm again. We are not told by what route the man travelled; but Sturm's biographer describes his return with the hermit to Fritzlar as *via* Seelheim near Amöneburg. This could well mean that the Saxon penetration was by that time endangering the area immediately to the south of Fritzlar and Büraburg.

The messenger had found Sturm and his two companions at Hersfeld again. They had returned thither after unsuccessful attempts to find 'God's appointed place' further up the River Fulda. Boniface, on hearing the story, is said to have expressed the firmest conviction that such a place was to be found. Sturm, after discussing 'many things' at Boniface's wish, returned once again. This time he told his two companions at Hersfeld to look after themselves, and travelled alone – an act of deep faith. Every night he built a fence round his donkey, but entrusted himself to God! Disentangling the narrative of his 'life', we may guess that he proceeded almost to the source of the Fulda on the side of the 'Rhön-gebirge' before returning to a place downstream which he suddenly discerned to be the site determined by God. His travels involved him in an unexpected encounter with Slavs, who were bathing; they did not harm him, but he found them 'offensive' in other ways! He also had a profitable spiritual exchange with a lay Christian travelling from west to east, from 'Wetterau' to 'Grabfeld' (the districts on either side of the forest of Buchonia). The layman helped Sturm in some way or other towards the disclosure of the God-given spot.

Archaeological research has shown that the predestined site was not merely a feature of the forest country but held the ruin of a Merovingian castle or fortress dating from the time of the original Frankish conquest of Thuringia.

Sturm hastened back to his two companions at Hersfeld, where the Saxon danger must indeed have been near. His subsequent journey to Fritzlar, where he joyfully announced to Boniface the discovery or revelation of the spot, was presumably as circuitous as before: 'the journey' we read, 'took several days'.

Boniface and Sturm spent 'a few days' together in deep satisfaction and thanksgiving. The relation between these two was somewhat similar to that between Boniface and the successive popes whom he served. Strong personalities, they sought to fulfil the will of God, each making allowance for the particular interests of the other. Boniface took account of Sturm's ascetical leanings by planning a monastery which would, in its first phase at least, be a little stricter than most Benedictine houses, and would be started with just a few men. Sturm adapted his nature from that of a near-hermit to that of a potential leader and guide of a considerable number of men as time went on, simply because that was the desire of his beloved father-in-God.

The immediate order which he received was to return to his two companions, accompany them to the site and occupy it; while Boniface would set about procuring the freehold of it through the good offices of Carloman. The archbishop had accepted on the basis of Sturm's description that this place, known as Eichloh, on the right bank of the Fulda, was that for which they had so long prayed. It may have occurred to him that the ruined castle might be considered royal property, and that this would make it simple for Carloman to make a conveyance of the site. The hand of God might be seen in that.

The visit to Carloman, which the archbishop would have made in any case at the conclusion of the campaigning season, now had this additional and weighty purpose to set alongside that of promoting the programme of reform where it could and should be done. Of their progress in the latter cause we have practically no evidence, nor of the methods which they chose to try to gain obedience to the decrees of April 21st. But as far as Boniface's particular and heartfelt interest is concerned we know something of the story. Carloman recognised the site which Boniface described, and readily agreed to its use for a special kind of monastery, a spiritual fountain-head close (but not too close) to the Saxons at the present time. He was also aware that the local lords, unless carefully handled, might prove difficult; so that he arranged to call them to confer with him and other nobles about the matter.

Meanwhile, Sturm had attempted to carry out his part of the plan, only to find that he and his two companions were frustrated by those very same local leaders of whom Carloman had spoken to Boniface, or perhaps rather, by forces stationed at their command to guard the site from these interfering churchmen. The three were compelled to take up their dwelling some distance away at 'another place called Dryhlar', where they remained until midwinter. Whether Sturm himself went to report this state of affairs is not quite clear from our sources. But in any case Carloman secured the attendance of the local lords at his court, and after explaining his own intentions, convinced them of the rightness of his plan. This was, that a circle of land around Eichloh, four miles in radius, should be made over for Boniface's purpose; and that they, the lesser landlords, should give up their small portions within that circle while he signed away the much larger area of 'royal' land involved. The matter having been decided, a charter was drawn up, signed by Carloman and confirmed by the others. This happy conclusion was reached before the end of the year.

Five monks of suitable disposition and calibre were found, to add to the two who were already with Sturm. These joined them at Dryhlar in the New Year, and 'on the twelfth day of January in the year . . . 744, . . . the brethren set foot for the first time on this holy spot', all opposition having been removed.

Boniface himself was still not able to travel to the site. It was not that age or health deterred him in mid-winter, for at this period of life he did not have reason to complain as he had done some seven or eight years before. We are left to suppose that the normal business of church life, coupled with such necessities as were contingent upon the reform programme, kept him continuously occupied in other parts of the realm until after the March assemblies. Sturm and the seven, despite the fact that it was winter, set about clearing the site, and established a regular round of prayer and psalmody and an ascetic discipline, after a pattern which in general conformed to the Benedictine custom and in some particulars had been specially agreed between Boniface and Sturm.

The thought of all this was an encouragement and consolation to the archbishop who, as 'the man sent from St. Peter', now prepared himself to face the additional challenge of Pippin's Neustrian reform plans, while learning to keep patience with the slow progress of affairs in Austrasia itself. The March assemblies were to be held at Les Estinnes (Carloman) and at Soissons (Pippin) two days apart, on March 1st and 3rd, the Sunday and Tuesday in the second week of Lent. Each was to involve a synod for church affaris. The brothers had co-ordinated their political and military aims for the year, and had doubtless conferred about the ecclesiastical problem for the purpose of which they were holding their gatherings on different days. Although it seems hard that Boniface should have been expected to attend two meetings separated by a distance of eighty-five miles with only one full day's travelling time between, it is even more unreasonable to suppose that he did not see something of both.

At Les Estinnes, the church business may have been kept fairly brief by reason of a decision not to issue a whole new set of decrees but to republish the decrees of 743 with appended paragraphs dated 1st March 744. This in turn may have reflected the unfortunate fact that the bishops in attendance were no more representative than in 743. The provenance at the western end of Austrasia had not made any difference, unless Wera of Utrecht was there; and he was not at all like the 'Old Franks', who again mostly stayed away. The edicts of Les Estinnes, 744, nearly all underlined or interpreted the earlier ones, a fact which revealed by implication the difficulty of applying such regulations. Clergy were urged to abide by the canons both in their moral life and in the conduct of their ministerial office. Monasteries must take the Rule of St. Benedict quite definitely as their pattern of living. Specific punishments were ordered, most particularly for immoral conduct, graded according to the clerical order of the offender and the seriousness of the offence. Heathen practices (listed in great detail in an appendix added not much later) were to be punished by heavy fines as ordered some years earlier by Duke Charles. Of considerable interest and significance is the paragraph concerning the impropriation of church possessions and rents. In view of the unsettled character of the times, and until a period of peace might supervene, these were not in general to be returned; but a system of taxation or regular levy was arranged, whereby the churches and monasteries would gain some benefit. There was a reversion clause also, but the effect of this could be negatived in a national emergency. (It was to be a characteristic of the 'Middle Ages' that affairs of Church and State were almost inseparably interlocked.) The one fresh subject which was brought to the fore at Les Estinnes was the standard of Christian marriage, an issue which Boniface had very much at heart: 'We order that adulterous and incestuous marriages are to be prohibited and corrected under the judgement of the bishop, accordingly to what has been decreed in the canons.'

It may be suggested that the churchmen left Carloman to ensure that the enlarged edict was published in due course, and that while he and his optimates worked through the normal business of their March gatherings, Boniface was already on his way south, and the other bishops were returning to their sees. Assuming that the archbishop was travelling light, and that security and hospitality had been arranged by the two Mayors, he could, with the help of a good horse, cover about twenty miles in the last few hours of daylight on the Sunday, and forty-five miles on the Monday, which would bring him to Laon. The royal palace of Quierzy lay on the River Oise not far from Laon; so that Pippin may well have welcomed him there, through his representatives if not in person. If their life-style was such as to meet with the archbishop's disapproval, this was an example of Boniface's difficulty in having to reconcile himself to 'court-ecclesiastics'. Be that as it may, the last stage of the journey to Soissons can be envisaged as having taken place in Neustrian company, during the morning of Tuesday, 3rd March. If Pippin had arranged to conduct the regular business of his March assembly in the earlier part of the day, and to keep the synod for Church purposes until the afternoon, then we have a reasonable picture of the course of events, justifying the supposition that Boniface attended both synods.

Because Pippin was shrewder than his brother, and because there had been no Anglo-Saxon mission in any part of Neustria, the views of the clergy and nobles had not become polarised as in Austrasia. Out of about thirty episcopal sees in Neustria proper, twenty-three were represented at Soissons on March 3rd, 744.*

We have no list of the names or sees of attending bishops. No edict has been preserved, only indirect reports. It appears that the several decrees were broadly similar to those of the two Austrasian synods taken as a whole, and somewhat cautiously drawn up to avoid repercussions. Most important was the genuine attempt made to reconstitute church provinces along with metropolitan sees. Three were designated, and their archbishops nominated. Somehow Grimo had already been appointed to Rouen as a bishop in favour of reform. Now, a certain Hartbert was brought into the scheme to occupy the vacant see of Sens, also as a metropolitan-elect. He may well have been an Anglo-Saxon rather than a Frank. More impressive still is the fact that in the case of the third place, Rheims, Milo (of Trier and Rheims) was left out of account and an Anglo-Saxon, Abel, was designated.

Boniface may well have come away from Soissons well satisfied on that and other counts. The documents available to us affirm that Pippin followed his brother in dating the edict by the year of our Lord's incarnation, and went further in copying English habits by mentioning the year of the local king ('the second year of Childeric III', puppet Merovingian set up by the 'Mayors' early in 743) and the day of the lunar month (the 14th, a practically full moon: 'luna XIIII'). Boniface himself, on the supposition that the archbishops were duly appointed and approved at Rome, would not be required to supervise the detail of reform in Neustria, but only to keep a general oversight as papal legate. The threefold metropolitan plan was being sent to Rome for approval, and he saw this in itself as a great step forward. At the same time he could hardly repress the feeling that the coming months of military involvement might see the evaporation of any enthusiasm for reform that had been aroused at Soissons. Pippin would be dealing with the Alamannian revolt, and Carloman making a serious bid to carry conquest deep into Saxon territory. How much energy would be left by September in either of the two-part kingdoms, for restoring Christian standards and proper church structures? One thing could be said. A decisive victory over the Saxons might

* This is the most favourable picture, admittedly: if Burgundian bishops had been invited, the total possible would have exceeded fifty; but many of these were in the far distant south. The dependencies, Aquitaine and Alamannia, were both in revolt.

open a way this time for conversions and baptisms among them. Such a thought would brace the elderly archbishop as he travelled back the three hundred miles from Neustria to Thuringia. Moreover, was not the object of his enterprise on the banks of the Fulda, where he was now going, to provide the best possible spiritual base for a Saxon mission? That was a positive aspect of his most cherished enterprise.

Sturm's biographer relates that it was about the middle of March, 744, two months after 'the brethren' had first set foot on the chosen site, that Boniface himself arrived there. On such longer and more encumbered journeys, thirty miles a day could be comfortably covered; so that with determination, and refusal to stay more than a night at any place on the way, a traveller could make the distance between Soissons and the Buchonian Forest between the 4th and the 14th of March.

Boniface, amid great rejoicing, raised a cross at the place which was to become known simply as 'Fulda', on a hill which gained the name of Bishop's Mount (*Mons Episcopi*). It was not until a year later, however, that the buildings were far enough advanced for Boniface, after journeying from another synod, to promulgate the full Rule which the inmates of 'Fulda' were to observe.

Chapter 19

DEALING WITH DISORDER

The extent of religious disorder among the Franks in the eighth century is vividly illustrated by the lives of individuals who gained large followings, misleading and dividing the people and sometimes 'deceiving the very elect'. The two most famous may have been a subject of discussion at the Soissons synod, since they figure in the subsequent correspondence with Rome alongside such matters as the metropolitan sees.

'Albert' is the name which we may give to one of the two chief offenders, (he appears in the literature of the time either as 'Adalbert' or 'Aldebert'). Quite early in his adult life, Albert claimed that an angel had visited him in human form, and had brought him relics of enormous sanctity from the other end of the world. Such was the potency of these objects which he carried about that there was practically nothing which he could not obtain from God with their aid, if it was something which he himself could see fit to ask. Whether with or without formal ordination to the presbyterate, he appointed himself a sort of travelling chaplain; and being a person of considerable charm, he was able to 'help' weak women to believe that they had God's forgiveness. He charged for his services, and began to amass a fortune. He impressed a wider circle by means of 'miracles', and successfully began to claim that he was similar to the Apostles. Significantly enough from the point of view of church life generally, he actually impressed at least three bishops, who consecrated him bishop in turn after the customary manner. He was not, of course, given a diocese, but was left to pursue his own free-lance career. Living a life of luxury, though not specifically (it ought to be said) of sexual immorality, he had enough money also to build and consecrate churches. Before his 'consecration' he had erected crosses and altars of his own, and occasionally even a small chapel, and had drawn people away from the regular churches. Now he was able to improve on this.* It was not his custom to dedicate his foundations to any of those Apostles with whom he liked to be compared. Averring that he himself was the saint of saints, proclaiming the names of 'angels' with whom he had had private converse, he had his churches dedicated in his own name. Gullible people were led to venerate pieces of 'Saint' Albert's hair and fingernails, which he (not without betraying his own superstition perhaps) exhibited along with a reputed relic of St. Peter himself.

Albert was, so we are told, of Gaulish origin. This may mean that his family were of the older, Celtic, strain of the population; or it may simply have a geographical significance, indicating that he did not originate from the Rhine basin but from the region of old Gaul. However that may be, his rival for fame is distinctly stated to have been a Celt, in fact an Irishman, although known by a name of Latin origin, 'Clement' (Clemens: the name of two early Christian saints, and, incidentally, the official name given to Willibrord by Pope Sergius I in the 690's). Some think him to have belonged to Austrasia rather than Neustria; but the balance of the evidence is the other way.

While our picture of Clement is not so full and clear as that of Albert, it can be said with confidence that he was far less vicious, although he undoubtedly represented a danger to the Church's life and teaching. Like Albert, he attained to episcopal rank. He expressly rejected the teachings of such great men of earlier times as Jerome, Augustine of Hippo and Gregory the Great. His leading tenet was universalism, the doctrine that all men without exception would eventually reach heaven through the atonement procured by Christ. As he expounded it, this left wide open the door to all forms of sin. In modern times he would be called an 'extreme liberal' in his theology. His mode of life was also much too liberal for such as Boniface and Pope Zacharias, since he kept a woman as his wife or concubine and had two sons by her. He excused certain moral practices that were disallowed in the canons, on the ground that they were allowed or even commanded in the Old Testament. One which is particularly mentioned is the requirement that a man shall take his brother's childless widow to wife. (We are left won-

* There can be little doubt that he added to his wealth by trading in 'ordinations' and benefices, supplying his 'churches' with 'clergy'.

dering whether the woman who gave him his two sons had in fact been the wife of his brother, now dead.)

Although the two men may be judged as of very different standards, as unattached or 'wandering' bishops they were both symptomatic of the chaotic state of religion in the Frankish kingdom.

Godalsacius, whose name appears with theirs at one stage in the exchange of letters with Pope Zacharias, is possibly the same as the 'indisciplined' schismatic bishop of disreputable origin, who was reprimanded at an earlier stage.*

Such men were popular and not easy to suppress. But the decrees of the synods eventually destroyed their careers. Pope Zacharias, who quickly identified Albert's so-called angels as devils, had Albert and Clement formally condemned (in their absence) in the Roman synod of 745, but they continued unchecked for at least two years after. What happened to them is not precisely known. Boniface's earliest biographer believes that both were brought to justice: 'The holy archbishop Boniface with the co-operation of Dukes Carloman and Pippin forcibly ejected them from the communion of the Church, and they were, in the words of the Apostle, delivered to Satan for the destruction of the flesh in order that their spirit might be saved in the Day of the Lord.' One later biographer claims that Albert was eventually deposed by Boniface at Mainz and put in the monastery prison-cell at Fulda, whence he escaped, and as a wretched vagrant was struck down and killed by a group of swineherds.

Inevitably the names of Gewilib and Milo come to the fore in this same period of years.

Gewilib, as we have seen, had grabbed the bishopric of Mainz after his father (or putative father) Gerold had lost his life in 737–8 fighting the Saxons. Revenge was evidently part of his philosophy. When at the March assembly of 744 it was determined that Carloman and the Austrasians would drive deep into Saxon territory and try to hold their gains, Gewilib determined that he would join this expedition. The fact that Carloman did not deter him reflects the impossibility of reforming church life all at once. As the story goes, the campaign reached a point at which the Frankish and Saxon armies were drawn up on either side of the River Weser, where Gerold had been

* Can he have been a man of *Alsace* who came near to identifying himself with *God*?

killed. Gewilib, or a man representing him, rode on horseback into the middle of the river and challenged the Saxon who had killed Gerold, if he were present, to come forward and parley in mid-stream. Rashly enough the man did so, and was promptly despatched by sword or dagger. After the battle which ensued, from which Gewilib emerged unscathed, the victorious Franks (even Carloman himself, according to one version) congratulated him: 'Not regarding the avenging of one's father as any sort of crime, they said he had repaid his father's death in kind.' Whatever Carloman's thoughts may have been in the flush of triumph, his more sober and long-term attitude was consonant with that of Boniface. He supported the latter in 'admonishing' Gewilib, who eventually gave way and resigned his see with a good will. He is said to have accepted a living some miles away, where 'he lived honourably for another fourteen years, and practised hospitality with much grace. He never came again to Mainz for a meeting or synod; but now and again on Maundy Thursday he would come to pray, on the occasion of the foot-washing ceremony.' The vacancy at Mainz had a significance for Boniface beyond anything he could have imagined at the time. Without knowing it he was carving out his own future.

Although in very different ways, Albert, Clement and Gewilib were all quixotic characters. Their very enthusiasms ensured that in the end they were defeated by the reformers. It was not so with Milo, bishop of Trier and Rheims. Apart from his sporting habits, he could not easily be brought under condemnation. He was a pluralist, certainly, and as his two sees straddled the boundary between Austrasia and Neustria he was a thorn in the flesh to Carloman and Pippin alike. But it was impossible to dislodge him. He had a strong enough following to challenge the higher authorities: in this he stood in the old Germanic tradition, in which the king had to reckon with independent nobles, and in which any man might rise to power if he could attract a following. Milo was, so to speak, the immovable object which successfully resists even the irresistible force. In the correspondence between the reformers and the Apostolic See his name appears again and again as the leader of a faction which must somehow be put down – 'Milo and his kind'. To Boniface as to the Mayors, the persistence of such a man in office was the source of ever-deepening disappointment. Such checks must be counted among the reasons for Carloman's resignation from political life. Pippin, more adaptable in diplomacy, was ready to change the Neustrian plan of metropolitan church organization when he found it impossible to substitute Abel for Milo in the see of Rheims. In planning for the future, Pippin faced reality by gradually diverting the initiative of reform into the hands of Frankish churchmen. Such factors help to explain the final stages of the career of Boniface himself, and to reveal the consistency which underlay his apparently sudden withdrawal from active leadership in the Frankish world, and his return to that field of evangelism which had originally drawn him to the Continent.

With these developments we may also link the names of other men who crossed the path of the great Anglo-Saxon in his middle and later sixties (744–8). It is not surprising to find several men of Irish stock among them. It is also understandable, in view of the strained and variable relationship between the Franks and Duke Odilo, that some were men working in Bavaria. Of them Boniface could have only second-hand information; but they appeared to him to be adversaries of the cause of canonical rectitude.

One, of whom we have neither the name nor any further description, was the subject of a complaint by Boniface to Pope Zacharias in 744, probably after the Frankish leadership had come to terms with Odilo in order to secure the defeat of the Alamannian, Theutbald, with whom he had allied himself. Boniface described him as a 'false bishop' who 'claimed to have been consecrated by the Pope'. Zacharias, in his reply (of November 744), uses rather careful language: 'Whomsoever you find deviating from the sacred canons, by no means are you to allow him to exercise a sacred ministry'. There is a strong possibility that the man concerned was a genuine bishop, perhaps not one whom Boniface would have chosen himself, who had been consecrated by Zacharias at Odilo's request to fill a vacancy which fell during the year (743–4) when there was no communication between Bavaria and the Franks;* or to supply a see which Odilo may have created at this time, and which two later writers affirm to have been occupied first by a bishop called Manno: the see of Neuburg, covering a part of the former Augsburg diocese. Boniface could well have assumed that any bishop who had not been consecrated nor installed

* Two of Boniface's nominees died early on: Erembert of Freising and John of Salzburg.

through his own good offices as legate of the Apostolic See could only be spurious. Suspecting that the Pope had acted without him he began to wonder whether the latter intended to relieve him of responsibility over Bavaria altogether. This suspicion is revealed in Zacharias' letter: 'And since you have raised the question whether you hold in the province of Bavaria that jurisdiction which was accorded to you by our predecessor, it is our intention not to diminish but to enlarge your area of responsibility. For we enjoin you, so long as the Divine Majesty shall prolong your life on earth, to speak in our stead not only in Bavaria but also throughout every province of Gaul; so that everything which you discover contrary to the Christian religion or the canons you are to endeavour to correct.' But what would the Pope have been able to say if Bavaria and the Franks had not ended their quarrel? The incident was a severe test of Boniface's own convictions. Had or had not the occupant of St. Peter's chair the right, even the duty, to override or bypass his own plenipotentiary when circumstances (e.g. of a political nature) appeared to him to necessitate such a step? Certainly, Boniface was so much identified with Carloman that at a time when Bavaria was totally opposed to the Franks his representation of the Pope had been incapable of due expression in that land.

The Pope's anxiety to reassure and even to exalt Boniface is clear from the letter: and doubtless he was sincere in wishing him not to abandon any part of the German world to which he had been sent by Gregory II and Gregory III. But Odilo, though formally at peace with the Franks, remained difficult, and himself chose to veer away from the Anglo-Saxon sphere of influence. He is thought to have leant towards the Pirmin-inspired centres of reform, perhaps through the alliance with Alamannia which inwardly he may have maintained. As early as 741, it may be, monks from Reichenau (on Lake Constance) came to the Bavarian monastery of Niederaltaich; and others followed, all with the Duke's encouragement. Although products of a Benedictine reform, they may well have been more broad-minded than Boniface and his disciples. Whether that was so or not, Odilo soon went further along his self-appointed way of drawing in clergy of Irish and strongly Gallican types. Surviving service-books of the Bavarian ducal house give evidence that the Celtic/Gallican type of liturgy existed alongside the Roman variety. Odilo's behaviour corresponds with this, and may be compared with that of Queen Elizabeth I of England, who after forbidding candles on the altars of churches throughout the realm, continued to use them in the royal Chapel of the Savoy because she preferred things that way.

It is unlikely that Boniface could visit Bavaria at this period. As with the 'false bishop', it was hard for him to make a proper estimate of personalities and issues at a distance. In the matter of the presbyters Feirghil and Sidonius he once again found himself at odds with the Pope. Feirghil, or 'Virgil' as a latinised approximation, was an Irishman, Abbot of Aghaboe, who came to the Continent and was received into the circle of court clergy at Quierzy in 743. Conceivably he was already there when Boniface travelled from Les Estinnes to Soissons. He was a great scholar, versatile and philosophical. Nicknamed 'The Geometer' in his home country, he put his classical learning to a rather different use from any which Boniface and those like him would allow. He taught that under the earth were normal people (cf. the Antipodes), not a 'hell'. Pippin came to regard him as an interesting and valuable man. When in 745 some sort of improvement was being attempted in Frankish-Bavarian relations, Feirghil was transferred to Bavaria. Along with a Gallo-Roman presbyter called Sidonius, who may or may not have been at Pippin's court with him, he took an active part in church affairs under Odilo. The two worked together, in what capacity it is hard to discern. Evidently they had some judicial and disciplinary powers over other clergy. In 746 they pronounced judgement in a case of baptisms performed by an ignorant clergyman. The cleric having practically no knowledge of Latin, had been baptising 'in the name of Fatherland and Daughter, and of the Holy Spirit'. (He had been saying '*Patria*' instead of '*Patris*', and '*Filia*' instead of '*Filii*'.) Feirghil and Sidonius declared that it was not necessary for the persons so baptized to be baptized again. Boniface hearing about this, objected strongly and wrote ordering them to re-baptize. They appealed to the Pope, who upheld their decision on the grounds that the clergyman concerned had the proper intention when baptizing. Boniface was amazed when he received a letter from Zacharias telling him to desist from instructing Feirghil and Sidonius to re-baptize, and that he must 'try to conform to the teaching and preaching of the Fathers of the Church'. In sober truth the instance was a border-line case. Boniface, we may suppose, like Mary after the visit with the child Jesus to

Jerusalem, had to admit to himself that there were some things which were hard to understand, and 'stored up these sayings in his heart', hoping that here or hereafter such puzzles would be resolved. He would never abandon his conviction that Gospel, Church, Traditions and Papacy all needed one another and formed together the wholeness which the word 'Catholic' signified. But there might come a time when, not merely out of age or failing health, he would find it right to leave in others' hands the working out of that union and to devote himself to the Gospel pure and simple.

He tended to become cautious as a result of issues which drew unexpected answers from the Apostolic See. On a later occasion he came across an Irishman called Sampson, who declared that baptism in water was not the essential sacrament of Christian initiation, but that the vital act was that of the bishop's laying-on-of-hands, namely, 'confirmation' as it has usually been called. He wrote to Zacharias about this, in the course of a letter about a number of issues. So cautiously did he word the paragraph that he gave the impression of regarding the issue as an open question. The Pope gave a straight answer, without suggesting that his legate ought not to have asked a question which had such an obvious answer. Zacharias, we may well suppose, had by this time come to understand the qualms as well as the strict tendencies of the Anglo-Saxon whom he continually addressed in highly respectful, even loving terms. It was not Zacharias but his successor who would tip the balance between Boniface the church-organizer and Boniface the evangelist.

Chapter 20

PIPPIN THE SHORT, PIPPIN THE STEADY

Men of short stature are not infrequently found to be inwardly sensitive, but outwardly assertive and even aggressive. The second son of Charles Martel, Pippin III, became known as 'the Short', to distinguish him from his grandfather (Pippin of Heristal) and his great-great-grandfather (Pippin of Landen). He did not, however, share the typical tendencies of those who lack physical height. To his shrewdness he added a certain balance and strength which enabled him to maintain principles and wholesome objectives in spite of the compromises which are necessary in politics, 'the art of the possible'. He had not the religious enthusiasms which his elder brother developed under the influence of Boniface, but his desire to see reform in morals and church order was basically as firm. Like Carloman he came to see the great Anglo-Saxon as the one who was needed to open the door to reform; but he knew from the start that to bring him into the Neustrian arena involved risks and difficulties beyond those prevailing in Austrasia. Whereas the non-Frankish population of Carloman's half-kingdom was mostly Germanic and akin to the Anglo-Saxons, that of Pippin's was predominantly Gallo-Roman and therefore ethnically alien to the leader of the reform. It was, in fact, a remarkable feat on Pippin's part to secure a good ecclesiastical muster at Soissons and to persuade optimates and senior clergy to adopt, in principle at least, the movement already begun in Austrasia. No doubt he made the most of the fact that the Frankish Kingdom might in due course become an Empire blessed by God if its citizens were willing to subscribe to the preferences of the Bishop of Rome. The fact that Frankish armies were prepared to cross the Alps to help Rome in the years which followed showed that the argument carried weight. As legate of the Holy See, the Anglo-Saxon Archbishop Boniface might be tolerated even by those who had a natural antipathy towards the foreigner. He was the proper channel of communication, by the will of the Pope himself. In the first instance, at least, proceedings of synods and other necessary information would be despatched to Rome through Boniface, and replies from that quarter could generally be expected to come through him.

Since we know well that there were strong opponents in Austrasia from the very beginning, it must be regarded as equally certain that an opposition party existed in Neustria, even if it chose not to be vocal at Soissons.

Boniface did not become immediately aware of the strength of opinion against him. When he forwarded to Rome, with a covering letter, the proceedings of the two synods of March 744, he wrote in an optimistic vein. On receiving these communications Zacharias was inspired to re-read as many letters from Boniface as were stored in the papal archives. Moreover he had living evidence before him of the achievement with which Boniface's mission and life-work were being crowned: the bearer of the latest group of messages to Rome (April–May 744) was one of the three designated metropolitans for Neustria, Hartbert.

His reply (Ep. 57), dated June 22nd, 744, is accordingly enthusiastic. Addressing Boniface as his 'most revered brother' and as 'your holiness', and greeting him finally as 'dearest', he surveys his whole career as in the tradition of Barnabas and Paul (Acts 13:2) and (of course) Peter himself, all three apostles to the Gentiles. God is to be praised for having, through Boniface, 'touched the hearts of Pippin and Carloman'. Judging from the order of the names of the brothers Pippin was already, after three years, regarded widely as the obvious leader.

Zacharias goes on to express satisfaction over the arrangement of metropolitan sees for Neustria, confirming it and saying that he is sending a *pallium* for each of the three archbishops-elect, Grimo (already known and approved by him, it seems), Hartbert (who will be their bearer) an Abel whose qualifications he accepts on Boniface's authority. In the same letter he deals with Albert and Clement, the two notorious offenders whose cases have come into prominence, and describes them as not merely 'false prophets' but 'pseudo-Christians', definitely to be rendered powerless and penalised. (He supposed that they were already in custody; but they were to give trouble for a few years yet.)

Zacharias was concerned that those receiving the dignity of the *pallium* should fully understand the responsibility laid upon them of properly organising their ecclesiastical provinces and maintaining Christian and canonical standards. Very likely he took opportunity to tell Hartbert more by word of mouth than he found space for in his letter. Possibly Hartbert heard more still from those around the Pope. He must surely have made the acquaintance of Cardinal-Deacon Gemmulus, a papal officer who had become friendly with Boniface and had sent a letter and gifts of spices about a year previously (possibly along with the important missive carried by Denehard in April 743). Gemmulus or another* may have explained to Hartbert that it had become virtually a custom for a thank-offering to be sent to the Pope when the *pallium* was granted. This piece of information, intended kindly, was to have serious repercussions in Neustria. The accusation of simony (*cf.* Acts 8:9–24), which Zacharias agreed was justified in reference to the notorious Albert, was brought against Rome by some of those around Pippin after Hartbert's return: the Pope, it was suggested, was trading for money in spiritual offices.

The speed with which suspicions and difficulties developed is reflected in a further exchange of correspondence later in 744. Within two months of Hartbert's return, Pippin's neat plan for the ecclesiastical subdivision of Neustria had proved impractical. Boniface was put in the embarrassing position of having to write again to Zacharias, reporting that the *pallia* for Sens and Rheims were no longer required. He evidently gave no clear reasons (the letter is lost), since Zacharias wrote back on November 5th (Ep. 58) saying that he was beside himself with amazement at this unexpected change. The sequel makes it uncertain whether even Rouen was totally approved, after this, as a metropolitan see by the Roman authorities. It appears that the whole question remained open for a while; although in Neustria itself Rouen may have been regarded as having the proper status.

What the precise reasons were is not clear. Certain influential people may have suggested that not too much should be done at once in re-organising according to the Roman canons. It may have been pointed out that Austrasia was managing with one archbishop only. At Rheims the party of Milo doubtless did its best to thwart the plan. Abel failed to secure the government

* *eg* Theophylact, a Greek like Zacharias, appearing later as Archdeacon of Rome, and a correspondent of Boniface who had evidently met him earlier.

of the church there. Hartbert retained the see of Sens which unlike Rheims had been vacant when he was appointed. There and elsewhere, there may well have besn strong opposition to any 'foreign' bishop being given the dignity and authority of archbishop. The second subject of Zacharias's letter of 5th November deals with the accusation of 'simoniacal heresy' which Boniface had reported as having been raised against the papacy in the matter of the *pallium*. We are bound to conclude that there was still a powerful anti-Roman lobby in Neustria which would grasp any possible advantage. Certainly there was no definite fee involved (though this was to become the position in a later age). Zacharias in some indignation wrote, 'It is entirely alien to us and our clergy that we should sell for a price the gift which we have received from the Holy Spirit: those three *pallia* . . . we handed over without seeking any consideration whatever.'

It was in the same letter that the Pope reassured Boniface over the question of his standing in relation to the Bavarian church, while not giving a perfectly explicit answer to his question about a biship consecrated at Rome to serve in Bavaria. Boniface thus had to face unwelcome developments in two directions at least during 744; and his trials were not to diminish as time went on. However, he had obtained Zacharias's unmistakable support and encouragement as 'legate of St. Peter' in relation to Neustria as well as the German lands. He found Pippin worthy of his personal respect, cautious but clearly intent on reform; he could therefore trust that God's will would finally be done. He felt much closer to Carloman as a personal friend, but had to recognize in the younger brother a man to whom governing came more naturally. Boniface might occasionally inveigh against 'the Franks' in general, as well as against 'Milo and his sort' in particular, but, to judge from the surviving correspondence, he never so much as murmured against either of the Mayors.

In any case the year 744 saw him busy in Austrasia and beyond its borders, in ways that brought ample satisfaction to one whose deepest prayer was for the conversion of the Saxons. Not only had Fulda now been founded as a bulwark and buttress to the bishoprics of Büraburg and Erfurt, bordering on the Saxons, but also, by means of the campaign of that summer, a portion of Saxon territory was opened to evangelization, and many baptisms were in fact achieved. This was joy indeed for although conquest was not the ideal mode of entry, there was no question under Carloman of procuring baptism at the point of the sword, such as was the practice later of his nephew Charles, whom we know as Charlemagne. In spite of their hatred of the Franks who fought and conquered them, Saxon men and women responded to the preaching of men of their own race whom Carloman encouraged; namely, the Anglo-Saxon missionaries under Boniface.

By the autumn it was also clear that Pippin had achieved decisive success against Theutbald in Alamannia, and had been able to press Odilo of Bavaria into a separate treaty. By this Bavaria was shorn both of the annexed Alamannian area which included Augsburg, and of the Nordgau, the diocese of Willibald of Eichstätt. Boniface's own position in relation to Bavaria remained unclear in practice; so that it was a relief to have Willibald more definitely grouped with Burghard and the others. His attitude to the defeat of Alamannia is harder to judge. Beyond the thought that God's wider plan for the German peoples was being fulfilled in an indirect way, he may by now have been sufficiently positive in his approval of Pirmin's circle to regard its merging with Frankland as a help towards the achievement of reform.

During the winter there appeared a further source of hope and encouragement, in that a joint March assembly for Neustria and Austrasia was being planned, and a grand ecclesiastical synod of both provinces was projected at the same time. Since the secular objective of the assembly was to launch a joint expedition southwards against Aquitaine, it is clear that the initiative came from Pippin. Ecclesiastically, both the brothers may have been concerned over the question of a settled see for Boniface, concerning which their joint names might carry great weight at Rome. The death about this time of Reginfrid of Cologne gave an unexpected opportunity for the fulfilment of Boniface's longstanding desire, hitherto thwarted by papal objections. Not only was Carloman anxious to have his domain organised as a proper church province, but also Pippin might see benefit in having a good example of canonical arrangements in neighbouring Austrasia while the plans for Neustria were awry. There were other ecclesiastical matters which could benefit from the combined authority of a joint assembly. Obviously, the unashamed persistence of Albert, Clement and other offenders might the more readily be brought to an end.

There was the question of Bishop Gewilib at Mainz, whose presence and behaviour in the Saxon campaign could be seen in retrospect as a disgrace, even if in the excitement of the moment no one had objected and some had cheered. There was also the sensitive problem, as before, of revenues rightly belonging to the church at present being put to secular use. Did the victories of 744 allow any relaxation here? In the autumn the provisional answer might have been 'Yes'. As the winter passed, however, further pressures appeared from three directions. The treachery of Aquitaine was extended to an alliance with the Arabs, who thus presented a threat to Burgundy, and consequently to Neustria. Reactions to the Austrian success over the Saxons were twofold. Other Saxon tribes were showing their mettle: holding forces were needed, for example, in those regions near the Buchonian forest where similar pressure had been experienced in 743. Also the East Frisians had begun to take the part of their conquered neighbours, and were trying to push up the Rhine. In one of three communications sent by Boniface to Pope Zacharias during 745 he mentioned specifically 'trouble from Saracens, Saxons and Frisians', as is clear from the reply (Ep. 60) which Zacharias wrote to him personally in October of that year. (The Pope gave it as his view that troubles from the heathen were sent by God as a warning against the continuing malpractices in Christian Frankland, and that decisive victory on all fronts would be given only when these were ended.)

The joint assembly, when it met, was evidently an impressive occasion, as might be expected. No official pronouncement has come down to us, but its general import is fairly clear from what ensued. We do not know where the two Mayors held the meeting, nor how adequate an attendance of church representatives was mustered. The venue was possibly near the border between Neustria and Austrasia, e.g. at Laon or Cambrai, conceivably at the vacant see of Cologne. So far as Boniface's overall leadership was concerned, it was in any case one of the high points of his career. Conceivably the two brothers solved the problem of chairmanship in the ecclesiastical part of the proceedings by giving Boniface the lead. The impression which the latter gave afterwards in writing to Rome may be judged from Zacharias' comment thereupon: 'Concerning the synod which was held in the Frankish region (lit. 'province') with Pippin and Carloman, our most worthy sons, as moderators;

we have taken note of exactly how you carried it through, in your capacity as our personal representative and according to the instructions given in our letters: and we have given thanks . . . ' The Pope was conceivably thinking of Boniface as acting for the time being not only as his legate but as constitutional archbishop over Neustria as well as Austrasia; but if so, it was only expressed through a hint hidden in the word 'province'. The same term is repeated in his letter of about the same date (Ep. 61) addressed to leading Franks of church and state under both Mayors, to each of whom he had also written separately. Writing to senior clergy, nobles and civil servants he refers to 'the synod convoked in your *province* according to our instruction, with our sons your princes Pippin and Carloman as moderators and the aforesaid Boniface acting as our personal representative.'* The last phrase, used in both letters, was carefully and tactfully chosen.

These letters of Zacharias, seen as reflecting the communications sent by Boniface earlier in the year enable us to deduce the proceedings of the synod itself.**

Briefly the questions involved were roughly as follows. The subject of Neustrian metropolitan sees was not stressed. But for Austrasia the elevation of Cologne to metropolitan status was recommended in the strongest terms and it was decided to ask the Pope to alter his policy by allowing Boniface to occupy it as his permanent see. A discussion of the revenues diverted from the church led to the conclusion that it was impracticable to alleviate the situation as yet. Offending or false senior clergy were tried and condemned: these included Albert, Clement, Gewilib and, that other wretched bishop who may or may not have been the 'Godalsacius' of later correspondence. Confusion was also caused by clergy who claimed to have had earlier papal approval for what were obviously wicked and disorderly practices.

Boniface, forwarding the conclusions to Rome, enclosed further matter of his own along with his comments. He complained of men at court who were despoiling the churches further and who were themselves renegade clergy. No doubt he underlined the difficulties caused at the synod by those who claimed papal sanction for their evil ways. He may also have

* But he uses 'province' in the politico-geographical sense in the initial address, mentioning 'Gaul and the *provinces* of the Franks.'

** See Appendix B for a more detailed account.

asked the Pope to commend all that had been achieved, in such a manner as to encourage the two Mayors to persevere in holding yearly synods.

The political circumstances of 745 made it easier for the Pope to find time for these great issues. The readiness of the Franks to exert political pressure within the Italian scene had eased his position, and also made it more desirable for him to do all in his power to help in the development of a Christian Frankland. The specific question of Albert, Clement and others like them, was raised at a Roman synod, not unlike that which Boniface had attended for happier purposes some six or seven years before. In three sessions this venerable body debated in detail the cases of the named offenders, giving most thorough attention to that of Albert. He was, of course, thoroughly condemned, and all copies of his 'autobiography' were ordered to be consigned to the flames. Clement was put in an equally serious category. (The actual name of 'Godalsacius' does not appear until two years later.) The acts of this synod were dated 25th October; and it was as covering letters to these that the Pope sent the two letters, one to Boniface and one to the Frankish magnates, from which our knowledge of the March 745 all-Frankish synod is so largely derived.

The arrival of these from Rome towards the end of the year filled Boniface with satisfaction. He learned that the Cologne proposals had been accepted: he would be a wandering bishop no more! The other main decisions of the March meeting had been ratified. An effectual follow-up seemed assured, as the Pope had emphasised the necessity of holding a synod every year. But, as things turned out, there were great disappointments to be faced.

In spite of the Pope's reiterated insistence, there is no evidence that any Frankish synod was held in 746. The reasons for this can only be guessed at. To judge from later developments there were two main causes. One arose from diversions caused by the opposition, more notably in Austrasia than in Neustria. The other reflected the differing personalities of the two brothers Mayors, the younger a born ruler and the elder beginning to seek purely spiritual things. Carloman was increasingly offended by the contrast between Christian ideals and political practicalities. If he did not exhibit it publicly in 746, there can be little doubt that he confessed it to Boniface, for whom the news involved a strange mixture of joy and embarrassment. A further aggravation arose when those having power at Cologne refused to allow the fulfilment of the plan agreed upon by authority. Cologne was the ideal see for Boniface, close to the Saxon and Frisian borders, now that the sees of Hesse-Thuringia were well established and the development of Fulda seemingly assured. But his going to Cologne was effectually blocked. This was probably as frustrating to Carloman as to Boniface, perhaps more so. It brought into question his capacity to rule, at a moment when he faced an unwelcome external challenge from Alamannia. Alamannia had a direct boundary with Austrasia, but was separated from Neustria by a part of Burgundy, Neustria's dependency. Alamannia was more directly Carloman's concern, in principle, than Pippin's. Pippin had undertaken a successful expedition the year before, when (and perhaps largely because) Carloman had to deal with the Saxons. Now, when there was a revolt in that quarter, it fell to Carloman to put it down. He did so with consummate vigour. The decisive battle (at Cannstatt, near Stuttgart) has been described as a 'blood-bath'. It caused a revulsion in the mind of the unhappy Carloman. Early in 747 he retired to a monastic foundation in eastern Belgium.* From there he issued occasional directives until August, after which he retired to Rome and thence to Monte Cassino. Boniface was not unaccustomed to the phenomenon. Had not four English kings found similar destinies during his lifetime? Caedwalla of Wessex (resigned 688) had been followed by his successor Ine, the great lawgiver, thirty-seven years later; and during Ine's reign, two of his contemporaries in the Heptarchy had withdrawn similarly in one year (Coinred of Mercia and Offa of Essex, 709). Nevertheless, the departure of one to whom he had been so close was bound to be a grief to Boniface. It was as well that his respect for Pippin had continued to grow, and that the repeated references from Rome to 'Pippin and Carloman' had seemed to offer Pippin, as younger brother, the greater future.

Pippin himself, comparatively free from serious military enterprise in 746, had opportunity to assess the situation in his territory. He may well have foreseen the crisis that was about to break out in his brother's life, and have begun to prepare for possible eventualities. He perhaps put off a church synod while awaiting events. In the matter of church reform, in spite

* Stavelot-with-Malmédy, in the higher ground S.E. of Liège.

of all the difficulties which gave such acute pain to Bonifac and those who shared his feelings, Pippin saw several signs o hope. Reform did not depend entirely on the Anglo-Saxons They had made possible the renewed contact with Rome, whicl was a necessary factor in the whole movement towards a heal thy and unified church; but once the link was forged then th more its implications could be worked out by Frankish person nel, the smoother would be the road towards the desired goal The influence of Pirmin was penetrating into Frankland fron the east, and was basically similar to the influence of Bonifac while appearing less 'foreign'. Boniface himself could by nov see that this was so. Bishops of Frankish, perhaps even of Gallo Roman origin, could now be found who independently share the incentive to purify the church. Notably, across the borde in southern Austrasia, Chrodegang of Metz had a centre o renewal in and around his cathedral. He had been appointe by Carloman in 742. He had not attended the synods, bu nevertheless could prove a leader if the situation were rightl handled.

In detail, however, Pippin observed much that fell far shor of what was needed. There were many who offended agains the proper rules of church life and Christian conduct. He com piled a classified list of troubles. Whether he showed this t Boniface we do not know. However that may have been, h despatched the list, under twenty-seven heads, to Rome, askin the Pope for a ruling on each particular issue he had raised The list covered points of regular order, such as the relation between different grades and offices among clergy; the exten to which monks, and more particularly nuns, might take par in public worship outside the monastery; the treatment to b meted out to clergy and religious who ceased to observe thei vows; questions of all kinds concerning marriage, both clerica and lay (seven of these); others concerning sexual lapse, espe cially on the part of monks and nuns; and a few instances c criminal law, including one which involved the distinctio between premeditated and 'spontaneous' homicide. Zacharias replying in January 747, wrote direct to Pippin, giving suc answers as we should expect, and by-passing Boniface, so fa as the evidence goes.

In all this, Pippin cannot have offended Boniface seriously certainly the latter neither challenged him nor made complair either to the Frankish court or to Rome. There are those wh try to produce evidence that Boniface showed bitterness. They are too keen to counterbalance the idealistic tendencies of mediaeval biographers. It is equally necessary to avoid the pitfall of the 'Lytton Strachey' school, who pour scorn upon those of whom they write in order to show that the latter were 'real flesh and blood'.

Not without good reason is Boniface called a Saint. Like St. Peter and St. Paul he could be grieved or angry; but he also retained both the humility and the lovable nature which were his when he first started on his European journeys. One convincing piece of evidence is afforded by the story of his eight years' connection with Mainz, the former see of Gerold and Gewilib, in which he now found himself installed.

The possession of this see was the last great benefit which Carloman secured for Boniface. Mainz was admittedly 'second best' to Cologne, at least from Boniface's point of view; and neither the Frankish leaders nor the Pope were prepared to recognize it as a proper metropolitan see until well after Boniface's death.* Nevertheless it gave him a settled centre. A testimony to the genuine greatness of the man is the fact that, while Gewilib retained a degree of local affection after his deposition, Boniface built up such a reputation that its inhabitants desired to have him enshrined at Mainz, although they knew that his wish was to be buried at Fulda.

*The metropolitan question remained unresolved in both parts of the kingdom for the time being.

Chapter 21

FRANKLAND AND ENGLAND

At all times, and most especially at times of hardship and disappointment, Boniface had derived spiritual strength from hhis native land. Although his absence had been lengthy, the links with England by prayer and correspondence had been maintained. From the beginning of his jouneyings abroad he had thought of his home country as peculiarly equipped to provide missionaries to peoples as yet unconverted to Christ. England had been blessed with a firm Church organization, thanks to Augustine, Theodore and others. The different kinds of Christianity adopted in the early part of the seventh century had been brought within a united pattern, and the best of the traditions of the Western Church, centred on Rome, had taken root there. Anglo-Saxons who travelled abroad in the cause of Christ would not only preach to gain converts, but would see to it that the new Christians were gathered into a church properly organised and administered, a church respected and supported by secular authority, a church in union with the See of Rome and thus with the Christians of other lands. Missionaries from England had every reason to be proud of their home church and grateful to God for it. Faced with difficult tasks in the parts of the world to which their vocation led them, they had everything to gain by keeping in touch with trusted friends at home. Boniface had gained more than most because he was an exceptionally good correspondent. But he had also needed support more than most. He was at heart a humble man, called to an exceptionally weighty task. If he had unusual powers of perseverance and single-mindedness, he also suffered from periods of despondency occasionally bordering on the state known technically to-day as 'depressive': or so we may deduce as we have reviewed the course of his long ministry in Europe.

According to a theory which found favour in the 1930s the world's weather conditions vary over cycles of eleven years, and human beings can suffer changes of health or mood as a result. Whether there is any truth in this or not, the times of depression which Boniface endured were separated by intervals of approximately eleven years. It was in 735 or thereabouts, that he had declared in writing (Ep. 30, 33, 34) that he was in danger of being overwhelmed by the 'storms' of the 'Germanic sea'. But he had been not far from a similar experience around 724, not long after the success of Geismar, when he had complained of 'weariness from many trials' in mind and body (Ep. 27). With or without the theory, the elderly Archbishop Boniface around the year 746, once again underwent times of serious depression. Not all his personal humility could prevent the frustrations and disappointments of the years of Frankish reform from having this effect. Such moments, sometimes of near-despair, were the occasions when again he would express his feelings in letters to England. He was not far from such distress already in 744–5, when he wrote a letter of sympathy to Bishop Daniel (Ep. 63), now blind and retired from office and residing at Malmesbury (he died in 745 or 746): he informed the aged prelate of the extreme difficulties and unpleasantnesses which faced him among the Franks, and of his recurrent guilt-feelings over doing business (and even sharing in communion) with unworthy churchmen at court. As in 724 and 735. Abbess Eadburga was the recipient of an urgent message (Ep. 65) this time requesting earnest prayer for 'false brethren' as well as for the heathen. Other nuns of his acquaintance received similar pleas. To his dear cousin Leoba (Ep. 67), at Wimborne, along with Thecla and Cynehilda, he wrote from the depths of his sorrow: he asked whether he was not, in the end, 'the most wretched of all the envoys whom the catholic and apostolic Church of Rome has sent out to preach the Gospel', and expressed the fear that he would 'die without fruit of the Gospel, return without sons or daughters. . . .' Modern knowledge may help us to understand how Boniface could forget for a while the masses of converts of Hesse-Thuringia, in his agony over events in Frankland proper which he did not fully understand.

Consolation he did receive, and most notably from his old bishop, who wrote a letter as apposite to Boniface's needs (Ep. 64) as his much earlier letter (723–4) had failed to meet of them. Daniel wrote in a manner which revealed a clear understanding of the overall historical importance of the work of

Boniface and his colleagues. We may guess that other correspondents rose to the occasion, too.

Meanwhile a heavy weight was thrown into the opposite scale by other news from England: a Christian king was becoming notorious for his immoral, profligate life. Ethelbald of Mercia, who since the resignation and death of Ine of Wessex (725–6) had become the most powerful king in England, was the culprit. He had not married, but felt free to take women and girls as he chose*, not even drawing the line at nuns and novices. This last detail was related to yet further reports, which reflected very seriously on the condition of some English monastic houses up and down the land. To Boniface, while the English church was the basis, the rationale and justification of the Anglo-Saxon mission abroad, the Christian 'prince' and the monastic orders were the twin pillars of the church, in England as in any other settled Christian country. Alas now for England, and alas for Boniface's work! Matters must somehow be put right if the credibility of his own task and that of his colleagues, already at risk in Frankland, was not to be eroded even further.

At a time when his hopes of Cologne as a settled base of operations were being overthrown, and when the Pope's attitude to matters in Bavaria were causing him increasing puzzlement and anxiety, his sense of urgency about the condition of England was at its most extreme. Possibly this preoccupation was a factor which, along with Carloman's increased distaste for government, helped Pippin to take Frankish church matters into his own hands in 746 in the manner already described. The omission of any Frankish synod in the same year, while undoubtedly a further source of distress to Boniface, left room for a plan which he proceeded to put into effect in the interests of the English question. He called together those of his Anglo-Saxon colleagues who were in episcopal orders, to hold a solemn synod with him on subjects of concern to them in particular. Before the meeting took place he wrote firmly and politely to King Ethelbald on a personal basis, presumably with a view to preparing him for what was intended to follow. The synod itself, meeting perhaps at Utrecht and involving eight bishops had little difficulty in agreeing upon the terms of its message.

The admonition sent from the synod to Ethelbald (Ep. 73) began, somewhat in the style of a typical Pauline epistle, by

* cf. p. 40.

congratulating the Mercian king on those aspects of his rule which could be justly commended: firm government in general, good works in certain directions including the distribution of alms, and a considerable success in the suppression of crime. Next came the main subject of concern. The king's habits in relation to women were compared unfavourably, in a quite devastating fashion, to those of heathen nations who had their own clean codes of moral conduct. The 'Old-Saxons' were stern against adultery. The Wends (i.e. Slavs) from the east favoured such strong marriage ties as led widows to throw themselves on their husbands' funeral pyres. In such ways, in spite of excesses, the pagans could be said to have 'the law of God written on their hearts'. The letter concludes with a different sort of complaint, concerning another practice in Mercia which could weaken the impetus to reform among the Frankish churches: the seizing of monastic revenues for royal purposes. Boniface and his colleagues condemned this practice outright. It seems the decline in standards in the religious houses themselves was not directly mentioned. Perhaps it was believed that a new start by Ethelbald himself would quickly be reflected in the lives of his subjects. The assembled bishops* were not sufficiently certain of themselves to send their composition direct to the Mercian court. They sent it first with a covering letter (Ep. 75) from Boniface to the Archbishop of York, Egbert, to whom he in any case wished to write concerning certain books and papers. Egbert was asked to make corrections and improvements and then to send on the admonition to Ethelbald adding the weight of his own authority. Of Ethelbald's conduct and the situation in Mercia generally Boniface wrote, 'It is an evil unheard of in the past, and as my colleagues here who are versed in Scripture say, three or four times worse than the corruption of Sodom, when a Christian people, flouting the custom of the whole world, nay more, the command of God, turns against marriage and abandons itself to incest, lust, adultery and the seduction of veiled and consecrated women.'

In the other part of his letter Boniface requests of Egbert some of the treatises of Bede, and assures him that certain of the letters of Saint Gregory not yet known in Britain have been copied for English use from the archives at Rome and are being forwarded, along with gifts: 'a cloak, and a towel to wipe the

* For details of those attending see Appendix C.

feet of the brethren when you have washed them' (*viz.* at th ceremony on Maundy Thursday). Some years later, Bonifac was still writing for the Bede treatises, while thanking Egber for other books received in the meantime (Ep. 91). He alsc applied to Abbot Hutberht of Wearmouth for the same work of Bede (Ep. 76). The letters of Gregory the Great had been th subject of correspondence between Boniface and Pope Zachar ias, and in particular Cardinal-deacon Gemmulus.

How much other English support Boniface tried to obtai apart from Egbert's over the Mercian affair, it is hard to know A letter dealing with the matter to a certain presbyter Herefri (Ep. 74), probably Abbot of Lindisfarne, has been preserved There may have been others. Possibly there were several whicl were carried in one batch to England with the admonition, al in the good care of Ceola, a presbyter or deacon of Boniface' entourage.

It is a remarkable proof of the influence of the great monl of Wessex and his following that Ethelbald saw the error of hi ways. In the next year he co-operated in a reforming counci which was attended by representatives of Mercia, East Angli and the kingdoms to the south of them. This, and later th arrival in Germany of nuns from England, were two grea blessings, each of which in turn would uplift the heart o Boniface. He needed the encouragement. Fresh difficulties face him now, due simply to the onset of old age. Although he wa not so apt to call himself 'an old man' as he had been ten year earlier, he began to be afflicted by failing sight, so much so tha his outgoing letters had to be written for him. For this purpos Lull, whom he had already used as a close administrative col league more than a pastor, was admirably suited. Still only i deacon's orders, Lull was appointed arch-deacon when Boni face settled into the see of Mainz. He acted, among other things as his secretary and amanuensis. From 747 at least, letters ser out in Boniface's name show clear signs of the style character istic of Lull in correspondence which has come down to u under the latter's name.

Presumably Lull, or someone else, was now required regu larly to read to Boniface his incoming correspondence. Such reader might at times have opportunity, by his own tactfu comment, to enable Boniface to gain the most benefit from th news received. We can imagine this taking place in the colc wet weather of February 747, when a letter arrived from Pope Zacharias, dated January 5th (Ep. 77).

Zacharias opens by assuring Boniface of his constant spiritual companionship and the support of his prayers; everything that he can give, (in fact), apart from his actual presence at his side. His prayer is that God 'may strengthen you unto the fulfilment of your ministry'. The delicate situation and heavy responsibility faced by Boniface in the Frankish setting form the primary reference here. Nevertheless, recognising that the name and reputation of Boniface stand for evangelism at the most fundamental level, rather than for reform as such, he phrases the remainder of his prayer in these terms: 'that so in the day of his coming you may be found worthy to say, Behold me and the children whom you have given me: I have lost none of them' (cf. Jn. 17:12). So shall he hear, along with all the saints, the great words of divine welcome into the kingdom (Mt. 25:34).

The Pope then goes straight to the point. His object is to explain to Boniface his exchange of correspondence with Pippin, and thereby to reassure him of his own key position in representing Rome. 'You are already aware, my beloved, of the request that Pippin, that most excellent Mayor of the Frankish Palace, has made of us.' After giving a summary of the questions covered, Zacharias says that he has 'adapted our ear to his (Pippin's) prayers' by sending extracts of 'written apostolic documents' (*i.e.* conciliar 'canons', earlier papal decisions, and important statements from early Fathers). He has sent these direct, he suggests, out of a kind of courtesy due to the interest and initiative shown by Pippin, 'although your-holy-brotherliness (Boniface) is expert in all this': but he has also impressed upon Pippin, indeed 'commanded' him, that 'when these are published and explained in the sacerdotal college, your-holiness is to be called in.' It is a formal synod to which he refers; and he shows that he is aware of the difficulties which have continued in relation to the extinguishing of heretical fires in Frankland. 'When a council is gathered . . . those sacrilegious and contumacious men Albert, Godalsace and Clement are to be brought out into the midst, in order that their case may be traced out anew in detail and sifted through. If . . . they are convicted of a refusal to turn . . . you are to combine with the Prince of the province to do whatever seems good and satisfactory to you both, in accordance with the ordinances of the sacred canons.' If the culprits still persist and regard themselves as innocent parties they are to be despatched to Rome in the company of 'three or at least two well-proven and wise priests in order that their case may be examined in depth at the Apostolic See and that they may receive whatever finally they deserve'. (It was easy for a Pope to lapse into unrealistic recommendations!)

Zacharias did not criticise the Frankish authorities for having failed to hold a synod of (or with) churchmen in 746. In view of Pippin's co-operative attitude that would hardly have been prudent. Quite evidently, however, the Franks were under pressure, both from events and from the Pope, to hold a synod in 747. To do so in connexion with the March assembly (or assemblies) was not feasible. Carloman was on the point of withdrawing from his political responsibilities, at least to the extent of wishing to spend a trial period in a monastery. For almost a year the future of the Austrasian administration was unclear. Carloman had a son, Drogo, who might think himself able to take over, whether others (even his father) thought so or not. About the turn of the year, 747–748, an anonymous letter (Ep. 79) was written to a man in West Frisia, in which a request for certain garments to be supplied had appended to it the question – Does Boniface plan to attend Pippin's court or Drogo's? We have no other evidence, except that Pippin took over the administration without any trouble serious enough to have been recorded. Nevertheless the whole period from early 747 to March (at least) 748 must have had its political uncertainties. It is perhaps remarkable that Pippin managed to arrange any kind of church synod in 747.

In view of all his preoccupations, Pippin encouraged the clergy of both provinces to hold a representative gathering without the nobles and very likely without his personal presence. Presumably he arranged to have the Pope's reply to his questions 'laid on the table' at the synod. It seems that there was to be no question of formal declarations, or actual conviction of those offending grossly in religion and morals. It may have been necessary for Pippin to explain to Boniface that, if he held a meeting of all the bishops who could or would attend under his own leadership, and proclaimed as clearly as possible the principles of reform, things would steadily improve, as they were tending to do already. Such compromise could only be painful to the elderly legate of Rome: but Pippin was right in his expectations. None of the three chief offenders caused any further trouble after this date; although the indirect effect of their sectarian activities remained widespread, sufficiently for a letter from Boniface to give Zacharias the impression that 'false priests' generally 'outnumbered catholic ones'.*

A fair number of catholic ecclesiastics, including thirteen diocesan bishops beside Boniface himself, attended the 747 synod. Assistant bishops, presbyters and deacons were present with them. Although it has been supposed that the meeting took place at Mainz, where Boniface had recently settled, there seems to be good reason to suggest that in fact it was held in western Neustria, at Rouen.** If so, it was not only courteous to the one Neustrian see which was now intended as 'metropolitan', but strategic in terms of extending reform to fresh parts of Frankland. From this point of view it was possibly an advantage that eight Neustrian 'diocesans' came, while only five attended from Austrasia; though Boniface himself may have wished that more of his long-standing colleagues could have been present. (If Rouen did indeed provide the venue, distance was against those from Eastern Austrasia.) It is significant that Heddo of Strasbourg, reckoned among the Austrasians who came, was joined on this occasion by former disciple of Pirmin, namely Romanus of Meaux, one of the Neustrian contingent.†

Reginfrid, the new bishop of Rouen, appears first in the only list we possess of the thirteen diocesan bishops at the synod.‡ We take him to have been joint chairman with the Archbishop, as Wera at Utrecht the year before. Between them they drew the assembly into a close sense of unity. All present were impressed with Boniface's sense of the union of the Catholic Church with and through the See of Rome. All gained encouragement from him in their pastoral concerns, in the face of so much that had been amiss in the Church. They were heartened and inspired by his virtual equating of the pastoral and evangelistic aspects of ministry. A new sense of adventure came over them.

* See Appendix D.

** See Appendix D.

† Meaux had had connections with Pirmin earlier in his career; so that he came to be described erroneously as 'Bishop of Meaux'.

‡ i.e. in a letter of Pope Zacharias of the following year, 748.

The 747 synod was without doubt another of the high points in Boniface's career. The bishops and other clergy who came under his influence there were quite prepared to be reminded by his example as well as by his words of warning, that their new-found zeal for reform would draw the enmity, even the active hostility of others who did not share their enthusiasm.

It is clear from subsequent correspondence that more themes were prominent in the discussions. It can be taken for granted that the meeting also endorsed and re-affirmed the canons of church order approved at Rome. When, in the later months of 747, the Pope received news of the synod from the redoubtable bishop Burghard, he rejoiced at the thought that Frankish ecclesiastical leaders had so gladly 'turned to blessed Peter'. He must have felt very close to them in spirit. He could pray that they would be enabled to reckon a 'wealth of souls' to their credit in the Day of Christ.

But it was not immediately that the proceedings of the synod were taken to Rome. Exalted in spirit by the outcome, Boniface's first care was to write to England. Now that both parts of Frankland had reaffirmed the canonical decrees in a bold and unmistakable manner, he could make the maximum impact upon the English synod which was about to be held at Clovesho.* He wrote direct to the Archbishop of Canterbury, Cuthbert. The latter was a man of Kentish birth who had had four years in Mercia as bishop of Hereford (736–740), and was now elated at the change which had been brought about in King Ethelbald through the initiative of Boniface and his colleagues. The synod now planned was, indeed, in part at least an outcome of that change.

Boniface's letter to Cuthbert was designed to ensure that standards in England corresponded with all the aims of the reform movement on the Continent, and that no matter of importance was omitted. This was evidently not his first communication. The letter opens with thanks to Cuthbert for gifts received through Cynebert, a deacon of Canterbury, and the valuable conversation they had had together. In view of the Roman norm of an *annual* synod in every province, Boniface does not simply refer to the approaching meeting in the province of Canterbury, but writes on the basis of their 'equal status

* If we are right, the same place in North Kent at which a synod had been held in Boniface's infancy.

and responsibilities', inviting Cuthbert to share synodal findings 'at any time', whenever 'God shall inspire you or your synods with wholesome counsel'. The aim is an exchange of ideas in order that each may evaluate what the other has disclosed. So, 'we feel . . . you would like to be informed about the decisions we have taken here and so submit them to you for correction and improvement.'

His clear summary of points starts from adherence to the Roman Church as the guardian of unity and truth. Still impressed by the re-affirmation of the bishops of Frankland, he covers succinctly the familiar ground: metropolitan sees, archbishops therein gaining recognition from Rome by the grant of the *pallium,* an annual synod in each province under the metropolitan, synodal decisions to be lodged at Rome; the canons to be renewed each year at the synod, and the conduct of bishops tested thereby; every bishop to have his own diocese, properly defined, and to carry out an annual visitation, confirming, instructing, forbidding heathen, superstitious and immoral practices and ensuring that clergy, monks and nuns are conforming to their professions. Issues insoluble at diocesan level are to be brought to the provincial synod. Clergy and the monastic orders are forbidden to bear arms or indulge in field sports.

There follows an impassioned section in which the difficulties facing a 'metropolitan', in Frank-land or in England, are described by Boniface's favourite metaphor of the ship in the storm.

On practical matters that have arisen, Boniface advises Cuthbert to discourage women, whether 'veiled' or not, from undertaking pilgrimage to Rome: many have lost their virtue on the way, and are scattered about Europe, hardly a good advertisement for Christian England! He also, amongst the matters at issue in England itself, makes a further plea against the 'robbing of churches', viz. lay impropriation, which has already caused so much hardship in Frankish lands as well, and which in extreme cases tends to foster the decline in standards of other kinds.

Clovesho 747 became a significant event in the annals of England. It achieved most of its objectives and thus created or re-established a norm of Church order which had good long-term effects. When Boniface later came to evaluate the decrees that were issued, there was only one feature which would bring him genuine disappointment: the question of obedience to Rome was not given the direct and positive answer for which he looked.

However, as soon as he learned of the outcome of 'Clovesho', he wrote to Pope Zacharias, reporting on the two synods and including other matters which were weighing on his mind. To Burghard he gave not only this letter and the signed proceedings of the Frankish synod, but also the two statements of Christian doctrine which had been developed in the course of his labours: one of these may have been agreed in its final form by the Frankish synod as a whole. For both he sought the Pope's approval.

In the autumn of 747 the worthy bishop set off by one route or another from Würzburg to Rome, ready to spend the winter there. Boniface, no doubt, assured him that he would make sure that the affairs of the diocese of Würzburg were properly supervised during his absence. Having not been able to visit the present Pope, he regarded Burghard as far more than a mere messenger. He was to represent him in person. It was beneficial for many reasons, quite apart from those of age and health, that he should spend some months at the Apostolic See, as Boniface had done on earlier occasions. Certainly, in the event, this trusted colleague lived up to expectations, and more.

When at last he returned, he was to find a further joy and reward awaiting him, or near at hand. The advent of a large party of nuns from the home country in 748 'settled accounts' between England and Boniface's mission after the concerns over Ethelbald's lapse of two years before.

Chapter 22

A LIGHT SOMETIMES VEILED

The year 748, during which he completed thirty full years of untinterrupted ministry on the continent of Europe, brought to Boniface much consolation and encouragement. He had been relieved of intense anxiety about trends in England. His happiness for his home country was enhanced by a letter from King Elbwald of East Anglia, requesting fellowship in prayer. In Frank-land, Pippin's first year as sole effective ruler showed promise of steady development and consolidation in the years to come. Carloman had been a ruler and a friend after Bonifaace's own heart; but it had to be admitted that in comparison with his brother he was not a good politician. His resignation and departure from the scene had been a personal blow to Boniface. But from the monastery of Monte Cassino the ex-Mayor could maintain a fellowship of prayer parallel to that sought by the East Anglian King, and so help to set forward under God all that Boniface held most dear. To that same source of the Benedictine tradition, Cassino, he planned to send Sturm, so that the latter's rough-hewn, hermit-like monasticism could be tempered and moulded to the vocation of an abbot. In this year too, as an answer to many prayers over many years, there arrived those dear nuns from Wimborne, all thirty of them (one for every year of his continental mission . . .), under Leoba, Thecla and Cynehilda. For Leoba, too, Boniface had plans similar to those for Sturm, which (so her biographer relates) he had already outlined when applying to Abbess Tetta for help. His beloved cousin, whose friendship and spiritual companionship he had cherished by correspondence down the years, was to be no less than the greatest of leaders among the dedicated women to whom she would be 'mother' within the borders of the German mission. Therefore it was his wish and intention that she should first draw from the most wholesome spring of all that was best in monastic life. Near to Monte Cassino a convent had been founded by Scholastica, sister of

Benedict; she had kept in touch with him annually while he lived, and had been buried at Cassino itself some years before his death (*c.* 550 A.D.). Boniface envisaged a not altogether dissimilar pattern for himself and his cousin on her return. Meanwhile she and Sturm might have the opportunity to join in a bicentenary celebration of St. Benedict's death.

As mentioned in an earlier chapter, the details of the foundation and development of the three convents around Würzburg are not clearly known. But whether or not the house at Tauberbischofsheim was begun before Leoba went to Italy, whether or not that at Kitzingen was based on an earlier foundation (possibly inspired by Pirmin's movement) under Hadeloga, and whether or not Thecla governed Ochsenfurt as well as Kitzingen, such matters are of little importance beside the plain fact that Boniface was adding a new and shining facet to the previous jewel of his achievement among the German peoples. While he himself was more directly concerned with Fulda (two or three days' journey northward from the Würzburg district) he could safely leave the supervision of the nunneries to Bishop Burghard, who returned from Rome in the middle of the year.*

For the first part of the year, however, Burghard was still absent from his see, having remained in Rome until Zacharias saw fit to respond, by comment or reply, to the various matters which Boniface had referred to him. The Pope's careful response was completed on May 1st, ten days after Easter, and was accompanied by a letter to the Frankish bishops who had associated themselves with Boniface the previous year, the name of Reginfrid of Rouen heading the list. He sent also a letter of encouragement to Frankish laymen, twelve leaders being named.** There was yet another enclosure, a note to Boniface from Archdeacon Theophylact of Rome, who at Boniface's request had given Zacharias his own testimony to the soundness of everything that Boniface stood for, and to his constancy in support of all that Rome approved against 'opponents and heretics'. Theophylact, as we have seen, belonged with Cardinal-deacon Gemmulus to a steady group of friends which

* In character, as in age, Burghard was closer to Boniface than any other of his disciples and colleagues, even Sturm or Lull.

** Conceivably there was one leader for each diocese concerned in the 747 synod other than Mainz and Würzburg,: '. . . to Throand, Sandrad, Nanthere, (9 others named): and all, great and small . . .'

Boniface had made during his visits to Rome. Burghard was a sufficient witness to his master's qualities, if such was needed; but Theophylact, a Greek like Zacharias himself, could underline Burghard's remarks in a distinctive way. Anxiety may have been caused, in the Pope's mind, by one or two seemingly elementary questions concerning right and wrong teaching and practice which were scattered about in Boniface's letters; questions reflecting those extremely heavy pressures which at times could almost overwhelm the venerable Legate of St. Peter.

It is likely that Burghard travelled direct to Mainz on his return, because of the letters to clergy and people which would be forwarded (possibly in copy) to destinations a long way from there, southward, westward and to the north-west down the Rhine. Boniface, whatever his other concerns, was likely to be found at Mainz on greater feasts, and thus available there between Ascension Day (May 30th) and Whit Sunday (June 9th). As to the journey from Rome, it was possible for Burghard, starting on May 2nd, to spend Ascension Day at Mainz and proceed to Würzburg for Whit Sunday. Be that as it may, there was much fresh encouragement for Boniface when they met. Zacharias' opinion of them both shone out of the opening passage of his letter to Boniface, which he wrote that Burghard's presence in Rome had been to him as 'a breath of your own holiness'. He had written gratefully of all the 'affirmations' which Boniface had made to him, and used a word, '*affatus*', which could be a deliberate play on the name 'Boni-fatius'. These, taken as a whole, had impressed him with the magnitude of the 'great fight' in which Boniface had for so long been engaged 'on behalf of the Gospel which we have received through Peter, through the 'chosen vessel' Paul and the other Apostles'. It was his prayer that God would give Boniface strength, for as long as he was spared to this earthly life, to complete that task and 'bring in a wealth of souls'. No permission was given to him to resign: only death would remove him from office. Certainly no other '*sacerdos*' (for which Boniface had asked) would be sent from Rome to 'Francia and Gaul'. On the other hand, and this was more than satisfactory to him, he could have permission to consecrate to the rank of Bishop, though only as co-adjutor, the man whom he wished to follow him. In this way the government of the diocese of Mainz, which the Pope accepted as Boniface's see since Cologne had proved impracticable, could be properly maintained alongside the archbishop's other and wider interests and responsibilities. It is impressive that Zacharias saw the latter's work overall as concerned with 'the Gospel', although almost every item of the correspondence between them was concerned with church order. There was no dichotomy between these two aspects for either man.

As already mentioned, two statements of Christian doctrine had been sent to Zacharias by Boniface for comment. One, a concise handbook prepared by the latter 'for Catholic bishops, presbyters and religious', he found quite admirable: 'it is indeed acceptable . . . you worked it out by the grace of the Holy Spirit.' The other, a sort of 'charter', had been composed and sent by Boniface along with 'bishops, who are beloved by us, belonging to one part of Frankland'. After 'careful examination' of this the Pope had been 'filled with utter joy', particularly as it meant that God had 'seen fit to recall them unanimously to fellowship with us'. Perhaps it was a statement drawn up at Rouen by those bishops who had not previously been active in the 'reform movement', in answer to a challenge presented by Boniface. This, along with the 'proceedings' of the synod, and in particular the subscription of its members to the Roman 'canons', had inspired Zacharias to write the letter which he was now enclosing to be forwarded to the thirteen named bishops and their clerical colleagues. In a reference to the English synod, Zacharias expressed to Boniface his appreciation of the Anglo-Saxon Church, taking care to mention not only the missionaries sent by Gregory the Great but also Archbishop Theodore, who like Zacharias himself was a Greek ordained at Rome, and 'who was governing' (viz. the Church in England) 'within the span of your own life-time.'

Boniface was encouraged by the Pope both in the straightforward development of his work and in the correction of those who had erred. Presbyters of sound understanding and purity of life were to be placed where there was the greatest need for the hearing of God's word. Synods (as it seemed unlikely that Pippin would continue to hold the sort that Carloman and he had begun) were to be convened as and where possible, particularly because of the need to bring about the reform or else the deposition of erring bishops. Zacharias gave rulings on particular matters of false teaching and practice at Boniface's request. These were mostly related to the making of a Christian by baptism and laying-on-of-hands. The case of Sampson, already mentioned, was summarily dealt with. The Bavarian teachers who were at variance with Boniface were being handled with all circumspection by the Pope. It was here that he assured Boniface that he had not authorized the presbyter Feirghil to run a diocese; if it proved impractical for that man's views about the Creation to be examined on Bavarian soil, he was making arrangements for Feirghil and Sidonius to be sent to Rome. Because of the political situation these proved to be vain hopes; but in any case Boniface by now knew that his writ had ceased to run, in practice, in Bavaria. Although Odilo died in this year (748), things were to become worse before they settled down again. The young Duke Tassilo III came too much under extraneous influences to be able even to form a judgement for or against Boniface's point of view.

The news from Rome, giving so much cause for reassurance, arrived against the background of Pippin's successful attempts to weld the Frankish realm into a national unity. Boniface, after the resignation of Carloman, had prudently avoided siding with his son Drogo in the manner in which the anonymous writer to Andhun (see p. 170) had supposed he might do. He had given his allegiance to Pippin, whom he never ceased to respect through strained and difficult times. We may assume that Boniface and other church representatives attended the March-assembly of 748, which Pippin held on a national scale at Düren, on Austrasian territory and seemingly unchallenged in the end by Drogo. Presumably by the prior understanding between the Mayor and the archbishop, little or no formal church business was conducted. Certainly no decrees were published. We can well imagine that Pippin wished the emphasis to be taken off ecclesiastical reform by national pronouncements, while readily allowing that reforming measures already decreed should continue to be put into practice whenever and wherever this could be done without causing serious discord. He needed a few years to consolidate the life of the kingdom as a whole, and had to retain the political loyalty of subjects whose views (and lives) were opposed to everything Boniface represented.

Discussion of secular business at Düren between Pippin and his 'optimates' centred on the Saxon problem. As always this was of keen interest to Boniface. While never failing to support the authorities over military measures, he had been increasingly sorrowful that little other opportunity was offered for him to breach the spiritual walls of heathendom among his 'kin of blood and bone'. Preaching and baptism conducted in the wake of military conquest were not only hampered by the identification of Christian advance with political subjugation, but were apt to be of fleeting consequence because of retaliation from the Saxon side. However, Boniface continued to hope that a more widespread and lasting conversion of the Saxon tribes might not long be delayed. A further poignancy was added to the plans for the campaigning season of 748. Grifo, Pippin's half-brother, whom Boniface had approached with a letter of loyalty in 741, was now among the Saxons fomenting trouble. Unforgiving for his original overthrow, still rankling after six years in custody, unwilling to be grateful after Pippin had released him and had even given him lands in Neustria, he had joined the most troublesome enemy of the Franks. The Saxons had already been regaining ground in the Westphalian region after their reverse in 744. Their border with Hesse and Thuringia, lively before that but quieter since, had begun to show signs of renewed activity. It was hard to know what Grifo was planning, or where he would strike. Pippin, assuming that he could expect an attack, if anywhere, at the point nearest to where the March assembly was being held, quietly arranged to enter Saxon territory at the further end of the border.

Boniface may or may not have been a party to this plan. But in either case we can envisage him going to Fulda after Whitsuntide, to make further arrangements for Sturm's projected absence in Italy, and to meditate over all the news and advice from Rome; and in general to give thanks for many blessings, in spite of much continued opposition and a score of matters that puzzled his idealistic and in some ways too inflexible mind. At Fulda he found peace. Gaining inspiration from the austere and primitive type of Benedictine rule which Sturm and his companions preferred, he sometimes (so it is said) joined them in the actual task of construction, which would take a decade or more to complete. His sight was good enough for that, although for reading and writing he needed help increasingly.

The Frankish army under Pippin came through eastward and northward to the Thuringian border, and swept through the territory of the Saxons. Grifo, whether he joined in battle or not, escaped from Frankish hands and took refuge in Bavaria. The Frankish victory was extensive, and the enemy were severely punished. Boniface's preachers from the dioceses of

Büraburg and Erfurt, and perhaps from Fulda too, set out to take the Christian message to those areas which had fallen into Frankish hands. Once again there were a number of baptisms, a cause for joy accompanied by uncertainty as to how long these results could last. It was perhaps at the time of the 748 campaign that Boniface was given a sharp reminder of the other kind of enemy, more inimical to him than any Saxon. A bishop, one already having a reputation as a 'womaniser', was seen to be taking part as a combatant in the Frankish army, and relishing the experience. Boniface was shocked and shamed. The man was, indeed, later removed from office; but he created trouble for Pippin, as he was enabled by his friends to cling to the material benefits of the bishopric. Of the man and his 'see' we have no details; but Boniface determined that he would refer the matter to the Pope if Pippin did not manage to oust the offender altogether. (This matter was included in the next round of correspondence with Rome, in 751). The party of Milo was, alas, hardly on the wane. Gewilib had resigned and conformed, but another had risen in his place.

The following year saw a further serious challenge to the security of Frank-land, adjudged to be the last major obstacle which Pippin had to overcome. Grifo, whose mother was of the Bavarian royal house, had not only found sympathy but had gained influence over young Tassilo, and also, not surprisingly, over the dowager duchess Hiltrud, the sister of Pippin, whose marriage to Odilo had taken place against her brother's will. He had drawn also into alliance Siudger of Nordgau, thus removing the diocese of Eichstätt from Boniface's effective control. Further still, he had reawakened Lantfrid of Alamannia to the possibility of casting off the Frankish yoke. It was this formidable alliance which, by the time of the March-assembly of 749, Pippin knew that he had to defeat, if his united kingdom was not to suffer a fatal reverse.

We can conceive that he begged to be excused from all attention to church matters for the time being. There is no trace of a 'synod' or anything approaching it having taken place in the spring of 749; Boniface, disappointed, had to be patient. He and his colleagues had plenty to keep them busy. Sturm was away, and so, probably, was Leoba. Burghard was well occupied, having the nunneries to supervise alongside other matters which had accumulated during his stay in Rome. For Boniface himself there was Fulda to be fostered. The Saxon mission northward, arising from the 748 campaign, had to be maintained and if possible extended.

As to the diocese of Mainz, which required proper supervision constantly, there was a considerable set-back when Pippin restrained the old archbishop, now entering his seventieth year, from taking advantage of the permission recently given by the Pope. To make Lull bishop even in an auxiliary capacity, was considered by Pippin too much of a risk at this stage. Until the present crisis was over, until he had more time to use his own tact and influence with the opponents of Boniface's reform, the Anglo-Saxon presence along the Middle Rhine was to be as unobtrusive as possible. Partial preferment only was permitted for the time being. Strictly speaking, he had remained a deacon until now. According to the usage of the period, an 'archdeacon' was an administrator, quite literally a deacon over the other deacons, and affecting the presbyters only through the organising of diocesan work for the bishop. Lull, described as 'deacon' in correspondence up to this time, figured later (by 751) as 'presbyter'. Doubtless, if there were two grades of presbyter then, as seems likely, Lull was ordained (749–50) and authorized in the fuller sense, including the right to celebrate the Mass without any special or further permission from the bishop. This fell far short of what was needed at Mainz to cover Boniface's absences and to take into account his age and failing sight: Lull could not, as a presbyter (even a 'sacerdotal' presbyter), administer confirmation, still less any sort of ordination. With regard to the future of the see of Mainz itself, Pippin was known privately to be in agreement with Boniface's wish that Lull should eventually succeed him as diocesan. In principle, Pippin would very probably agree with the proposal that Mainz should be made a metropolitan see in perpetuity; but as yet there was no question of this in any precise sense, since the Pope himself had made no formal pronouncement, but had remained silent on that larger aspect. Here was another subject in the list of those which Boniface would refer back to Rome at the opportune moment.

Pippin's appeal for national unity in face of the Bavarian alliance was successful. It is possible that he had to use careful diplomacy to prevent supporters of Grifo from thwarting him. But he won the day. A costly campaign carried the Frankish army to the banks of the River Inn, but the victorious conclusion was decisive, so that the Bavarian duchy was strictly subordinated to Frankish overlordship for a long time to come. Grifo was captured and at first imprisoned. Later, whether out of generosity on Pippin's part or because of the strength of his supporters, he was again released. It was hoped that he would remain quiet as lord of a dozen countships in Neustria; but that was not the end of his treacherous activities.

The turn of the year 749–50 saw Boniface under very considerable constraint. It was as well for him that Fulda still needed his attention. Even the onset of problems in the Thuringian region could be an advantage, affording a diversion from the contemplation of his trying situation vis-à-vis the Frankish court. That he still attended the court from time to time is evident from the renewed pangs of conscience which he had concerning contact and communion with unworthy priests. As he recalled his oath under Gregory III, this subject was filed for re-submission to Rome in due course. But Pippin had advised Boniface that for a second year in succession there would be no synod of any kind, this time to aid him in the arts of peace rather than to ensure success in the conduct of war. It was his particular desire by now to exercise kingship in his own name, since he had united the kingdom, and since the 'reign' of Childeric III through seven years had served only to show more clearly the pointlessness of the present arrangement. To unite the nation in the recognition of Pippin as king, however, was an even more delicate task than to weld it together for military purposes. For this reason it was required that Boniface's part in public affairs be even less obvious.

Pippin did not think of trying to secure a change of dynasty by a sudden coup. The mystical quality of kingship was not to be transferred in that way. Spiritual authority was needed for such a move, in his estimation, and due solemnity must mark its accomplishment. This meant the involvement of the Church of Rome. Only the declared approval of the Pope could sanctify the procedure in such a way that the change would be recognised throughout the Christian world. By this time, probably, it would convince a majority of the people in Frank-land itself. Doubters would be the more easily brought round to the same point of view if the authority of Rome was not too exactly identified with Boniface the Anglo-Saxon. The situation was delicately balanced since the Pope had no other resident representative in the kingdom, and could not be expected to give his full blessing to the initiation of a new Frankish king and royal house without Boniface's ministration. All such questions, however, were merely theoretical until the views of the Pope on the basic issue had been obtained.

Events in Italy were moving in Pippin's favour, and he may have known it. The Lombards had become aggressive again under King Ratchis, after some years of quiescence following Liutprand's death in 744. Recently in 749 Ratchis, faced with the grand ambitions of his brother Aistulf, had retired to Rome and then to Monte Cassino. By 750 it was clear that Aistulf would drive all trace of Byzantine rule out of Italy if he could. Rome was still nominally 'of the Empire': in spite of the renewal of 'iconoclasm' under Constantine V, Pope Zacharias had been dating documents by reference to his reign. Rome was in danger and needed a protector. Already, once, a Pope had turned to the Franks. Rome's need would minimise any hesitation which the present Pope might have over granting an unusual and far-reaching request from Pippin.

In 750, therefore, the Mayor made his reconnaissance, through two shrewdly chosen representatives, both churchmen. Bishop Burghard, unreservedly approved by Boniface and already having a close rapport with the Pope, was matched by a purely Frankish cleric of the moderate reforming school and of the court circle, named Fulrad. The latter was senior chaplain at court. (Not long afterwards he was made Abbot of St. Denis, near Paris.) The two went to Rome directly by order of Pippin, and were to report back direct to him. Boniface must have known; he very likely gave his personal blessing, quietly, to the arrangements. (A private consultation between Pippin and Boniface on such a weighty matter would have been some compensation to the latter for the absence of any synod). Boniface refrained from writing separately to Zacharias during that year, although his list of questions over issues great and small was mounting up.

His consent to the co-operation between a churchman of his own school and a member of the third force which was arising in Frankish affairs represents a certain mellowing in his own outlook. Such a mellowing might be expected to come about towards the end of the earthly pilgrimage of a man of prayer, a man whose basic humility could temper his strong convictions and enable him to leave some questions open. Fulrad, though not himself known as a disciple of Pirmin, had the closest association with Chrodegang of Metz and others who had been in Pirmin's circle. We may see in the collaboration between Fulrad and Burghard the beginning of a rapprochement which, if tradition can be trusted, grew to the point where Boniface himself paid a personal visit to Pirmin himself (perhaps not until 753, a few months before Pirmin's death). If Boniface was yet to find himself questioning events happening in Frankland, it would not be because he resented the transfer of responsibility for reform out of Anglo-Saxon hands. Modern scholarship has been too swift to ascribe to him a narrow bitterness in this respect.

Zacharias gave audience to the two, and after due consideration, gave his firm assent to Pippin's proposal. We do not know how long they stayed. As Pippin was being careful, deliberate and unhurried about the whole affair, they may have had leisure to discuss a range of matters with the Pope. Synods and metropolitan sees were obvious subjects to be raised, over which the two would need to appeal to Zacharias for further patience. They could assure him that Boniface as 'legate of the Apostolic See' was not to be blamed for postponements and deficiences. Concerning the 'province of Mainz', not yet confirmed or defined, they may have agreed to advise the Pope to limit it to those dioceses which lay to the east and north of Mainz, leaving several southern Austrasian sees to be joined eventually to a Neustrian province. They could recommend such an arrangement as being politic for two reasons, the continuing activities of Milo (of Trier), and the independent outlook and initiative of Chrodegang (of Metz) in matters of reform. They may have needed to allay Zacharias' disappointment on hearing that Lull was not yet in episcopal orders. Burghard was in a position to give favourable reports on the development of the women's convents in his diocese, and on progress at Fulda: everything should be in good order for the return of Sturm and Leoba in a year's time. At Rome the two messengers doubtless felt the force of the Lombard threat, and could sense the need of the Papacy for an alliance (more than merely spiritual) with a strong Frankish power.

The ready response of the Pope did not deflect Pippin from his cautious approach, however deep his satisfaction at the clear reply. A full year, as it turned out, was necessary to mount the operation without too much danger of repercussion. After the winter, Boniface and Pippin needed to approach, together, a practical understanding as to how the inauguration of the new dynasty was to be carried through. Their deliberations (which again had to suffice in lieu of a synod) may still have needed to be somewhat private; and Boniface, though no longer restrained from communicating with Rome over the many matters which were on his mind, was discouraged from referring to this most delicate subject in writing. If he consulted Zacharias over the possibilities and proprieties of the change of kingship, it was by personal and verbal representation through Lull, whom he sent to Rome with a variety of items, some in writing and some by word of mouth. Zacharias' written reply was not given until November 4th, and it is an open question whether Lull returned in time to bring verbal confirmation of any proposals about king-making with which Boniface may have entrusted him.

With or without such satisfaction in detail, the whole affair was successfully concluded in the latter part of 750. Difficulties of all kinds were resolved by the decision that there should be an *anointing* of Pippin by 'the Frankish bishops', in addition to the handing over of the symbols of office. In the Old Testament, David had been endued with the kingship by anointing, and in such a manner that he was deemed to have ousted Saul in spite of the latter's earlier anointing. Much more surely could the new Carolingian house be deemed to acquire the royal character by anointing, in preference to the (now effete) Merovingians who had *not* been anointed. Anointing was thought to confer a mysterious, almost priestly quality. In David's case it had been not only his personal guarantee of God's intention for him, but (in spite of Saul's history) a factor in the expectation that his descendants would be likewise blessed. So it could be a fitting beginning for an enduring dynasty. Before long the Carolingians would describe themselves as reigning 'by the grace of God'. (That phrase, like the ceremonial act which inspired it, passed into English tradition and has remained there ever since.) Less certain is the dependence of this Frankish development upon earlier Christian examples. It is at least interesting to note that Boniface may have been aware of the place of anointing in Celtic traditions of kingship, particularly the Cornish; while Pirmin who originated in the area of the Pyrenees may have known of a similar tradition among the Visigoths (viz. Spain, *c.* 500–700 A.D.). Pippin overcame personal difficulties among doubting bishops and nobles with consummate tact. We are not told which or how many bishops took part in his anointing. He could defend Boniface's taking the chief part, both from the significance of Rome and from the fact that the latter was the only bishop as yet whose status as *arch*bishop could be regarded as settled. Probably by agreement between Pippin and the doubters, the contemporary chronicles did not mention Boniface by name or title. (In fact he had not once been mentioned in the palace annals!) Only a generation later was it recorded in writing that Boniface had anointed Pippin king.

The autumn of 751 thus saw what in effect was the 'swan-song' of the elderly Anglo-Saxon, now over seventy years old; or rather, the opening bars of that song. The sacring of King Pippin was, in public terms, the climax of his work in the Frankish kingdom as such. All that had happened in the ten years since 741 leading to that event could not have taken place as it did without Boniface and his commission from the Apostolic See. There is no reason to suppose that he had any regrets or reservations about this achievement. It may, on the other hand, have made him acutely aware that his contribution to the national life was completed in spheres in which the political and 'secular' impinge upon the spiritual. From now on so long as he might be spared to this earthly life, it was to the spiritual side that he was increasingly to turn.

Chapter 23

THE LIGHT SHINES AGAIN

Already, while publicly quiescent at Pippin's request, Boniface had taken his precious Fulda project one stage further, and in a manner which on the face of it seems strange. This stalwart upholder of church order in diocesan terms made a blatant exception of his model monastery. He had it put outside the jurisdiction of any diocesan bishop, or metropolitan archbishop as such, and set it in direct relation to the see of Rome. Pippin had presumably agreed to this before Boniface sent Lull to Rome in spring or summer 751. Perhaps he too could see it as the 'exception which proved the rule' so far as Boniface was concerned. Possibly the long delays over the definition of the province over which Boniface was supposed to be the metropolitan, and continuing uncertainties about the future, had engendered the conviction that without such an arrangement for Fulda the best of Boniface's work might have no certainty of enduring. Such an explanation enables *us* to retain the thought that Fulda was a 'monument' to all that Boniface had stood for, without supposing that *he* consciously envisaged this particular move in those personal terms.

His application in writing to Pope Zacharias for the 'privilege' or 'exemption' which he desired for Fulda includes words of introduction that are well worth quoting. They afford an intimate view of the old man himself at this stage, throwing light on his priorities and inclinations.

'There is a wooded place in the midst of a vast wilderness, situated among the peoples to whom I am preaching. There I have placed a group of monks living under the Rule of St. Benedict who are building a monastery. They are men of ascetic habits, who abstain from meats and wines and spirits, keeping no servants but . . . content with the labour of their own hands. This place I have acquired by humble effort through the help of pious and god-fearing men, especially of Carloman, formerly king (*sic*) of the Franks, and have dedicated it in honour of the

Holy Saviour. Here I propose with your kind permission to rest my aged body a little time, and after my death to be buried here.'

But he is thinking not only of rest nor immediately of death: 'The four peoples to whom we have preached the Word of God dwell . . . round about this place; and as long as I live and retain my faculties, I can with your support be useful to them. It is my desire, sustained by your prayers and led by God's grace, to continue my close relations and to remain in your service among the German people to whom I was sent.'

By Christmas, 751, Boniface was in possession of the 'privilege'. But also, now, with Pippin as anointed king, there was to be no question, from Zacharias' point of view, of his abandoning his duty to the established church in Frank-land. It had been necessary however to delimit rather carefully the province of Mainz. Zacharias sent back with Lull another document establishing Mainz as a metropolitan see in perpetuity, and including within its jurisdiction the four dioceses which Boniface had founded and the following besides: Tongres, Cologne, Worms, Speyer and Utrecht. It was a large enough province; but it did not contain Metz or Trier, and (also within Austrasia) Toul and Verdun were likewise excluded. On the other hand Worms and Speyer, along with Mainz itself, ensured that Boniface was not concerned merely with the Saxon-Frisian borderlands but had a considerable influence in Frank-land proper, quite apart from any duties he might have as legate of Rome in relation to the whole kingdom.

A long letter from the Pope, which Lull brought back along with the documents for Fulda and Mainz, was designed to put Boniface's mind at rest on the series of matters which the latter had referred to him in writing and by word of mouth. Some of these involve details of ritual and ceremonial, concerning which he might have had no need to refer to Rome had he not been often bewildered by the extraordinary activities in parts of the Frankish church, and were he not suffering sometimes from the extreme pressure of opinions diverse from his own. Zacharias by now has understood his situation more completely, and nowhere hints (as in 748 he had done) that he ought to have known the answer already. Points of interest in the letter, applying to the areas of Boniface's most cherished endeavours, include a reference to persecution from the heathen, over which Zacharias quotes the Gospels, saying that Christians should if possible hold on and convert the heathen, but if not should 'go to other towns'. Had the Saxons by now, while Pippin was busy securing his kingship, begun causing trouble of an acute kind along the frontier? Very likely so: they were shortly to burst their bounds (752). Another item involves the Slavs, who have begun settling in groups in Frankish territory (presumably Thuringia, and not far from Fulda in the forests, where Sturm had encountered a few): there seems no question, in 751 as in 719, of the Anglo-Saxon missionaries evangelizing them; the question concerns the dues which the Slavs ought to pay, especially church dues. The Pope suggests that groups which have not formally acknowledged Frankish overlordship should not be pestered for payment, but that those who have should pay.

No reference was made, in this correspondence of 751, to the change of dynasty. Nor was the question of Lull's consecration to the episcopate raised afresh, at least in writing. Pippin, having achieved the kingship and placed the Merovings in monasteries, still found it necessary to be exceedingly prudent in promoting the cause of Boniface and his followers. He did not, in fact, allow the Pope's establishment of a metropolitan province of Mainz beyond Boniface's lifetime. Perhaps as a partial compensation for the disappointment thus caused, he allowed Boniface to elevate Lull to the rank of bishop, strictly as assistant to himself (*chor-episcopus*) at Mainz and without any guarantee (as yet) that he would follow him in the see. Boniface had to exercise great patience still. He remained loyal to Pippin in spite of much perplexity. The year 752 brought further shocks of one sort or another; but on the whole it was for Boniface a time of gradual restoration within the Frankish scene.

The death of Pope Zacharias in March, 752, was an unwelcome and unsettling event for Boniface. His immediate successor, Stephen, lived only a few days, to be followed by another of the same name, a Roman by birth. This latter has been known by some as 'Stephen III' and by others as 'Stephen II', in consequence of this very rapid succession. Boniface had had reason to bless the name 'Stephen' almost thirty-four years earlier, when Bishop Daniel had appointed one of that name to be abbot of Nursling. The advent of this other Stephen, late in Boniface's life, was to bring him little but doubts and questionings in a situation already holding potential enough for embarrassment. It was now fourteen years since Boniface had visited

Rome. We cannot tell whether he was acquainted with Stephen. For every reason, and above all because of Fulda, he would wish to establish cordial relations. This aim, so it appears, was not achieved.

His intention to write immediately to the new Pope as he had to Gregory III and Zacharias was thwarted by another grievous blow. The Saxons on the borders of Hesse and Thuringia, taking advantage of Frankish pre-occupation with the crisis which was arising in Italy, made raids of unprecedented proportions, and burned down about thirty churches in the dioceses of Büraburg and Erfurt. His energies were wholly taken up with the problems thus caused; and when, some few months later, he found time to write to Rome, he apologized for the delay, describing what had happened and giving it as his excuse. In his letter he recalled the relationship in which he had stood to three preceding Popes over "thirty-six years", and pledged his loyalty to Stephen, without making any explicit assumptions or requests about his position under the latter. If he did not receive a reply, it was either because Stephen was preoccupied with the Italian scene, or because by now the interplay of forces in Frank-land was well understood at Rome, making the new Pope reluctant to identify himself with one party in case the Papacy needed to rely heavily on the Franks in the near future.

Stephen had certainly inherited trouble. Nothing less than a suzerainty over the whole of Italy would satisfy King Aistulf of Lombardy. In 751 he had completed the occupation of the former Byzantine Exarchate by finally taking Ravenna itself. He had by now the overlordship of the southern duchies of Spoleto and Benevento. In 752 he was making clear threats against Rome, which still nominally stood in relation to Constantinople. Less than ever was it of any avail for the Pope to seek help from the Emperor. Constantine V was reasserting 'iconoclasm' more narrowly and severely than ever. (A synod that very year at Hieria, near his capital, failed to draw representatives from Antioch, Alexandria, Jerusalem and Rome.) Objections made in writing by Constantine to the Lombard king were not matched by any attempt at a show of force. Rome was isolated, and appeared to be in even greater danger than at the end of Charles Martel's reign when for the first time help had been sought from the Franks. Yet the new Pope did not at once request their aid against Aistulf; and this was an advantage to Pippin. He had the opportunity to prove himself in his new role of king, and to quieten the doubters. Pro-Merovingian factions had time to dissolve. Respect for the royal will and judgement could meanwhile grow to the point where further dealings with the Papacy would not divide the kingdom, should Stephen decide to call for assistance across the Alps.

Boniface, unsure of his standing with Stephen, and willing to work inconspicuously for many reasons (including Pippin's welfare), refrained from court appearances and went about his business in an uncontroversial way. The wearisome job of clearing up after the Saxon inroads led him to consider further the conditions under which his presbyters were working, especially in the northern borderlands. In winter great hardships could be suffered, with or without invasion or persecution. His own absence from Mainz at this period caused him to feel more strongly than ever the need to ensure that his successor in that see (and if possible, in the archbishopric) should be a man possessing the necessary sympathy and experience: he must have an intimate understanding of those whom he, Boniface, had nurtured for so long. He determined somehow to draw Pippin's attention to his own old age, of which he was increasingly aware as he travelled among his stricken congregations. Having now, through Burghard, made friends with the royal chaplain, Fulrad, he decided to write to the latter rather than direct to the king. He framed a letter to Fulrad in the most friendly terms, at a time when his argument could be more forceful because of the extreme physical weakness which he felt just at this time. Through the chaplain he begged His Majesty the King 'to indicate, while I am still alive, what future provision he is willing to make for my disciples.' He drew attention to the fact that nearly all were foreigners, and that most had other needs irrespective of the distance from their homes: '. . . presbyters . . . in lonely places, . . . monks in cloisters, or children learning to read . . . men of mature age who have been my helpers and companions for many years.' He expressed anxiety that this noble band might have to disperse after his death, unless King Pippin ensured their support. Particularly, 'people near the border of the heathen may lose their faith', since 'presbyters . . . near the border . . . lead (even now) a bare existence.' These clergy 'can get enough to eat, but cannot procure clothing without help and support from elsewhere, such as until now they have had from me. For this reason I earnestly beg your gracious Highness to have my son, assistant-bishop Lull, appointed in my place as preacher and teacher to the presbyters and people.' The words 'in my place' cannot be taken to show that Boniface was asking to be released from office, but must be seen in relation to his request for 'future provision'. He would not be inclined even at this stage to go against the declared wish of Pope Zacharias that he should persevere in office unto death.

Fulrad did his best in pleading with Pippin, so that Boniface received partial satisfaction by the end of the year. Lull was named as his successor in the see and diocese of Mainz. But no assurance was given that he would rank higher than diocesan bishop. At this level there would be little chance indeed of his becoming 'legate of the Apostolic see' whereby alone he could have some oversight of Fulda; and without the rank of arch-bishop (or metropolitan) he could not supervise the border dioceses of Büraburg and Erfurt in the same way as Boniface. Once again the old man had to be thankful for small mercies, and to leave many open questions to be solved in God's good time.

About the turn of the year, 752–3, something happened which brought about a restoration of confidence on Boniface's part in relation to his standing in the realm. Pippin may have given some indication that Boniface could now fulfil his duties more openly. Pope Stephen may have sent a message, which has not been preserved, encouraging him to return to court, while suggesting that conciliatory gestures should be made and provocative moves avoided. Boniface himself may have felt stronger in health. However it came about, he wrote to the king in person, in a tone of thanksgiving that Lull had been appointed as his successor at Mainz, stating that 'by the grace of God I can enter once more into your service' and asking him therefore 'to let me know whether I may attend the assembly to carry out your wishes.' If these slightly sycophantic words were inspired by Pope Stephen, one may wonder whether in some corner of Boniface's mind a doubt may have begun to lurk about the exercise of papacy by the new occupant of the Roman see. But his confidence vis-à-vis Pippin was now firm enough: with the same letter he could send back peremptorily to the king a man, Ansfrid, belonging to the church of Mainz who had told lies about him (Boniface) to the king and had come to Mainz again with a royal letter requiring the archbishop to 'do him justice'; 'I am sending him back to you with my letter and my messenger: you will then see how much he has lied to you. I beg you in your own interest to defend me against such liars and to give no ear to their falsehoods.' Ansfrid (the name is Frankish) was presumably one of those who still preferred bishops like Gewilib!

In view of the above, it is possible that Boniface attended the March-assembly, 753, although again no formal 'synod' is recorded as having been held. On that occasion the Frankish leadership decided on yet another punitive expedition against the Saxons. Once again the aged archbishop would have heard this decision with mixed feelings. Whatever the military necessities might be, he no longer believed that the true conversion of the tribes of the 'Old Saxons' could be promoted by military conquest. It took only a timely reminder to bring into his mind once again a familiar train of thought: the door to the Saxons lies in Frisia. Indeed, his thoughts were turned to Frisia at this very moment by an unforeseen and painful development. Not without cause had 'Milo and his sort' continued to figure in Boniface's correspondence with Rome up to 751. They could still cause a riot here and there if they did not get their way. Cologne, one of the cities in Boniface's ecclesiastical province as defined by Pope Zacharias, contained a strong group of their supporters. Quiescent for a while, this faction was stirred into life after the death of Bishop Agilolf. Perhaps it was in view of such a possibility that Pippin earlier had not endorsed the arrangements approved by Zacharias. He bowed to local feeling, inflamed as it was, and allowed a certain Hildegar to enter the episcopal see. Assuming that he was already in bishop's orders, we may be permitted to wonder whether he was that war-like and notorious bishop who had been deprived after fighting the Saxons in Thuringia in 748. Hildegar was ready enough to take up arms, and did so in the summer of 753, losing his life as a consequence; but not before he had done other things which forced Boniface into action.

The church of Cologne, which had declined metropolitan status when it was a question of Boniface taking the see as archbishop, began during Hildegar's brief period of office a power game whereby the see of Utrecht would be subordinated to it. The two sees would, by implication, become one unit, independent of Mainz. The claim was made on supposedly historical grounds. There had been a church at Utrecht long before Willibrord the Northumbrian had come to Frisia, and that church had been founded by missionaries from Cologne. Boniface wrote promptly to Pope Stephen, giving the whole history, and pointing out that Willibrord had found the earlier church in ruins at Utrecht, and that the diocese of Cologne had never taken any further initiative in that direction even when the possibility had existed. Pope Sergius had established Willibrord's Frisian mission, which had lasted over fifty years (689–739) and had been fruitful in conversions and church-building. Boniface had had an interest in Frisia since 716, and had worked with Willibrord for a time. It was fitting that the area, having lost the status of a separate 'province', should be one with the Anglo-Saxon mission area founded by Boniface east of the Rhine. Pope Stephen accepted Boniface's argument. Pippin, to whom Boniface may have applied in person (hiding his indignation at the appointment of Hildegar), also took the point, and pressed the matter home. Utrecht, in fact, was placed in a rather special relationship to Boniface himself. If Wera had been thought of as diocesan bishop, his successor, Eoba (another Anglo-Saxon) as regarded as '*chor-episcopus*' only; presumably it was at this same time that the succession took place. If anyone could now be called 'diocesan bishop' of Utrecht, it was Boniface himself. As with Fulda, the old man's sentiments here seem to have outweighed his loyalty to strict canonical traditions, and to have been respected by those in authority (Pippin and Stephen).

It was not inappropriate that Boniface should spend time in 'his' new diocese. In the event of his death, and in view of the recent challenge from Cologne, he needed to have made firm arrangements which would last. Having Abbot Gregory of St Martin's as well as Eoba, one Frank and one Anglo-Saxon, between whom the administrative duties might be shared, he organized Utrecht in such a way as to make full use of both. The local count was also an admirer of Boniface, whom he must have seen as the spiritual successor of Willibrord: he may have had boyhood memories of him from the period 719–721. He would have been dismayed if Cologne had prevailed, and would do his utmost to repel any danger from that quarter in the future.

It is tempting to think that Pippin's punitive expedition took place while Boniface was attending to matters at Utrecht, and that Pippin chose to enter Saxon territory this time at the western end, crossing the Rhine around Cologne where the border was not far distant. So Bishop Hildegar would most easily take up arms and follow to the fight. The thought of this military enterprise, and of its uselessness as a prelude to evangelism, brought with it a more firm conviction than ever before that Christianity would best enter the Saxon region by peaceful penetration of the East Frisian area. Boniface resolved to try out a preaching expedition immediately. He mustered a party of presbyters, monks and lay servants, and selected books for use and relics of the saints for spiritual protection. The journey is represented in most of our sources as via the Zuyder Zee, though there is a suggestion that the party went round by the open sea.* Arriving in a landscape then as now intersected by waterways, they had a varied reception from local groups of inhabitants. Bearing in mind, perhaps, Pope Zacharias' reply to his question about persecution, Boniface approached local leaders tactfully, and proclaimed the Gospel only in those parts where a welcome was offered.

It is hard to guess what length of time was spent in Frisia. The party were reasonably encouraged by successes achieved. No violent opposition was aroused. When the first autumn rains brought the expedition to an end, much more than a reconnaissance had been achieved. A larger expedition would be worth trying after the winter. Those natives who had been baptized but not yet confirmed when the party left, were told that Boniface intended to return after Easter next year, and would confirm them then, along with such others as might be ready for baptism by the week of Pentecost.

The expedition of 753 was an example of a normal type of activity on the part of a Christian diocese with a heathen border. It involved little more danger than some enterprises from Büraburg and Erfurt during the preceding years. During the winter which followed, the project altered its aspect and proportion, and took on a momentum and excitement which gave it a deeper significance, not least for Boniface, who saw in evangelism the end as well as the beginning of his mission.

Though some historians dispute this, it makes sense to suppose that he returned to Frank-land from September 753 to May 754, and attempted as many of his usual and proper duties

* Perhaps different routes applied to the two different years, 753 and 754: the fact that there were two distinct visits was almost lost to sight in the tradition.

as his health in winter allowed. The revival of his physical strength since 751 enabled him to return not only to Utrecht (as scholars suggest) but to Mainz, Fulda and the Würzburg area, and conceivably to the southern part of his province and beyond. For it was now, if not before, that he visited his celebrated contemporary Pirmin at Hornbach, half way between Speyer and Metz, shortly before the latter's death on 3rd November, 753. The mellowing of Boniface's movement and its partial merging with less rigidly canonical ways of thought had been illustrated in another way not long before, when Burghard, in response to popular feeling, had the bones of St. Kilian enshrined in the cathedral at Würzburg, and allowed him to be thought of as the founder of the church there. Now, in 753, the worthy Burghard had died and Boniface, in considerable sorrow at the loss, may have officiated with fellow bishops at the consecration of Megingaud to the see. At Fulda he found Sturm, two years after his return, fully capable as abbot, and rejoicing that he was no longer at Cassino now that the Lombards had sway in southern Italy. The same was true of his cousin Leoba at Tauberbischofsheim. Lull, of course, was well in charge at Mainz. Boniface had accepted the situation in Bavaria before this, since the Frankish victory of 749 had done no more than restore Eichstätt, with its bishop Willibald, to Boniface's province. Perhaps, now that he understood Pirmin's attitude better, he could with less concern let Bavaria go its own way. If a Pope had not been able (or willing?) to set things right at Salzburg, what business had *he* to try any more to intervene or even to object?

But what of Pope Stephen? Christmas was overshadowed by reports that he was coming to Frank-land through Burgundy, in the company of Bishop Chrodegang and Duke Autchar, after failing, with their help, to make any impression on Aistulf at Pavia. Boniface was troubled. His view of the authority of the Bishop of Rome over the Church of Christ rested, perhaps more than he had hitherto realized, on the location of the papal see 'alongside the tombs of the apostles', particularly Peter's. It rested, too, on the fact tht Rome was the centre to which issues had been referred from far and wide, where there was a repository of conciliar and canonical decisions upon which the Pope could draw. Away from the city of Rome, could the 'Vicar of St. Peter' speak properly on behalf of St. Peter? He could, perhaps, if one imagined a Pope attending a General Council away from Rome: but in fact, Popes had sent legates to such meetings, from Nicaea (325 AD) onwards. But for a Pope to leave his see in order to secure its physical and political safety was something which disturbed Boniface deeply. Illogical though it might appear, it almost seemed to him as though Pope Stephen was 'trespassing'. So far from his arrival being a triumphant vindication of everything for which Boniface had stood in the Frankish realm, it simply appeared as an irresponsible action. In truth, Boniface did not know what to think. All previous problems were dwarfed by this. He distanced himself from the court as the course of events unfolded. He began seriously to wonder whether there was anything further which he could contribute to the progress and organizing of the Frankish church and kingdom.

Chapter 24

THE TRUE GLORY

Pope Stephen had endured the threats of King Aistulf for nearly a year before sending a message of extreme urgency to Pippin. A preliminary reply had been taken to him by a Frankish cleric, Abbot Droctegang of Jumièges, who had brought back letters to Pippin and to the Frankish nobles, at the end of the summer of 753. These negotiations had taken place, in fact, during Boniface's period at Utrecht and in East Frisia. In the early autumn Pippin despatched two Frankish representatives to Rome. From what followed, it seems that he did not expect King Aistulf to be appeased (though an attempt might be made), but took it for granted that the Pope would soon need to be rescued. That would mean having him at the Frankish court for the winter of 753–4. Pippin made out a timetable of arrangements for welcoming Stephen into his dominions. He could hope, through such a visit, to impress his people, cement the unity of his realm, and make the future of his dynasty yet more secure. The Pope was almost bound to be a willing agent in all this, while the way was prepared for the Lombard enemy to be overcome.

As already mentioned, the two who went to Rome were Bishop Chrodegang of Metz and a certain Duke Autchar. A representative of the Byzantine empire, despite all quarrels, arrived about the same time. On 14th October, the eastern and western envoys set out for Pavia with the Pope. The latter was accompanied by two bishops, four presbyters, and two who had corresponded with Boniface as friends, namely Arch-deacon Theophylact and Cardinal-deacon Gemmulus. This weighty company, duly arriving at the Lombard capital, spent a week or two vainly endeavouring to gain concessions from Aistulf. For his part Aistulf, while totally unyielding, did not wish to appear provocative. He had his own secret plans for reducing the Frankish power, and he did not want an open rift with the Apostolic See. He allowed the Frankish representatives to conduct the papal party through his territory into Burgundy unmolested. The imperial legate returned to Constantinople having gained nothing: rather, the parting of the ways at Pavia was virtually the end of all connection between the old Rome and the new, *viz.* Roman.

Despite the onset of winter, the group started out from Pavia on 15th November and travelled by easy stages westward and northward over what became known later as the Great St. Bernard Pass, and so into Burgundy. (It was a journey which Boniface had made in the opposite direction). They certainly stopped at the Alpine monastery of St. Maurice, where they may have rested a day or two, perhaps over Sunday, December 9th. Waiting there to welcome them were Fulrad, now abbot of St. Denis, and Duke Rothard. The enlarged company continued its deliberate progress, over the Jura mountains and down into the Saône valley, to reach the Burgundian castle at Gray about Christmas. There, as a further stage in the Pope's welcome, Pippin's elder son Charles, a lad of twelve years, joined up with him. (At Christmas forty-seven years later (800 A.D.) he would be crowned as 'Emperor' by Pope Leo III in Rome: Charlemagne, 'Charles the Great'.) There was comfortable time for them to reach the palace of Ponthion in the Champagne by Epiphany. The events of 6th and 7th January, 754, must surely have been envisaged and agreed in advance. On the Feast of the Epiphany itself, as the Pope was arriving, King Pippin led his horse a certain distance, holding the reins himself. On the following day Stephen, dressed in a hair-shirt and with ashes on his head, appeared before the king as suppliant, begging protection. Pippin thereupon swore an oath of friendship and guaranteed aid and defence to the papacy. A formal treaty was signed. Already Pippin was 'restoring' to the Pope the Exarchate of Ravenna. To fulfil this he would have to deal with Lombardy himself. The ceremonial adopted on those two successive days, and the assumption that at least part of Italy belonged by right to the Apostolic See and could therefore be 'restored', must be associated with traditions (resting on no firm foundation) concerning the Emperor Constantine the Great and Pope Sylvester I, which later crystallised into a wholly spurious document entitled 'The Donation of Constantine'. For centuries this fictitious deed was used as a basis of support for the temporal power of the popes. The story concerning Constantine and Sylvester may have been familiar to

Boniface, as it was to Aldhelm and Bede. It may have formed part of the literary background of his strong adherence to the Papacy. That still need not mean that he approved of a Pope consenting, gladly as it seemed, to abandon his see and the tombs of the Apostles in order to win the earthly security which (as it was thought) Constantine had sought to provide for the Bishops of Rome.

During January and February of 754, while we envisage Boniface attending to the wants of his most necessitous clergy, ordaining and consecrating to vacant posts, and generally going about the business of his province, travelling between Mainz and Fulda, we find Pippin trying strenously to fulfil his promise to the Pope while avoiding, if it were possible, the necessity of a military expedition over the Alps. He sent swift messengers with letters couched in the strongest language, but all to no avail. Aistulf replied with actions already planned, playing his trump card. He had for months been fomenting feelings against Pippin's regime amongst the former supporters of Grifo, who had tried to go over to the Lombard cause but lost his life in the attempt. Now he tried to rouse another sizeable section of the Frankish populace in Austrasia. He had secured the overlordship of the land south of Rome; so he put pressure upon the Abbot of Monte Cassino, removed Carloman from the number of his monks, and had him returned to Frank-land where he might most quickly gain support. He had not counted, however, upon the effect which Boniface had had in rallying respect for the Roman See. Pippin and Stephen, with the combination of civil and spiritual authority which they together could exercise, quickly and successfully declared Carloman to be a monk and a monk only. Pippin, at his March-assembly held near Soissons, gained overall support and approval: Carloman was apprehended and taken to a monastery at Vienne, on the Rhone, where in fact he died six months later.

Boniface, finding his old friend being treated as a pawn in a political game, and partly against the very cause (the Frankish-Roman connection) which that same friend had so energetically and originally espoused, can only have been further dismayed at the whole trend of events.

By Easter (April 14th) Pippin had further quelled the doubts of any of his nobles who in March had expressed opposition to a major military offensive against Lombardy. He held another general assembly, at Pfalz-Quierzy near Laon, and gained acceptance for a plan to enter Lombardy when there was least snow on the Alps, using a route which would further minimise the effect of the journey.

While Boniface never allowed his disillusionments to break his faith, Easter 754 saw him convinced that the only aspect of his vocation which he could pursue with any hope of positive fulfilment was the strictly evangelistic one which had first taken him to Europe, and which he had followed for a while during the previous year. Such enterprise in heathen lands had always involved danger. Now, after Easter, he had an inner awareness that he would very shortly meet his destiny, be it at the hands of pagans or from old age. Going a final round of his province, he spoke to the two who were closest to him amongst his compatriots, Lull and Leoba. Leoba's biographer gives the impression that these two attended him at Fulda at his request. Privately he spoke first to Lull 'and entrusted everything to his care, impressing upon him a solicitude for the faithful, and zeal for preaching the Gospel and for the preservation of the churches which he himself had built in divers places. Above all, he ordered him to complete the building of the monastery of Fulda. . . . He commanded him also to remove his body there after his death.' Then he spoke to Leoba alone, and begged her to follow his example by remaining at her post at all costs and avoiding the temptation to return to England. (Had he also had such temptations of which we know nothing?) Then he spoke jointly to Lull and the seniors of the monastery together, asking them to 'care for her with reverence and respect' and stating once again his declared wish 'that after her death her bones should be placed next to his in his tomb.' Boniface's own biographers speak of him literally prophesying to Lull the manner in which he would shortly die. We may perhaps imagine this, or whatever lies behind the account, taking place during a final interview with Lull at Mainz, rather than at Fulda. On that solemn occasion the old archbishop's final words are given as follows: 'Carefully provide everything we shall need on our journey, not forgetting to place in the chest in which my books are kept a linen sheet in which my aged body may be wrapped.' His earliest biographer, who frequently drew comparisons with St. Paul, here recalls (implicitly) the scene at Miletus in Acts 20.37f.: 'At these words Bishop Lull could not restrain his tears.'

Lull might indeed be sorrowful, principally at the thought of losing his dear master, but also because, above and beyond his own feelings, the latter's desire that he (Lull) might be able to carry on his work was by no means certain of fulfilment.

Boniface quite deliberately gathered around him, or allowed to join in his enterprise, as many as cared to come and could reasonably be spared. Even this latter limit may have been overstepped. His magnetic personality, as well as his mission, drew men after him. Fulda ... Mainz ... Utrecht ... other places, too, contributed missionaries and lay followers. At the last stage, even Bishop Eoba could not be withheld from going along with him. The party eventually numbered fifty or more. Inspired by all that Boniface had reported of his success the previous year, they joyfully followed him into those regions where the converts were expecting him at Pentecost. The two bishops were accompanied by three presbyters whose names we know: Ethelhere, Walthere, Wintrung. There were three deacons: Botha, Hahmund, Scirbald. Four monks of no stated clerical degree are named: Gundaecer, Hathowulf, Illehere and Wachar. So twelve of the total number are accounted for. Of others, including servants, we know only the name of the archbishop's personal attendant, Hildebrand, who was brother to the deacon Hahmund. (These names in general sound Anglo-Saxon.) Whatever route they took, and whatever preaching and baptism they managed on their way, by Whitsuntide they had reached the district for which Boniface was aiming. There he arranged with those waiting to be confirmed, whether baptized the previous year or more recently, that on the Wednesday after Pentecost, the 'Nones' (5th) of June, there would be a muster for the rite of confirmation. The appointed place was near the river Boorn, which divided two areas known as 'Westerach' and 'Osterach', and close to an inhabited place called Docking (in modern times, Dokkum).

Encamped by the river, the missionary band were awakened at first daylight on June 5th by harsh and violent sounds. The unconverted of the region, and renegades among the baptized, conceivably instigated by those hostile to Boniface in Cologne or further afield, were physically attacking this exposed contingent of the spiritual army of Christ. Hildebrand leapt out of Boniface's tent on hearing the noise, ran to see what was wrong, and was hacked to death. His brother Hahmund followed and met the same fate. Others jumped out after them, taking up weapons to resist. The old archbishop, breaking off his prayers, ran out and shouted to them not to render evil for evil. They put their weapons down. Boniface held up a large book, which he had seized in his hands as representing the armour of the Spirit; somewhat as Moses had held up his arms that Israel might prevail, but to signify, in this instance, a heavenly victory through an earthly defeat. In a matter of minutes the whole band had suffered martyrdom. Boniface, protected till the last by others, finally fell, his skull shattered by a Frisian sword. The book, held high above his head as witness to his foes and encouragement to his friends, was torn by the weapon which slew him.*

* His biographers call it a Gospel-book: it was in all probability a volume of theological tracts, surviving even today under the title of the 'Ragyntrudis Codex', and showing the effects of a blow from a weapon. The tribes and clans of eastern Frisia did not all yield to the Christian Gospel until the Saxons had undergone military conquest at the hands of Charlemagne, a conquest not completed until fifty years later (804). Some of those who preached to them in the meanwhile were apt to threaten them with the sword of that mightiest of Franks. When they accepted the Gospel, willingly or unwillingly, their Christian adherence was subjected to vigorous laws of conformity, as happened to the Saxons also. It was as well that both Saxons and Frisians knew of one great evangelist who had lived and died close the pattern of the Christ, a genuine Christian who refused to associate the Gospel with the sword, one whom they, akin to him in blood, could honour and imitate. (See ch. 25)

Chapter 25

SEQUEL TO MARTYRDOM

The attackers, goaded on by their own stupidity or the encouragement of others, were expecting a reward for their brutal and cold-blooded butchery. They imagined that the party's boats, moored on the river, held much treasure, and that further valuable booty might be found in the camp. Looting the tents, they soon found wine. Drunkenness began to aggravate the confusion and violence. Opening the boxes which they discovered in tents and boats, they were dismayed to find neither gold nor silver, but books, and relics of the saints, valueless to such as themselves. Their anger and frustration led to quarrelling. By evening their weapons were in use again, and at nightfall their own dead lay strewn about, not far from where the bodies of the martyrs lay.

The next day was one of awe and fear on all sides. Local people who still regarded themselves as Christians, and others too who had had respect for those distant kinsmen who had preached to them felt bitter, angry at what had happened. Not pausing to consider whether the faith of Christ was compatible with vengeance, they took action on the third day, killing or routing any of the original murderers who remained alive and within reach.

'Evil news rides post', as Milton wrote. Martyrdom may have a glorious result, but the act of murder is an evil deed. The news of the blood-bath of Dokkum travelled quickly. (This is shown by the fact that the first recorded donation in memory of Boniface was signed by a friendly Frankish noble in favour of Fulda, as soon as June 15th, 754, only ten days after his death.) Meanwhile the church of Utrecht, supported by an official Frankish force, sent men to recover the bodies, along with whatever belongings still remained. Punishments and warnings were to be handed out as might seem necessary, (The Franks appear to have regarded E. Frisia as their territory, though they were not able regularly to police it nor have formal relations with its leaders.)

Some of the local people assisted the faithful Utrechters in the work of recovery. Half of the bodies were buried there and then. Twenty-five more they conveyed in stately progress to their city: Boniface, with broken skull, Eoba, whose severed head could not be found; the three presbyters, three deacons and four monks already named, and thirteen others among whom we may be sure was Hildebrand, the archbishop's 'man'. Then and later some of the books were recovered, including, apparently, the one which Boniface had held up as he died; and perhaps also a number of holy relics and other items.

The company arriving at Utrecht was greeted with a blend of deep solemnity and mystical joy. A notable choir, which had owed its foundation to Willibrord almost sixty years before, came out to meet the incoming procession with psalms and hymns. Under the direction of Abbot Gregory, to whom Boniface and Eoba had entrusted the administration of diocesan affairs, holy burial was given to all the bodies except that of Boniface himself.

Not all at Utrecht, however, were ready to acknowledge that the body of the venerable archbishop was to be taken further. The local Count, who (as already explained) had been a great enthusiast on Boniface's behalf, may have deceived himself into thinking that Pippin's (and the Pope's) decree of 752 gave Boniface at least as sure a footing in the Utrecht see as in that of Mainz. It was announced that the king had 'ordered' that he should be buried there. It was, after all, the place with which he had had connections since his interview with Duke Radbod in 716. It had been duly constituted a metropolitan see earlier still, under Willibrord before 700, a measure agreed between the earlier Pippin (with his assembly) and the Pope of that time. At Willibrord's death its status had somehow been lost, and its province absorbed into the (somewhat ill-defined) archbishopric with which Boniface had been endued. But the latter had held synod there, in Utrecht, not long after the see of Mainz had been designated at his centre of operations. It was proper pride which led the Utrechters to covet the body of Boniface, all the more earnestly in view of the fact that the remains of Willibrord were at Echternach and not at Utrecht. When a party of men from Mainz arrived to carry the bier of Boniface away, an impasse was reached. This state of affairs lasted, so it is said, until the men of Utrecht tried to lift the bier but found they could not move it. Then astonishment turned to terror when a church bell was heard to ring insistently without human agency. After these portents the Count and his followers gave way. The men of Mainz took charge, lifted the body without difficulty, took it to the boats which they had ready at the riverside, and began their solemn journey up the Rhine.

In spite of delay at Utrecht, they were days ahead of their expected schedule. Lull had given them four weeks, starting on 15th June, for the lengthy journey, three hundred miles each way. But their enthusiasm was such that they had completed the whole distance downstream in six days. Having recovered strength while the argument proceeded at Utrecht, they tackled the upstream journey with super-human strength, inspired by the thought of the sacred cargo they were carrying. (One might reflect that it was already three weeks since Boniface's death, and that little or no embalming is likely to have taken place.) We may wonder what sort of reception they had at Cologne, amongst the various stopping places they are likely to have used. There is no rumour that they were shunned or molested anywhere. They arrived at Mainz in triumph on July 4th, and declared that the divine spirit had propelled them all the way (later legend took their words literally, and claimed that no oars had had to be used).

Rather to their surprise, Lull's return took place not long after theirs. For he too had been away, at the court of Pippin. Originally it had been suggested that Sunday, July 14th would be the day upon which the people of Mainz would have an opportunity to pay honour to the mortal remains of the old archbishop; but inevitably the arrangement had been a flexible one.

It is not clear whether Lull had been summoned to the court, or whether he simply decided to go after hearing of the martyrdom of Boniface and his companions. If the court was at St. Denis, near Paris, three hundred and fifty miles away, he too had a strenuous programme if he was to complete the whole arrangement in four weeks. He, also, however, had his reasons for speed. On the way to St. Denis, his mind was burdened not only with human sorrow at the loss of his dear master but also with deep uncertainty about the future. At St. Denis were not only King Pippin but also Pope Stephen, in safe keeping there until he might be taken back to Rome, that is, until a successful issue to the Lombardy campaign, which was due to begin almost immediately. Such was the agony of suspense that Lull rode fast, and arrived at St. Denis on June 26th; or it may be that he knew that a great event was planned for the 27th. On that day, in the presence of representative bishops and nobles, the Pope anointed Pippin afresh, and with him also his two young sons, Charles and Carloman. Thus, in exchange (as we might say) for the protection and support of the Frankish power, Stephen was giving further confirmation to that dynasty which his predecessor had set up through the hand of his legate Boniface. It was with mixed feelings, certainly, that Lull witnessed such an act. He could not but share that sense which had come over his master some months earlier, that the Pope was somehow 'trespassing'. Would not Zacharias have supposed that the one anointing had been enough, and that (as with baptism) a second was worse than meaningless? Lull might perhaps have hidden his feelings and let the matter pass. But other matters came to light which caused him to hasten back to Mainz as soon as he could with courtesy do so. Mainz was quite certainly not to be allowed that full status of 'metropolitan' see which Zacharias had desired for it. No city, in fact, was being yet allowed that privilege. But a person, a bishop, was being granted the *pallium* in place of Boniface; and that person was Chrodegang of Metz.

Leaving St. Denis on the morning of the 28th June, Lull felt it necessary to travel as quickly as possible, and arrived back at Mainz after only seven days' travelling, on the evening of 4th July. It was as well that he did so. In a matter of hours, since the boats from Utrecht had tied up at the wharf, a clamour had arisen for Boniface to be buried at Mainz. Lull, himself exhausted, had some difficulty at first. He tried to appease the people, so much so that he was accused (in retrospect) of having himself forgotten his master's express wish to be buried at Fulda. He found release from his dilemma when a certain deacon named Otbert reported that he had had a vision, in which the holy Boniface had appeared to him and made it clear that his remains were to be laid to rest at Fulda. Otbert was not believed at first; but when he persisted under an ordeal of solemn oath-taking, the people reluctantly accepted, and the river journey was resumed.

The unusual funeral procession continued on its way, turning eastwards up the river Main. The last few days' journey were accomplished on foot. People came from all directions to join the company. A large crowd eventually arrived at Fulda. There, in the monastery chapel of the Holy Saviour which Boniface had dedicated, his body was laid, in accordance with his wish. There, in the precincts of the monastery, it has remained ever since, though moved more than once to allow for developments within the site. A vast number of pilgrims have, down the generations, visited his shrine.

Before the assembly dispersed after the ceremony of entombment, a meal was provided for all. (According to later legend this was made possible by a miracle, somewhat similar to those in the Gospels, involving a huge draught of fish.) Miracles of other kinds, especially cures, were associated with Boniface's shrine through the ages which followed. This was true also of other places at which his name was invoked for heavenly intercession, notably Mainz and Utrecht.

Boniface's martyrdom was not blazoned abroad for all to hear or read. His fame depended upon those who appreciated him personally. No entry was made in the annals of the Frankish court. No contemporary reference is to be found in the proceedings of the Papacy at Rome. Only over the passage of centuries was his sainthood given universal recognition, and only more recently still has his importance in the history of the Church and of Europe been discerned and duly acknowledged.

In his own native land a genuine attempt was made to do justice to his memory. A start was made at the first opportunity after the news of his death was received. Bishop Milred of Worcester wrote immediately to Lull, as he had been on the Continent the previous year and had met Boniface and some of his colleagues. Writing with vivid recollection of that encounter, since which 'hardly a year' had passed, he described the shock of hearing of the events at Dokkum, and went on to remark: 'Though we lament with bitter tears the comfort we have lost in this life, yet he who is now consecrated a martyr to Christ by the shedding of his blood, the glory and crown of all those whom this country has sent forth, soothes and relieves our saddened hearts by his blessed life, by the fulfilment of his noble work and his glorious end.' He begged Lull to make sure that the story of Boniface's life would be committed to writing. His letter was followed by one from Archbishop Cuthbert of Canterbury. The archbishop was equally enthusiastic, while writing in his official capacity: a synod had been held, he explained, at which Boniface was given an honourable place in the English calendar of saints and martyrs, his name being linked to the date June 5th. Boniface was to be accounted, alongside Augustine and Theodore, among the 'chief patrons' of England.

These two letters afforded consolation to Lull at this time of grief, embarrassment and frustration. They doubtless inspired many others also, among those who remained of Boniface's disciples after the events at Dokkum. Lull saw to it, sooner or later, that a biography of the martyr was compiled by one of these, a presbyter of Mainz named Willibald (not to be confused with the first bishop of Eichstätt). Lull also made the first collection of his master's correspondence, to which others have since added, providing us with a source of knowledge and understanding better than any biography on its own.

The character of Lull himself is hard to judge, in view of the immense confidence which Boniface had in him, and by contrast, of the evident jealousy which dogged him as a temptation. He was in any case left in an unenviable position, between Chrodegang of Metz on the one hand, and Fulda and Sturm on the other.

Pippin commited to Chrodegang the task of continuing the reform of the Frankish church, much along the lines set out by Boniface. They conducted a series of synods, beginning already in 755, the year after Boniface's death, and after an interval of eight years. Lull had to attend these as ordinary diocesan bishop. But he was not altogether ignored as Boniface's successor in a wide sense. He was allowed general oversight of the eastern Austrasian dioceses which Boniface had founded. He was given considerable discretion. As the dioceses of Büraburg and Erfurt became vacant by death, he absorbed them into his own, and no further bishop was appointed to either. Fulda came, of course, in that same area. Lull may be excused, perhaps, for having felt that its 'exemption' in favour of Rome was a doubtful asset in view of Pope Stephen's general behaviour. Whatever Sturm may have thought about the Pope, he resisted Lull's long-drawn-out attempt to bring the monastery under Mainz. Eventually the abbot appealed to the king, and the monastery was taken into royal patronage. Rome was hardly in a position to object in view of all that it now owed to the Frankish power. Pippin, in 754 and again in 756, had defeated the Lombards. He had fulfilled his plan to make over the 'Exarchate of Ravenna' to the Bishop of Rome as a 'papal state'. (This opened, as things turned out, a new and long chapter in the history of the Papacy.)

The disappointment over Fulda caused Lull to concentrate on the monastery at Hersfeld, a place which had figured in Sturm's original journeyings in search of Fulda (see p.138). His attempt to promote Hersfeld as a great monastic foundation in the diocese of Mainz was countered, however, by Chrodegang. The latter, with large benefactions, created a rival foundation at Lorsch in the same diocese. Boniface would neither have taken nor approved such a high-handed action.

The situation appears gradually to have eased as time went on. In 762 Lull is known to have co-operated with Chrodegang and with Heddo of Strasbourg, the three of them jointly being given charge of a synod of twenty-seven bishops and seventeen abbots. The Frankish church was gaining by degrees those qualities and features of which Boniface had approved. Not until Charlemagne's reign, however, and in his thirteenth year (781) was its constitution properly worked out. The elderly Lull at length received the *pallium* in that year, and Mainz was made a metropolitan see in the permanent sense. Whereas Boniface had been 'Archbishop *at* Mainz', the elderly Lull could be styled the first 'Archbishop *of* Mainz'. (Chrodegang had died some years before.) Lull lived five years in enjoyment of his new status, and died at Hersfeld in 786, one of the last of Boniface's colleagues to survive. In the end he was appreciated sufficiently to be admitted to the company of recognized 'saints'. Before his death he may have begun to see a greater value placed on Boniface's life and work in official Frankish circles: for it was in 781 that Alcuin (Alchwine) of York became Charlemagne's adviser in religion and education. The clash of personalities of the 740's and 750's had been forgotten with the passage of time; so that, as already pointed out, Boniface could now be looked back to with respect as the archbishop who had anointed Pippin king.

It is both relevant and interesting to notice other developments in the period between Boniface's death and that of Lull, and in some cases beyond that date, before drawing conclusions as to the value and significance of all that the martyr-monk of Wessex had achieved.

The monastery of Fulda, when Sturm died in 779 and was succeeded by Eigil, his biographer, was Boniface's greatest memorial, as well as his shrine. It survived the difficult period of Charlemagne and rose to great fame and honour in the ninth century. During Charlemagne's wars of conquest this monastery, along with Hersfeld, Lorsch and Fritzlar, formed a base of operations for the evangelization of the Saxons under duress: all four were under royal patronage by that time. In happier times later on, under Rabanus Maurus who had been brought up at Fulda and then trained by Alcuin, 'the abbey rapidly developed spiritually and intellectually as well as materially'. Its material advancement inevitably altered the form of its spirituality, taking the emphasis off that asceticism for which Sturm had passionately striven. Rabanus, master of the school at Fulda from about 810 and abbot 822–842, after five year's retirement for prayer and study became Archbishop of Mainz (847 to 856). We may see in this the forging of a link between Fulda and Mainz. It is worth observing that Rabanus is said to have promoted the *evangelization* of the German people from both centres; so that clearly this process, begun several centuries earlier, took many years to complete.

The diocese of Würzburg and the much smaller one of Eichstätt had straightforward histories from the time of their foundation. The convent at Tauberbischofsheim was blessed with Leoba as abbess until her death in 780. There is no reason to doubt the excellence of character (nor the physical beauty) ascribed to her by her biographer. A truly great woman, she became friend and counsellor to Hiltigard, queen-consort of Charlemagne. She had the unique privilege of being allowed to visit Fulda annually to pray, leaving her companions outside the gates; and when she did, the monks would gather to confer with her and learn from her. She was buried at Fulda as her cousin had requested, although not precisely next to him as he would have preferred. The double monastery at Heidenheim near Eichstätt progressed under Wynnebald, who died in 761, and thereafter under his sister Waldburga until her death some eighteen years later; while their brother Willibald, who was also their diocesan bishop, outlived them both, dying in the same year as Lull (786). Our detailed knowledge of Willibald's life, including his journey to the Holy Land, is due to Hugeburga, a nun of Heidenheim, one of the later additions to the Anglo-Saxon mission in Germany.

The diocese of Utrecht continued the evangelistic work which Boniface had begun, and was successful in some degree. For the first twelve years no bishop was working regularly in the area, although presumably Lull visited for necessary occasions. Gregory the Frank, Abbot of St. Martin's, was for most purposes in sole charge. He was joined by an Englishman from Ripon, a presbyter called Liafwin ('Lebuin'), who went to preach on the banks of the river Ijssel. The church which he built at Deventer was burned down by the heathen about 773, and he died about the same time. The wrath of the local population had been aroused by his having threatened them with the sword of the Franks if they did not respond to his message.

More than one of the Englishmen working with Gregory (who still owed much to the Northumbrian, Willibrord) was sent back for training to York, where the great teacher Alcuin worked until about 780. One of them, Aluberht, was there consecrated bishop in 766, and went back to perform episcopal functions for Gregory although not appointed diocesan bishop. A Frisian, Liudger, was also sent to York. After his return, and when Charlemagne had failed to persuade the Saxons of Westphalia by coercion, Liudger became missionary to them and had great success: he finished life as duly constituted bishop of Münster. He was a man of whom Boniface would have approved and it is a pleasing thought, in relation to Boniface's ambitions, that Liudger broke through to the Saxons with spiritual weapons, from Frisia. As for Utrecht itself, the irony of history was displayed in 781: when Lull was granted the *pallium* at Mainz, Cologne was given parallel dignity, becoming the metropolitan see for north-west Austrasia and the Saxon borderlands. So Utrecht was subordinated to Cologne. By then, of course, old animosities had begun to be forgotten. Boniface, we may safely say, would have been glad to see the 'canonical' arrangements taking shape.

Chapter 26

AUTHORITY AND ALLEGIANCE

It was as an evangelist who gave his life for the Gospel of Christ, that Wynfrith-Boniface was remembered by the German peoples to whom he preached, and amongst whom he worked for the building of the church and the recalling of those who had fallen away. The three outstanding moments, dramatically conceived, were his abandonment of his native land for Christ's sake, his courageous felling of the Thunderer's Oak at Geismar, and his martyrdom in the Frisian fields. It was facts like these, along with the memory of his charm and power, which caused diocese after diocese to adopt his name into their calendars. The odd turn of events at the end of his life in relation to the Roman See resulted in his remaining a 'local' saint rather than one of universal recognition. But his 'locality' was broad indeed, extending as time went on beyond the boundaries of the German and English world. The southern or Gallo-Frankish parts of the Western Empire were reluctant to follow suit, for reasons which are plain enough. It has taken objective assessment of historical study, characteristic of the modern age, to enable the world at large to honour Boniface. In 1874 (twelve hundred years from the date of his birth as some would hold), he was at last formally 'canonized' by the Pope. The wave of romanticism which swept Europe alongside the scientific approach (but in total contrast to it) ensured that the German nation which was built up in the mid-nineteenth century took him to its heart. He became 'the Apostle of Germany'. This is a concept which would have been inconceivable in the age in which he lived: yet it is not unfair to consider him the greatest of that long line of missionaries of many nationalities, who preached Christ to heathen Germans over more than four countries.

The modern research which has retrieved his memory and broadened his appeal, has in its own strict discipline tended to minimise the evangelistic side of Boniface's achievement and to exalt instead his function in the foundation of mediaeval Europe as a whole. There is no need, however, for one aspect to detract from the other. Boniface, an evangelist at heart, also occupied a key position in the 740's in the Frankish kingdom. He became the agent of a *rapprochement* between Rome and the Frankish leadership. This in turn resulted in the 'twinning' of Pope and Emperor as powers in Europe in the centuries which followed. His significance here is undeniable. His behaviour throughout that fateful decade gives further evidence of the greatness of the man. His acceptance of the sufferings into which his endeavours for Carloman and Pippin led him testifies to the quality of his character and the depth of his devotion to God. On the other hand, in spite of his anxiety that all branches of the Church should look to Rome, it must be stressed that the eventual outcome in terms of rivalry between Pope and Emperor was not what he had hoped for, and that by the end of his career, he had reservations about the direction in which King Pippin and Pope Stephen were moving.

Two other aspects of his life have been regarded as of high importance. One is his enthusiasm for the Benedictine form of monasticism. His conviction that the moderate and humane approach of the Benedictine rule made it superior to the extremer ascetical disciplines, his practical genius and fundamental wisdom in seeing it as a 'handmaid' to church life in its outward movement and its inward order, his own embodiment of the Benedictine ideal in his personal life and in the monastic foundations which he inspired, all this has appeared to some as his great contribution to the church of the early Middle Ages. In a year (1980) in which the birth of Benedict of Nursia (480) is being celebrated alongside that of Boniface two centuries later, it is certainly right to draw attention to this notable feature of the latter's career.

The other emphasis which, according to their convictions, certain writers have wished to make, lies in the witness which the life of Boniface provides to the Roman allegiance of the Anglo-Saxon Church. This has been stressed as against the tendency since the time of the Anglican reformers, Archbishop Matthew Parker in particular, to proclaim that the Church of England before the Norman Conquest had taken little account of papal claims. As a matter of factual history, the more recent emphasis may have been necessary to redress the balance of truth. That does not prevent us from considering, finally, whether the question which Boniface asks of the church in the twentieth century may not imply a rather different estimate of his overall attitude to Roman authority.

The monk of Wessex crossed to Europe with a four-square concept of authority in church life. There was the authority of the Gospel which the church proclaimed. There was the authority of Church decisions, the sum total of 'canons' which defined the order of the Church's life in terms of doctrine, morals and ministry. There was the peculiar authority of the Bishop of Rome, holding all together. Lastly, there was the need for the Church to work in partnership with the civil or 'secular' authority, another item of God's creation and one without whose goodwill the Church could not in practice survive. He imagined these forms of authority to be fairly easily compatible. During the course of his long career, he found that in a variety of ways these different aspects could readily conflict with one another. Eventually, just when the harmonising of the Papacy with a great world-power might have seemed to herald a solution to the problems of church order and provide thereby an easier opening into the territory of unconverted peoples, he discerned a confusion creeping in at the highest level. He saw the bearer of supreme spiritual authority not merely seeking a worldly alliance with secular power, but preparing to accept that kind of power as his own. Boniface, and ourselves after him, may well ask: What does such a basic misjudgement on the part of the 'spokesman of St. Peter' imply? Can Christians rely on pronouncements from such a source without checking by other means, most of all by the content of the Gospel which the Church exists to set forth? Furthermore, do Christians not have the right and duty to use their own minds, in prayerful reasoning, as 'authorities' in weighing one against the other?

Boniface's final venture into Frisia, whether consciously or unconsciously, involved in some real sense his turning his back upon ecclesiastical and temporal authority as he had understood them. It represented an act of private judgement such as the soundest of 16th Century reformers could have approved, and an assertion of the supremacy of the Gospel.

The various movements towards unity with which Christian bodies have concerned themselves in the twentieth century, and which make only sporadic progress as the years go by, depend for their successful conclusion upon a proper resolution of the problem of authority. Boniface, so far from encouraging us simply to look to Rome for that happy consequence, illustrates just how much subtler, yet wider and more all-embracing a subject it is with which we have to deal. A devotion and a perseverance equal to that which he so nobly exhibited will be needed if our fragmented Church is to become that one true family which the Saviour himself desired it to be.

APPENDIX A

An alternative view of Pope Gregory III's plan in 738
(cf. Chapters 12–14)

On this theory, neatly expounded by Dr. Theodor Schieffer 25 years ago, the plan was much more restricted. The letter to five named bishops had to do with re-organisation in *Bavaria*, after the pattern proposed in 716 under Gregory II and Duke Theodo. The words 'region (strictly, *province*) of Bavaria and Alamannia' are taken to mean the enlarged duchy of Bavaria, *i.e.* including Augsburg and district with its populace of Alamannian stock. The name 'Wigo' is supposed to refer to Wikterp, whom most agree to have been an uncanonical (monastic) bishop in Regensburg. 'Liudo' is held to mean Luiti, similarly a not fully Catholic bishop in Salzburg. The correspondence of names in these two instances forms a considerable part of the argument on this side. 'Rudolf' is assumed, on this theory, to have been at Freising in a similar position. The name given to the form 'Adda' in the Pope's letter is not regarded as a variant of 'Heddo'; Adda is said, hypothetically, to have been bishop of Augsburg.

This way of looking at things does not regard Boniface as having had any dealings with Alamannia as a whole, and is in accord with the silence of the biographers on that subject. The journeyings envisaged in Chapter 13 of the present book around the borders of Alamannia, are on this basis out of the question.

The argument is attractive in many ways. But we must regard the correspondence as a more primary source than even the earliest biography; and the general tenor of the Pope's letters gives the plan a bigger build-up than a mere fulfilment of the Bavarian proposals *plus* an episcopal organisation of the northern territories would justify. It is hard to see why the Pope wrote, 'on the banks of the Danube or at Augsburg', when he intended (as on this theory) 'Passau, Regensburg or Augsburg'.

It is even harder to envisage the Pope having written to five bishops, three of whom were known to Boniface already as men most unlikely to obey the instructions of the Apostolic See.

In face of all the arguments which can be adduced on either side, it has to be admitted that neither view is wholly convincing. In choosing and developing the larger, which is also the traditional one, the present author may have laid himself open to the charge of tending towards sentimental 'hagiography'. He does really believe, however, that this larger view is more likely to be correct. If it displays Boniface in the most splendid proportions, that is because the man was of that size in reality.

APPENDIX B

Proceedings of the combined Synod of 745, points from Zacharias' reply

(*cf. Chapter 20*)

1 System of metropolitan bishops in Neustria

This may have been omitted from the agenda as being too sensitive a subject. (Zacharias however, while speaking of one 'province' of the Franks, does refer to 'metropolitans' with whom Boniface may come into conflict when calling a future all-Frankish synod: this is a little mysterious.)

2 Metropolitan see in Austrasia

The synod definitely put forward the proposal that the vacant see of Cologne should be recognised at Rome as of metropolitan status, in the strict sense which ensured the perpetuity of the arrangement, and that its province (in the strict ecclesiastical sense) should extend to the whole of Austrasia; Boniface to occupy the see as soon as papal approval was obtained. (To this the Pope gave positive approval, giving high regard to the wishes of the two Mayors in the matter and seeing a change of policy at Rome as fully justified by changed circumstances.)

3 Lay impropriation

The synod evidently did not find it possible to make any further alleviation of the position regarding church assets in civil use. (Zacharias suggested that the church should be thankful for small mercies, at a time when the Frankish realm still had dangers to face from at least three neighbouring peoples, all of them heathen.)

4 Erring bishops and presbyters

Albert and Clement were strongly condemned, and Rome was to be consulted further about their appropriate punishment. Gewilib's condemnation was also secured. The case of a fourth bishop, the 'completely indisciplined son of an adulterous clergyman and a murderess', who had ordained his own clergy, consecrated churches and so forth, was likewise to be referred, along with similar instances involving men of either episcopal or presbyteral rank (*Sacerdotes*). (Could the notorious one be 'Godalsacius', whom Zacharias was eventually to link with Albert and Clement as having been formally condemned at Rome?) A query was raised about former offenders who claimed to have received papal absolution on the borders of Frankland. (Zacharias dealt summarily with this sort of claim in his reply!)

5 Troublesome ex-clergy

Whether or not these were mentioned at the synod itself, Boniface reported to Rome that some former clergymen were now courtiers who were (openly or secretly?) despoiling the churches. (Zacharias made it clear to Boniface that he had brought this up with the two Mayors.)

6 Future synods

Possibly the main concern was whether the magnificent accomplishment of March 745 could or should be attempted again annually. Conceivably the necessity of annual convocations was in dispute, and the question raised whether regional or more local gatherings were not more practical and convenient. (Zacharias, doubtless bearing in mind the confusion over the Neustrian metropolitans, stressed to Boniface and to the leading Franks the canonical necessity of an annual gathering, and ordered an all-Frankish representation at such gatherings for the time being at least.)

APPENDIX C

Reconstruction of the Synod of 746

(cf. Chapter 21)

Although we are possessed of documents arising out of Boniface's Anglo-Saxon synod, including the corporate letter of admonition issued to the Mercian king under the names of eight bishops, the following (or any) reconstruction of the occasion itself necessarily rests on a number of assumptions. What is set down as fact is therefore in considerable measure speculative, but may have value.

The synod, if such it could properly be called, took place (possibly) at Utrecht. Wera was bishop of Utrecht, and unlike his successor Eoba, had full diocesan status. Boniface made him co-chairman of the gathering. Utrecht was a convenient place from which to send messages to England, using the route which Boniface himself had taken in 716, in reverse. To hold a synod there also accorded with the intuition in Boniface's mind that Frisia was the divinely chosen door into the 'Old Saxon' mission field. (The Saxon area conquered by the Franks in 744 was not held securely for more than a few years; and in the Thuringian region the Saxons were making repeated inroads.) There was a diplomatic reason, too. Before Willibrord's time there had been a church at Utrecht, in ruins when he arrived in 689 or thereabouts: that church was, while it lasted, under the care of the ancient see of Cologne. In view of the hostility shown towards Boniface by the local leaders at Cologne, it was important to try to forestall any claim which Cologne might make to have the oversight of the church in Utrecht. (Such a claim was indeed made not long after.) For all these reasons, and in spite of the long journey involved for some, this most north-westerly of all the sees under Frankish dominion was selected for the solemn conference.

All four of the sees which Boniface had set up in the eastern Austrasian region were represented at Utrecht. Of their bishops, Burghard of Würzburg was given pride of place. He and Witta of Buraburg were accompanied by Liafwine who had succeede Dada as bishop of Erfurt. Willibald of Eichstätt, with hi impressive life history, was an honoured member of the grou which assembled. From Neustria came Hartbert, Bishop (nominated as Archbishop) of Sens, and Abel, who had been dul consecrated similarly for Rheims but was still powerless t unseat Milo and was beginning to speak of resigning.

It was the sort of conference which could take place at table, being quite unlike the great gathering of the nationa 'March-assembly'. Even if the bishops brought presbyters wit them, as is highly likely, there may have been no more tha two dozen men present. The proceedings are likely to hav consisted not so much in debate about the issues involved as i working out how to compose the most effective letter to Kin Ethelbald. The letter which eventually emerged has the name of the bishops present in the following form and order: '. . . Boniface, legate in Germany of the Roman Church, with Wera Burghard, Hartbert, Abel, Willibald, Witta and Liafwine, hi fellow-bishops'. In this list (as given here) 'Hartbert' is a reconstruction from 'Werberht' on our mss., a person of whom ther is no other evidence. The name could have arisen because of scribal error after 'Wera' earlier in the sentence. The precis order of the names may be explained if during the meeting th bishops signed either an attendance register or some form o agreement to the policy on which the letter was to be based Suppose they sat as in the illustration, at a long table such a was characteristic of the Anglo-Saxon 'hall', for example, the they signed one after another as indicated by the arrows.

The arrangement shown puts Willibald, as slightly extraterritorial from the Austrasian point of view, alongside the tw bishops of Neustrian sees. On the other side of the table Liafwine the most recent is flanked by his two seniors from th eastern Austrasian area. Wera is the single representative of th western end of Austrasia, and Boniface of the central portion Their precise geographical location was not, however, of firs importance for the matter in hand.

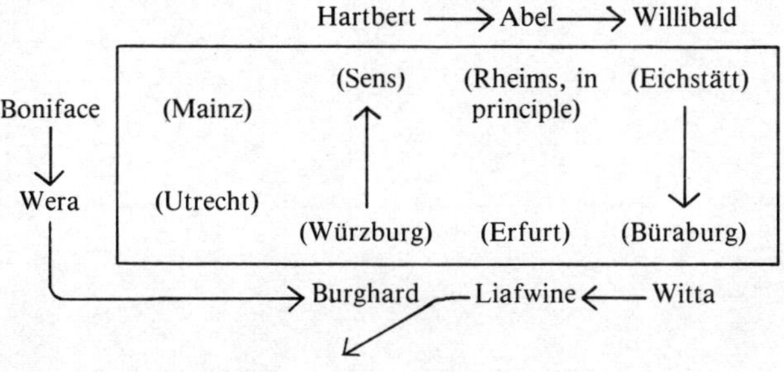
Hartbert
Abel
Willibald
(Sens)
(Rheims, in principle)
(Eichstätt)
Boniface
(Mainz)
Wera
(Utrecht)
(Würzburg)
(Erfurt)
(Büraburg)
Burghard
Liafwine
Witta
(And so back to the 'chair')

APPENDIX D

Reconstruction of the Frankish Synod of 747
(*cf. Chapter 21*)

'he names of the diocesan bishops who attended were given ·y the Pope in a letter of May 748, presumably in the order in vhich they had put their names to whatever report was sent to ıim after the meeting. (See the end of this Appendix.) As in the ۱nglo-Saxon gathering of the previous year, an attempt can be ıade to reconstruct the arrangement of seating by dioceses; ut in this case the further hypothesis is needed, that more ishops were expected than in fact came, especially from the astern and western ends of Austrasia. Indeed, the synod must .ave been a hard experience for Boniface, with so few of 'his ·wn men' present. This, and the order of the names, lead to ıe speculation that the *venue* may have been Rouen, a long ·ay to the south-west. Reasons can be suggested for such a hoice. Pippin found it hard to interest those parts of Neustria ·here ethnically the Franks were fewest and the old Romano-Gallic population had hardly been disturbed. Rouen was one f the sees which had been designated to be 'metropolitan', and ıerefore was in any case a worthy meeting place. Its new ishop, successor to Grimo who had died, was another Frank f reforming tendencies, Reginfrid*. It stood on the edge of the Gallic portions in the south and west of Neustria. If the aim ·as to interest their church leaders, it failed. On the other and, Pippin secured a more than fair attendance from the arts to the north of the Seine, though there were notable bsences.

Our possible reconstruction is as follows. Apart from any ·duction in numbers caused by unexpected 'apologies', Boni-ıce was to expect eighteen diocesan delegations besides his ·wn from Mainz. Nine were to be from Neustria, nine from ·ustrasia. Pippin, or his agents in church and state, had at least

* Not to be confused with the (earlier) bishop of Cologne.

ensured that the Neustrians would not be seriously outnum bered. In the event it was the Austrasians who were the fewe in number. Of the four dioceses founded by Boniface, onl Würzburg was represented directly, though Burghard was redoubtable enough bishop to speak for the other three as wel Utrecht was also unrepresented: conceivably Wera was ill o had died. Of those expected from Neustria, Hartbert of Sen was not present. (Abel, it may well be supposed, had by no decided that he could not go on pretending to be in charge o Rheims.) The accompanying diagram shows the relative pos itions at table of the bishops (and their delegations?); and, onc again, the arrows indicate the order in which the bishop signed, or recorded their names, as reflected in the Pope's lette of the following year.

This guesswork (for such it surely is) does at least enable u to fit together the likely arrangement of the delegates in geo graphical groups, and the very 'ungeographical' order in whic the bishops' names appear in the correspondence. In Austrasia Mainz and Speyer represent the 'Middle Rhine': Bürabur (*absent*), Erfurt (*absent*) and Würzburg represent 'Hesse-Thu ringia region': Tongres, Cologne and Utrecht (*absent*) represen the 'Lower Rhine'. Eichstätt and Strasbourg were on the bor ders of Bavaria and Alamannia (Alsace) respectively, but coul be counted as belonging to Austrasia. In Neustria, Rouen alon had to stand for the Seine valley and all to the south of i 'Western Picardy' could be the title of the group comprisin Beauvais, Amiens and Thérouanne: 'Eastern Picardy' that o Noyon, Cambrai and Laon. Sens (*absent*) and Meaux belonge to the 'Champagne'. An association across provincial bounda ries is also worth noting, namely between two disciples o Pirmin, Romanus and Heddo.

This account makes sense of the opening address in th Pope's reply: 'To our beloved [fellow bishops] Reginfrid o Rouen, Deodatus of Beauvais, Rambert of Amiens, David o Speyer, Aetherius of Thérouanne, Heliseus of Noyon, Trewa of Cambrai, Burghard of Würzburg, Folcric of Tongres, Gen baud of Laon, Romanus of Meaux, Agilolf of Cologne an Heddo of Strasbourg; and to the others beloved [of us], assis ant bishops, presbyters and deacons, and all clerics of th churches who are orthodox and maintain the apostolic do trine, Zacharias, by divine grace high priest set upon the Apo tolic See, yet a servant of the servants of God, gives greeting i the Lord.'

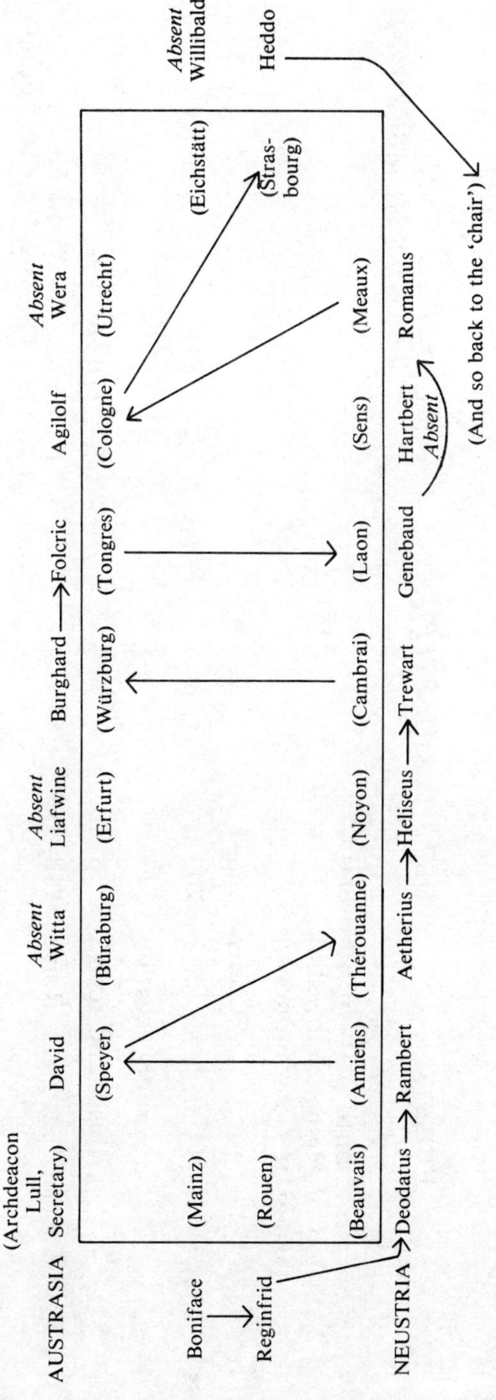
AUSTRASIA
(Archdeacon Lull, Secretary)
David
Absent Witta
Absent Liafwine
Burghard
Folcric
Agilolf
Absent Wera
Absent Willibald
(Speyer)
(Büraburg)
(Erfurt)
(Würzburg)
(Tongres)
(Cologne)
(Utrecht)
(Eichstätt)
Boniface
(Mainz)
Reginfrid
(Rouen)
(Stras-bourg)
Heddo
(Beauvais)
(Amiens)
(Thérouanne)
(Noyon)
(Cambrai)
(Laon)
(Sens)
(Meaux)
NEUSTRIA
Deodatus
Rambert
Aetherius
Heliseus
Trewart
Genebaud
Hartbert
Absent
Romanus
(And so back to the 'chair')

APPENDIX E

Time Chart: Events, Chapter References and Correspondence

EVENTS	*DATE*	*CHAPTER*	*'EPISTLES' INVOLVED (TANGL'S NUMBERING)*	
Birth of Wynfrith	680	1		
(Synod of Hatfield/Clovesho)				
(Synod at Constantinople)				
Exeter	685–6	2		
Nursling	702	3		
Canterbury legation	713			
Frisia and return	716	4	9	Wynfrith to Nithard
Rome	718	5	11	Daniel, for Wynfrith
			12	Pope Gregory II to W., 'Boniface' from now on
Bavaria, N. Germany, Frisia	719	6	15	Eadburga to Boniface
(With Willibrord)	719–21			

Rome: made bishop	722	7	16	Consecration oath	
			17–19	Pope Gregory II, commendatory, to groups in Germany	
			20	Pope Gregory II to Charles	
N. German mission continuing		8	22	Charles to leaders	
			23	Daniel to B.	
Thunderer's Oak	723–4		24	G. II to B., 4.12.723	
			25	G. II to Thuringians, 724	
			27	B. to Eadburga, c.725	
(726,730: Iconoclastic Edicts, Constantinople)		9	26	G. II to B., 22.11.726	
(Death of Pope Gregory II)	731				
Made Archbishop	732	10	28	Pope Gregory III to B. with *pallium*	
			29	Leoba to B.	
(Charles' victory at Poitiers-Tours)					
Bavarian visit	734				
			30,35	B. to Eadburga	
			32	B. to Pecthelm	
(Anxieties)	735–6		33	B. to Abp. Nothelm	c.735
			34	B. to Duddo	
			36	Sigebald to B.	

EVENTS	DATE	CHAPTER	'EPISTLES' INVOLVED (TANGL'S NUMBERING)	
Rome	737	11	40	B. to Fritzlar
			41	B. to colleagues
Rome: Synod	738	12	42–44,21	G. III to various German groups
N. German mission resumed		13	46	B. to English bishops
			47	B. to Torthelm
			38	B. to Aldhere
(Alamannian tour)	739	14	45	G. III to B., 29.10.739
Bavarian bishoprics			[49	Denehard, Lull and Burghard to Cuniburga]
(Death of Charles, G. III and Emperor Leo)	741	(15)		
		16	48	B. to Grifo
			50	B. to Pope Zacharias
Hesse-Thuringia bishoprics	742		51–53	Z. to B. with confirmation of bishoprics
Sturm's search (→ Fulda)			54	Gemmulus to B.
'German' Synod (Würzburg)	743	17	56	(Synodal decrees) – first part
Synod of Les Estinnes	744	18	56	(Synodal decrees) – later part
Synod of Soissons				

Event	Year		Letter	Description	Date
		(19)		(*cf.* 58–61, 68, 77, 80, 87)	
Combined Frankish Synod	745	20	58	Z. to B., 5.11.744	
Rome Synod			59	Acts of Rome Synod	
			60	Z. to B.	
			61	Z. to Franks	October 745
			62	Gemmulus to B.	
Boniface at Mainz		21			
Anglo-Saxon Synod (Utrecht)	746		63–64	B. to Daniel and reply	
			65–67	B. to English nuns, including Leoba	
			69	B. to King Ethelbald	
			73	Synodal admonition to Ethelbald	
			74–76	Accompanying letters to Herefrid, Abp. Egbert, Hutberht	
Pippin writes to Rome direct			77	Z. to B.	
			[85	Theophylact to B.]	
Frankish Synod (Rouen)	747			(*cf.* 80, Z. to B., 1.5.748)	
(Carloman's retirement)			79	*Anon.* to Andhun	
English Synod (Clovesho)			78	B. to Abp. Cuthbert	
Burghard's Rome visit					

EVENTS	*DATE*	*CHAPTER*	*'EPISTLES' INVOLVED (TANGL'S NUMBERING)*	
(Arrival of 30 nuns, including Leoba)	748	22	80	Z. to B., 1.5.748
			82–83	Z. to Franks
(Lull as arch-deacon)			84	Theophylact to B.
			81	King Elbwald to B.
Burghard and Fulrad at Rome	750			
Anointing of Pippin	751			
Exemption of Fulda		23	86	B. to Z.
(Lull made presbyter)			87–89	Z. to B.: Mainz; Fulda
(Death of Zacharias)	752		92	B. to Fulrad
Cologne/Utrecht question	753		107	B. to Pippin
Boniface to Frisia				
Return to Mainz and Fulda				
Pope Stephen to Pavia and Ponthion	753–4	24		
Boniface to Frisia	754			
Martyrdom 5.6.754				
		25	111	Abp. Cuthbert to Lull
			112	Bp. Milred to Lull

Epistles mentioned in square brackets have some relevance to the story but have not been used in the text.

Epistles not mentioned are omitted as marginal, *i.e.* not contributing any significant additional information.

BIBLIOGRAPHY

(With acknowledgements)

Primary Sources

'Lives' of Boniface: In original Latin (notes also in Latin), collected in the series *Monumenta Germaniae Historica,* among *Scriptores Rerum Germanicorum,* ed. W. Levison, 1905.

(1) By Presbyter Willibald of Mainz, pre-768.
(2) As in Fulda martyrology, about 900 AD.
(3) By Radbod of Utrecht, between 899 and 917, incorporating material pre-850.
(4) Also from Utrecht, between 917 and 1075.
(5) From Mainz, shortly after 1000 AD.
(6) By Otloh, monk of St. Emmeram (Bavaria) while in exile at Fulda, 1062–6; including all or most of thirty of the Letters.

Correspondence: Letters of or concerning Boniface and Lull, in Latin with Latin notes; also found in the *M. G. H.*, in the 3rd volume of *Epistolae,* ed. G. Dümmler, 1892. (English translation of the Letters, E. Kylie, New York, 1840.)

Modern Works in English

Bright, W. *Early English Church History* (3rd ed., Oxford, 1897).

Browne, G. F. *Boniface of Crediton and his Companions* (London, 1910).

Duckett, Eleanor S. *Anglo-Saxon Saints and Scholars* (New York, 1948).

Greenaway, G. W. *St. Boniface* (1955).

Levison, W. *England and the Continent in the Eighth Century* (Ford Lectures, Oxford, 1946).

Parkes, M. B. *The Handwriting of St. Boniface* (article in *Beiträge zur Geschichte der Deutschen Sprache und Literatur,* (98 Band, 2 Heft; Tübingen, 1976).

Talbot, C. H., (ed.) *The Anglo-Saxon Missionaries in Germany* (London, 1954).*

Williamson, J. M. *Biography* (Ventnor, 1904).

* Talbot's English version has been followed in nearly all cases in those letters which he included and in the earliest 'Life'. Otherwise the present author has made his own English renderings.

For General History:

Canton, N. F. *The Life and Death of a Civilisation* (2nd ed., London, 1969).

Deanesley, M. *A History of Early Mediaeval Europe*

Fisher, H. A. L. *A History of Europe* (London, 1936).

Continental Works:

Angenendt, 124A. *Pirmin und Bonifatius* (in *Vorträge und Forschungen,* Vol. 20, 1974, p. 251ff.).

Nottarp, H. *Die Bistumserrichtung in Deutschland in Achten Jahrhundert* (Stuttgart, 1920).

Praue, L. *Das Dom-Museum in Fulda* (in series *Ars Sacra,* Kassel, 1973).

Schieffer, Th. *Winfrid-Bonifatius und die Christliche Gründung Europas* (revised ed., Darmstadt, 1972).

Sankt Bonifatius Gedenkgabe zum zwölfhundertsten Todestag (Fulda, 1954).

Schüling, H. *Die Handbibliothek des Bonifatius* (in *Archiv für Geschichte des Buchwesens,* no. 4, 1961–3, p. 285ff.).

For General history:

Decarreaux, J. (transl. fr. French) *Monks and Civilisation* (London, 1964).

Duruy (ed.) *Histoire du Moyen Age* (vol. in *Histoire Universelle,* Paris, 1902).

For art and craft:

Backes, M. and Dölling, Regine (transl. fr. German) *Art of the Dark Ages* (New York, 1970s).

Notes and Acknowledgements:

There is a massive literature in the German language, of which many details are given by Schieffer (pp. 295–299 *op.cit.*). To Schieffer the present author owes much by way of fact, if rather less by way of interpretation.

The author is grateful for the use of the John Rylands Library of the University of Manchester, Deansgate, Manchester, and of the Manchester Central Library.
Also to the Rev. Bruce Duncan, Vicar of Crediton, for the loan of source material.

INDEX OF

PERSONS AND FAMILIES

including groups and movements named after persons

abb. = abbot abp. = archbishop bp. = bishop emp. = emperor kg. = king pr. = presbyter

INDEX OF

GEOGRAPHICAL NAMES, TRIBES, NATIONS AND LANGUAGES

INDEX OF

SUBJECTS

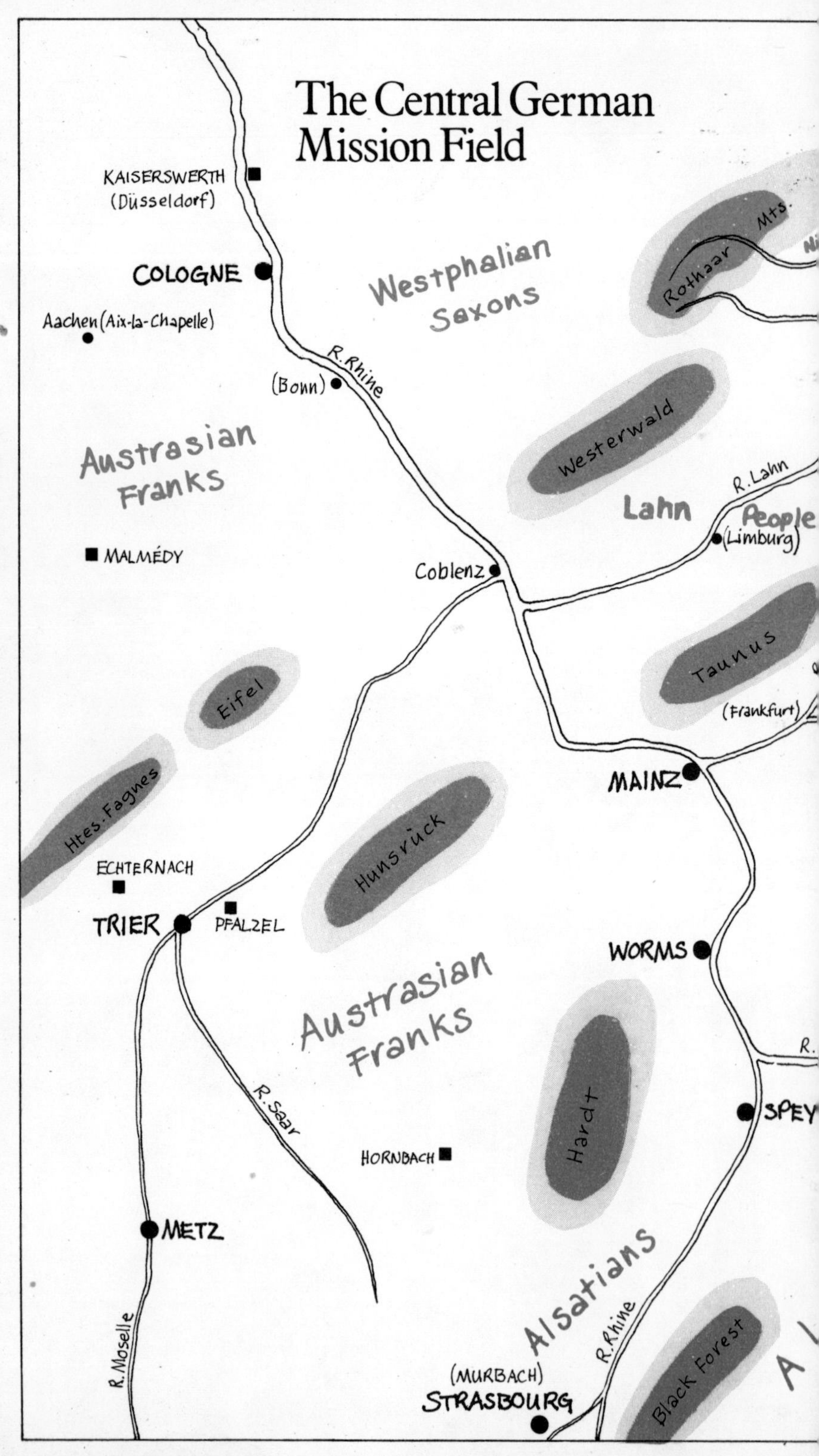

The Central German Mission Field
KAISERSWERTH
(Düsseldorf)
COLOGNE
Aachen (Aix-la-Chapelle)
Westphalian Saxons
Rothaar Mts.
R. Rhine
(Bonn)
Austrasian Franks
Westerwald
R. Lahn
Lahn People
(Limburg)
MALMÉDY
Coblenz
Taunus
(Frankfurt)
Eifel
MAINZ
Htes. Fagnes
Hunsrück
ECHTERNACH
TRIER
PFALZEL
WORMS
Austrasian Franks
R. Saar
Hardt
SPEY
HORNBACH
METZ
Alsatians
R. Moselle
R. Rhine
Black Forest
(MURBACH)
STRASBOURG